BE GREAT TODAY! NO DAYS OFF!

DARNELLE CUYLER

EDITOR: WILLIAM BODDEN JR.

DARNELLE CUYLER

Darnelle Cuyler was born in Orlando Florida on November 19th. He was raised in Altamonte Springs with his siblings and nieces. He has a bachelor's degree in Applied Mathematics from Louisiana State University as well as his master's Degree in Applied and Computational Mathematics from Florida State University.

His favorite things are playing or watching sports, having out with friends and loved ones, as well as working out. In his down time, he love binge watching shows, playing with his dog, and eating Oreos a row a time, otherwise known as sleeving.

He's a very passionate person that's always striving to bring his best and bring the best out of others. Being a hype-man is what he like to phrase it.

One of his biggest goals is to be a motivational speaker and being inside the Olympic stadium during the Olympic games.

BE GREAT TODAY! NO DAYS OFF!

IN LOVE MEMORY

KATHERINE L. CUYLER MANDY

THE ONES TO NEVER BE FORGOTTEN

HODGES J. CUYLER
ZACHARY WOOD
ANDREW SUN
DR. JOHNATHAN DOWLING
DR. TROY D. ALLEN

DARNELLE CUYLER

This book is for those who have dreams, goals, and aspirations of achieving greatness. Those who have passion that is resilient and have accepted that hardships will not prevent their triumphs. Those who conquer adversity through their own growth and development. Those who find others who are unforgettable, inspire you, and helps you enjoy the journey along the way.

PREFACE

I've always knew I would write a motivational book one day, but I was unsure of how much of my life I would include in it. It was odd, but I always felt authenticity and transparency are the only ways of truly getting your point across. not knowing how much of my life would be incorporated into it. This book is an expedition from spring 2011 to the beginning of 2021.

I will share with you how my life was and progressed from the end of high school, going through my undergraduate experience, and sometime postgraduation. I will navigate you through my successes, my failures, my trials, and my triumphs. Essentially, you're going to feel a lot emotions as you read my story. Ultimately, I want to motivate you and light a fire that can never be dimmed.

Along my journey, I share a lot about my time as a student at LSU and Florida State University. I really dive into my struggles as a boy growing into a man, a black man dealing the stigma of inequity, and prevailing no matter what came my way. I want to show you the strength of preservation, the people who came into my life and molded me into the man I am today. You'll notice I emphasize passion, hard work, and work ethic on a daily basis. Those were the ingredients needed to propel me forward, live the life that I want, and achieve goals that was once viewed as impossible.

Motivating people is a strong passion of mine. It pretty much makes me who I am. Every day I strive to deliver motivation to others around me that could help them be the best that they can be. This is including myself.

I hope you enjoy reading my journey, and it helps you find the strength to get through yours.

DARNELLE CUYLER

Table of Contents

Intro

Life is full of mysteries and unanswered questions. As humans, we're always trying to figure something our or at least understand what happens, how it happens, and why it happens. There is one question I hear people ask often.

What is life?

"Is that a rhetorical question," I'd ask out of curiosity. "Because everyone knows ball is life!"

That was funny, but all jokes aside. There are three questions I get from people consistently.

What keeps you motivated?

What keeps you going when you have nothing left?

How do you continue to beat the odds when the deck is stacked against you?

Depending on the person that meets me, they're usually shocked and amazed when we converse and I tell them bits and pieces about who I am, what I've done so far, and what I've been through. Some of them have left our in-depth conversations with more questions due to us not having enough time. To me, I believe writing this book is the best way for to answer those questions. I believe it would enable others to not only a better understanding of

DARNELLE CUYLER

who I am but understanding the journey that made me into who I am today.

Are you ready?

My name is Darnelle Cuyler. Although I was born in Arnold Palmer Hospital in Orlando, Florida, I was raised in Altamonte Springs, Florida. I grew up in a single parent household with my mother, Jackie. However, I wasn't an only child. I have an older brother name Arthur, and also an older sister name Candice. Then there's me and my twin sister, Danielle.

Currently, I have six nieces. In order, it's Lyric and Rayven, who are the daughters of my sister Candice. Then I have A'laya, Aubrey, and Naomi that belong to Arthur. And lastly, my great niece Londyn, who is the daughter of my niece Lyric.

This is my family, and just like any other family we're loving but we do fight a lot from time to time.

Well, they fight a lot. I mind my business while ignoring their bullshit as much as I can. Usually when they're going at it, I just go workout.

Once I left home for college, I never came back consistently or often. I was a rare sighting like a lunar eclipse. So, whenever I did come home, we kept the peace. If it is one thing I can attest to about my family is that we are all very comical.

If you're wondering who is the funniest out of all of us, which is a dumb question I might add, the obvious answer is me. I'm naturally a funny person. I could be thinking of something stupid or funny to say and I would just start laughing out of nowhere. Depending on whoever was around me, they'd start laughing too! For some reason, whenever I laugh, it triggers other people to laugh with me, even if they don't know why I'm laughing.

That's enough about them. Let's get back to the purpose of this book.

As my senior year in high school was approaching an end, things were beginning to change for me. Life became more apparent during this time. It was this tangible and intangible entity that haunted you. At the least expected moments, life would whisper softly in my ear questions that seemingly were harmless, but it incited fear or chaos in the mind.

BE GREAT TODAY! NO DAYS OFF!

"What's next?" Life was not shy nor apologetic for its role.

Truth is I didn't know. I knew I didn't really want to start working right away, and I knew I wanted to go to college. As the spring semester of my senior year of high school started, Seth, one of my closest friends, and I would talk about what universities we wanted to attend.

He'd always say, "I'm trying to go to Florida State."

"We can slide up there," I responded. "Besides, I like their colors."

There was nothing wrong with other schools in Florida. But Seth and I just felt that Florida State University would be the best move if we stayed in Florida.

"Man, you know what'll be fire," I asked to him. "If I went to LSU."

He said, "Oh, yeah? You'll be a Tiger! And their football team so damn raw. That's a real good school academically as well. I think you'll like them."

"Yeah, and I'll also be partying with Boosie!"

We laughed.

Despite the plans made, life took things in a different direction. It wasn't too long after when Seth announced he was going to Bethune-Cookman University on a football scholarship. Do not get me wrong, I was extremely proud and happy for him. That's my boy. But I was faced with the reality of his decision. While the stars were aligning for him and his path became clearer, I still needed to figure out what my next step was going to be.

If I can be truly transparent with you, it was tough. Despite having really good grades and being involved in extra-curricular activities (sports, clubs, etc.), it wasn't enough. My options were slim-to-none. Although I did take the SAT and ACT, I was only able to take it once. I couldn't afford it on my own and the only source of income I had at the time was my mom. Unfortunately, I was stuck with those low scores and no way to better them.

I know what you're thinking.

Oh, you could have done this. You could've done that.

Relax Einstein. I did all I could at the time. Honesty speaking, I didn't think the tests were hard at all, but the timing did trip me up. I took them at the time to see what it was like and planned

DARNELLE CUYLER

on taking them again. But with limited resources and money, it wasn't happening.

Despite the odds stacked against me, I still went on and applied to big-time schools anyway. It was getting expensive, and my mom was getting tired of it. There were a lot of universities that were sending interest letters in the mail that can cover all four of my bedroom walls, but none of them were acceptance letters. It became apparent to me that I was not going to school on an athletic scholarship, so academics was really all I had going for myself.

The summer after graduation I was stuck in a constant limbo of despair and anger. I didn't know what I was going to do with my life. Like, was this it? Was this it for me? No matter how low I felt, I refused to accept that.

I was having a random conversation with Seth, and he blurted out, "man just come to Bethune. You'll get in easy. I'm playing football for them. So, try out for the track team."

Not too long after I graduated from Lyman High School in 2011, I went to Bethune-Cookman University in Daytona Beach, Florida. I was only there for a semester as a math major. I had a great time, and I met some amazing people who later became good friends. But I could not help feeling that I wasn't in the right place. I remembered what this old man said to me when I was younger.

Just because the door opens for your does not mean you should walk through it.

In other words, not every opportunity is the best opportunity for you. Sometimes, you have to learn when to say no. So, I took a leap of faith and reapplied to a couple of schools. I was going to transfer to the school I felt a sense of completeness.

This shouldn't have come at such a shock, but it did. Florida State University turned me down for the second time. Despite my feelings being hurt, they at least told me why and what I needed to do in order to be accepted. The old saying of when God closes one door, another door opens is true because LSU took a different approach. They required 30 credit hours for me transfer. Once I fulfill that requirement, I would be able to transfer over as a sophomore.

BE GREAT TODAY! NO DAYS OFF!

"Bet! Say less!" For those of you who do not know, this is Florida slang.

I kept thinking to myself that maybe I was meant to be at LSU instead of FSU.

While I was at Bethune, I had a roommate from Tampa, Florida. His name was Jaquell, and just like me, he was in the process of joining the track team for the university. We both rode the struggle bus during that first semester, but we overcame it, nevertheless.

"108B!"

That was one of things we used to shout to each other whenever we saw one another in public. It was our dorm room number. It still holds significant value to me still to this day. If you know anything about college kids, we don't necessarily sleep. We used to be in our dorm talking up a storm. We would bounce ideas off of each other and we would even talk about our goals. As a black man it was refreshing to be in a comfortable setting and be vulnerable. That's not something the world allows.

"Yeah, I think I'm going to head back home in the spring man," I blurted out. I had a plan, and I was going to see it through. "I'm trying to go to LSU."

I thought I would receive some pushback on it but surprisingly, he was hyped for me. He supported me on this without conflict, or backlash. We became friends on social media to keep in touch and we're still friends to this day.

So, I moved back home in December 2011. I did not want to move back for personal reasons but to get to where I wanted to go, I had to do what I had to do in order for the plan to come into fruition. As they would say, it is what it is. There were a lot of negativities brewing from family drama and to avoid being caught in the crossfire, I lived with my grandmother to stay sane.

In January I set a few goals for myself, and one way or another, I was going to accomplish them. So, boom here's the plan. Move back home, transfer to Seminole State College to get the credits I needed, and then transfer to LSU. Simple enough, right? As the Spring semester started, I was enrolled at Seminole State-College in Sanford, Florida. Some people thought of SSC as a place where some people that didn't graduate from high school

DARNELLE CUYLER

with good grades or didn't go off to a major college, would go there and would eventually give up on pursuing a better life.

Thankfully, that was not the case for me.

I was focused and seen my enrollment to SSC as an opportunity and a steppingstone. I knew my goal was to go to LSU, so I wasn't listening to the naysayers or even worried about if people saw me there on campus. I didn't have a car so my only means of transportation was either catching the bus or catching a ride from my friend Trent.

Trent and I have been friends since middle school. We had always hoped for the best and stayed supportive of one another other throughout our friendship. During Spring 2012, mainly February of that year, things became rough in Seminole County. SSC was right near where the Trayvon-Martin shooting occurred. I remember being stressed out of my mind because of the shooting and because I was emailing LSU every other day, and I wasn't getting a response.

I remember there were times when I wanted to give up, but something just kept telling me to hold on. One night, I'm unsure if it was God or not, but something was telling me to make sure I check the mailbox tomorrow. I was a bit stubborn at the time and I was restless for majority of the night. I was filling my head with negative thoughts and creating things that I knew weren't true. I was also stressing out because I had an exam the next day and I was failing that class. I don't know why I was being that hard on myself, and for some reason, even after noticing I was, I never let up.

"Man, fuck it. I'm going to just drop out and that'll be the end of that."

I didn't expect my subconscious to talk back to me as I was falling asleep.

"You're going to get up tomorrow, study, take the exam, and then go home and check the fucking mailbox!"

It was aggressive, but the next day, that's literally what I did. When I got home, I checked the mailbox immediately to find a big package and a letter from LSU.

BE GREAT TODAY! NO DAYS OFF!

Keep working hard and it'll happen. You know, some motivational stuff.

Man, you don't even know how much of a power up that gave me. I was so focused after that. It was unbelievable. I know this may sound weird, but for the next five to six months, anytime I got super down or super low on myself I would see a sign that encouraged me to keep going.

And I did.

I'm not trying to bring religion into this because I don't know what your personal beliefs are, but there were always signs from God that things were going to happen for me. For example, the very next day I would see writing on cars that said, 'Congratulations on getting into LSU! I'm proud of you!' Or I would be in the store and see someone with an LSU shirt on. I knew it was sign because I've never in my life seen someone wear an LSU shirt in Orlando until they sent me letters in the mail. I kid you not!

I knew if I was going to LSU, I was going to need money. I needed a job. So, prior to the upcoming summer term, I worked at a nursing home as part of the kitchen crew. This was a big thanks to CJ, who was my neighbor at the time. We worked for this man name Joe, and, in my opinion, Joe was really good people. Between working and being enrolled in the summer term, I think it was safe to say, it was ass long summer.

I didn't like the job I had, but I always felt eternally grateful for having one. I kept a smile on my face at all times, and I always kept the crew laughing. No one knew I was laughing a lot in my head because I knew I was going to quit at the end of the summer. LSU was calling and I was going to answer that call.

With all of the negativity going on in the city, which felt endless since it seemed to occur on a day-to-day basis, I needed to find a way out. I needed to find a place that I felt peace.

That's when I chose the back street of Sanford Avenue.

The Trenches.

Every day I would run on Sanford Avenue to keep my mind strong and focused. One day, all that running, praying, and speaking to it into existence finally paid off. I remember the day my life changed for the better. I came home one day from class and checked my email. I had an email from LSU, but before I clicked on it, I noticed the mailman pulled into the driveway. I don't know why but I ditched my computer and immediately went to the mailbox.

I had a letter from LSU as well.

I didn't open the letter right away though. After I got settled again, I clicked the email and my eyes widened.

Congratulations! You have been accepted into Louisiana State University.

"OH SHIT!"

This prompted me to open the letter from LSU and it confirmed that I got in.

"I GOT INTO LSU! OH MY GOD!" I was so hyped!

No one was home, so I couldn't share the great news immediately like I wanted to. This wasn't a bad thing though. I figured I'd wait a day or so to plan everything out accordingly. I had to think about what's going to happen if I didn't pass my summer class. Tears of joy covered my face all afternoon and again before I fell asleep. I responded back to LSU via email letting them know I accept as well. I informed of the situation currently and they let me know I would have to attend the summer term the following year.

I can't tell you how hyped I was! Eventually, I started sharing my excitement with everyone!

"Y'all, I'm going to LSU!"

People thought I was playing, but little did they know, it was the truth, and I was dead serious.

When I told my mom I was going to attend LSU in the fall, her initial reaction was not quite what I was expecting or could've ever imagined.

"Oh, I don't have the money for you to be going way out there."

Luckily, I wasn't expecting her help. Truthfully, I didn't plan on it. I pulled out of the money I had saved up to that point.

"Here is my acceptance letter," my demeanor was stern and serious. "I got money saved up. Whether you take me or not, on August 14th, I will be going to LSU."

She didn't say anything, nor did she try to stop me. My mom knew once my mind was made up and my heart was in it,

BE GREAT TODAY! NO DAYS OFF!

there was nothing she could do or say to change it. I planned everything accordingly and gathered all the supplies I needed. From the money I saved in a Reebok shoebox and the money from working with CJ, I paid for everything I needed alone. I didn't expect anyone to help me. Hell, I didn't expect anyone to believe in me. But I was going to bet on myself every single time because I know at the end of the day, nobody got me like I got me.

A door for new beginnings opened and I walked through it.

The Trenches

Now, *The Trenches* take place on a street called Sanford Avenue. It's between Magnolia Avenue and Ronald Reagan Boulevard. At first, I used to come to this street, and just run for extra conditioning during track season. I would've never thought this particularly road would be the place where I discovered my life's purpose that defined my existence.

Every day I went for a run, and when I did, I always ran on Sanford Avenue. And every single time I would run past this dude name Peanut while he was at the shop. I would always tell him that I was going to make it, and that I'm going to LSU.

I'm not bullshitting.

When I tell you I ran on Sanford Avenue every day, I really mean I ran on Sanford Avenue every single day.

I told Peanut the same thing for months, and he would just laugh me off as I ran by.

"I hear you boy," he said. "Just keep doing what you're doing. You gon' make it. I'm already proud of you."

Peanut's real name was Earl. I've known him most of my life.

Peanut & his wife, Stevan, have literally supported me since day one. I've been friends with their sons Edward, Keith, and Kelvin since we were six-years old at Altamonte Elementary running around the sandbox.

They're literally my second family. I promise you on everything, blood really couldn't make us any closer. Even though I told Peanut the same thing every time I seen him, there were times I felt like no one was really hearing nor understanding me. I remember this day like it was yesterday, and I remember going through men-

BE GREAT TODAY! NO DAYS OFF!

tal gymnastics of my mind creating so much doubt. I knew I needed to shake the thoughts despite how heavy they were. Whenever I wasn't at school, work, or slaving away for my grandmother, I was running through Sanford Avenue creating goals and dreams that I planned to make a reality.

My running sessions had three different phases.

Phase One:

I would think of all the things that went wrong in my life. There wasn't really a parameter or a criterion for this logic, but I would just think of a time in my life whether it was a certain minute, hour, day, or even week that things weren't going the way I'd hoped it go.

Regardless, it was something in my past.

I would get so down on myself thinking about the situation, that my emotions would sometimes go from sad to angry to full blown tears in the matter of minutes. Even after the sudden changes in emotions to the tears overflowing on my face, I would continue to think about all of the negative things that happened to me.

I would question God about my circumstances and proceed to cuss him out in the same breath.

I would do this until I couldn't do it anymore, until I couldn't think of anything else to beat me down with. Until there was nothing more to say.

Nothing.

This part of the run was probably the worse because, at times, remembering all the trials, tribulations, the adversity happening to me made question myself.

"Why don't I just give up?" I would ask myself again and again.

Phase One was a way to help me bring everything that was bothering me in the dark to the light You can't heal what you won't reveal, and I didn't want to hold onto all that anger, stress, and doubt. So, this was the perfect place to get it off my chest. Once the weight of failure, denials, and adversity had been lifted, I gained the ability to move forward.

DARNELLE CUYLER

But right before *Phase Two* would start, I would slow things down and walk for a bit. Take a sip of water to rehydrate myself. Most of the time, I forgot my water bottle and would just be dying of thirst in the blazing sun. I did manage to find shade depending on where the sun was located during the day.

Then, *Phase Two* would happen.

Phase Two:

This is the session where I would begin to shift my mindset. I would look at every situation from *Phase One* for what it really was, and then come up with solutions to fix what went wrong, if possible. And I say 'if possible' because I would only focus on creating plans to fix the situations that I had control over. Like the old folks would always say, "control what you can control."

These sessions were the most relaxing for me. The weather would seem calmer, the sun wasn't abusing me as much, and I could feel myself getting back centered. Even though I'm LITERALLY STILL RUNNING up and down the road, I felt centered, hydrated, and at peace. To me, I could feel my mind and heart getting back in sync, no longer battling one another, and giving me the serenity I was longing for.

However, I could feel my hamstrings shaking and I remember telling myself that once I was done with this session, I would take a break. The breaks were never really long. Very brief, so to speak.

After things calm down a bit, I would be feeling like I can go home, relax, or chill for a bit.

But nah.

Phase Three would begin.

Phase Three was a different ball game. A different tempo, I should say.

Phase Three:

This phase brings out a different attitude in me.

BE GREAT TODAY! NO DAYS OFF!

I can be dead tired, and I mean deadass tired, but once *Phase Three* begins, all that shit goes out the window.

Phase Three is when I bring my best to the table.

This where my subconscious expands my will, my will amplifies my motivation, and my motivation goes into overdrive. Hence, a different me emerges from the brink of exhaustion and I become something more than I already am.

Unstoppable.

During this part of my run, I notice this is where the tempo changes from a cross-country championship type of run to full-blown sprints. I'm not going to lie, this part of the run takes the most energy out of me but it's also when my adrenaline is the highest. So, it's cool.

The purpose of *Phase Three* is me seeing myself accomplish every goal that I set for myself. It's to pray to God and thank him for everything that I've been through and put faith into where I'm heading. This is where mental exhaustion, doubt, and fear from *Phase One* become motivation, determination, and faith.

I come into *Phase Three* with the appetite to train my mind, body, and spirit on a different level.

This is where I train myself be consistent and disciplined. This is where the essence of aggression and belligerence become dedication and passion.

To tell you the truth, I love *Phase Three*. I love *Phase Three* so much because I'm performing at my best, uplifting those near and dear to me, and supporting and inspiring the goals and dreams of others. I envision myself getting the job done with relentless effort. Not only striving but thriving.

Phase Three makes the goals I set for myself and the dreams I want to see come into fruition change from mere fairy tale to reality. From the impossible to the possible.

Another thing I love so much about *Phase Three* is that no matter what the weather looks like or how dark it is on the avenue, I can see my dreams clear as day. I'm talking 80-degree weather, no clouds in sight, and a light breeze kind of clear. I become so focused to the point that I can see every detail from start to finish.

It may be a dream, but I can see it. And if I can see it, then I will achieve it.

DARNELLE CUYLER

At its core, I had to see it through because despite the odds that were against me, and no matter the circumstances, I overcame all the adversity.

Still, I rise.

Seeing myself push through the obstacles and make it through hard times only reminded me that this path was worth it, and I must keep going. A man could still meet his destiny on the same road less traveled. Pep talks with myself kept me going because I didn't have anyone to hold me accountable. I had to do it for myself.

"This shit mandatory Darnelle," I would say to myself. "You're going to put in the work and you're going to make it happen! You will get the job done by any means necessary!"

This is the part of *Phase Three* that I can get lost in for hours and not care. I would pray the same prayers to God, repeat the same affirmations to myself, and see myself accomplishing all the goals I prayed for. I heard an old man say while I was running one day, "if you can see it, then you can be it."

That glorious feeling is incredible. The part I hate most about *Phase Three* is coming off that addicting high and feeling depleted. I could feel the soreness creeping in and my muscles preparing to cramp up. It's worse when all of it is happening simultaneously and I kind of just black out from the exhaustion. There's been times when I've done my run at night and whenever I felt like this, my pride went out the window.

"Fuck it," I said after I took a deep breath. "I gotta lay down." I would literally lay down in the road until I had enough strength to get up and walk home. Sometimes, I would even tell myself, "Alright, that's enough. Time to slide to the crib."

Phase Three always manages to make me cry tears of joy because each time I ran, I found new strength that kept me fighting towards my goals. It kept me going some days when things were hard, and I kept doubting myself.

"Is it worth it?"

"Why should I even keep going?"

Despite how I felt, I'd still say it's worth it and worked harder.

BE GREAT TODAY! NO DAYS OFF!

Running has always been a passion of mine because of the physical demand it requires, and competitiveness it comes with. I always felt that I was a strong-minded person, so I never thought using running as a mental health practice for myself. But running and creating these phases really helped shape me into the person I am today.

Also, just a little more insight on the phases. They can be done at any given time of the day. There's not a time frame of when it has to be done, but it had to be done every day for me because it was mandatory. So, some days I'd only do two phases, other days I'd do all three. I can never do *Phase One* alone, but *Phase Three* can be done alone. Sometimes I do it alone to help me keep the faith in my goals. If I did do two phases, I always chose either *Phase Two* or *Phase Three*. Understand this concept, because if I am constantly going through so much adversity why would I add negative physical stress to do that. The purpose of the phases while I run is to move forward. So, when I am running, I'm developing different aspects, perspectives, growth, and strengths to be better in life. In all honesty, it's really rare that I would do a *Phase One* and *Phase Three* together as a duo. I think I only did that session once or twice, give or take, but definitely not more than that. I remember the day I did Phase One and Phase Three together. That is a day I will never forget.

Although I don't remember the exact date, I know it was a Friday night. I was running like I usually do, and I was trying to figure it all out. I was still sending emails to LSU, but they weren't responding at the time. I was concerned because I wasn't doing too well in one of my classes, and I wasn't sure how to go about moving forward if I didn't get a passing grade. I needed 30 credit hours, and at that time, it was nonnegotiable.

"It'll all work itself out." I kept telling myself that as I was running.

I was so lost in my thoughts, and so focus on my run, I never noticed that it got super dark and there was a shoot-out happening a few blocks away. It was a full-blown drive by happening and my only concern was finding positive reinforcement to combat the doubt trying to fight its way through, while I was mid-stride.

DARNELLE CUYLER

Peanut and Stevan came down Sanford Ave and stopped me.

Stevan yelled, "boy is you crazy? Don't you hear them over there shooting and you out here running? Go home!"

"Nah, but I'll be alright. I gotta get my mind right. I gotta execute these plans to get to LSU and make y'all proud."

Peanut looked me dead in my eyes and said, "you gon make it. Alright? You gon make it, but I need you to get home and stay safe. Alright? Just go home tonight, and then run tomorrow when they stop."

"Take your ass home! I ain't saying it again." The concern in Stevan's was admirable.

"Alright, alright."

And then they drove off.

Now, you know damn well I didn't go home. I kept running. I'll die behind these dreams. That's how bad I wanted to go to LSU, and I needed to see myself doing it.

I said a quick prayer.

"God if a stray bullet hit me and knock my brains out, please let my life flash before me and let me see what I could've done before my body hit the ground. Amen."

And then I ran for a little longer.

My mind started to get clouded again, and I started asking myself, why am I putting my life at risk for something that might not happen? What did I do wrong? How come I'm always struggling and failing at everything? I don't want to live here. I don't want to go down the same path as everyone else. Why am I such a failure? I put in so much work and have nothing to show for it. I sat on the side of the road, and I started crying.

Tears were rolling down my face and bullets were still flying a few blocks over. I disregarded them like they were equivalent to fireworks. I was still questioning God on everything. Why am I such a failure? I don't have nothing or nobody to talk to about my problems. All I'm doing is struggling.

Then there was a voice in my head.

"Get up! And go home! Come back tomorrow and go harder!"

BE GREAT TODAY! NO DAYS OFF!

At first, I didn't know what to do, but it gave me chills. I wasn't tired anymore, and my heart rate picked back up. The fast-twitch muscles started moving in my hamstrings, and I just knew it was time to go home.

I couldn't wipe me face because my shirt was drenched in sweat, but I still made my way home. I knew one thing though, when I come back here tomorrow, I'll meet that aggressive ass voice again. However, the next day I was hesitating on running through *The Trenches* again because I wanted to chill, and I honestly didn't have time for another shoot out. When Saturday night came, I went to the Ave and started running again.

This was probably one of my most memorable running sessions. I was running towards Magnolia first, then I turned around to run towards Ronald Reagan Blvd. By the time I got there, it was completely dark. As I was coming down the Ave, it all the negative thoughts I suppressed in the back of my mind were coming to light.

God, how come I put in so much work to end up in this situation?

How come nobody wanted me to make it out of high school?

People always say they want you to succeed, but they don't really put forth the effort to help you succeed. I mean, I excelled at sports, I had a great grade point average, and I never got in trouble. I didn't smoke, I didn't drink, and yet, here I am. Hell, my senior year of high school, I had over a 4.0 grade point average, I was setting personal records in Track & Field for myself, and nothing came of it.

I'm going to this community college, and ironically, I'm on the brink of failing out. I feel like I was fed nothing but lies all throughout high school.

"Oh, make good grades."

"They'll pay for you to go to college!"

"Oh, you're Black! that'll definitely help you get in."

All bullshit.

And yet, here I am still running up and down the street in the hood.

God, why won't you help me? How does my success in life depend on whether somebody else deeming me worthy to make it?

DARNELLE CUYLER

Why the fuck is my life at the mercy of someone else? You mean to tell me, I can't make it in life if my family or the people around me don't want to support me?

That's crazy!

I worked so hard to do everything right and yet I don't have anything or anybody in my corner helping me get there. And this is not a shot at anyone, but I don't want to be like the people around here that didn't make the most of their opportunities.

The tears were running down my face again as I passed through Magnolia.

"God, I promise I'll do anything you ask. I promise I'll give my last if you get me away from here. People here don't do anything but talk bad about one another and degrade each other."

I was pleading with God heavy this day.

The people I seen go to college never wanted to have anything with drugs. In fact, they despised it. But when they dropped out and had to return home, they started selling dope just make ends meet or to fit in. The crazy part about it, I don't think they were ever offered any help with getting back into school. In my hood they make it seem that if you didn't get offered a scholarship in whatever sport you were in, you were either a bum or you just weren't going to amount to anything!

But that's in every hood, I feel like.

If people feel like you're an easy come up, and they can profit off your success, they'll ride behind you the whole way. If they can't do a quick scheme to get rich off you or see that you won't be able to produce a promising return on investment, you can pretty much go to hell in their eyes.

I'm a living witness to this. I've seen it with my own eyes.

When I made that turn and was running to Ronald Reagan Blvd, I kept thinking how I don't want to end up like them and I do not want people who aren't for me around me. Most of the people here have nothing but envy and malice in their hearts when it come to the next person doing better than them. The sense of power they feel parading throughout the neighborhood, killing people loved dearly by others, and bragging about it.

That's so dumb to me.

BE GREAT TODAY! NO DAYS OFF!

We all come from the same neighborhood, we have the same home, and even ate off the same plates growing up.

I turned around and ran the opposite way once I got to Ronald Reagan.

How you brag about killing your own family member? You're flexing in front of the same people that'll set you up and kill you, just so you can seem 'real' in their eyes. That's dumb as hell if you ask me. The way people think around here is so ass backwards. They'll give everything they own to the streets but wouldn't put forth that same energy to provide for their own household. Expose they own siblings to the brutalness of the streets instead of trying to protect them. Some shoot at their own family members and not think twice about it. I'm tired of it.

You can't even mind you own business without potentially running into or from a stray bullet.

As I got to Magnolia and prepared to turn around to go the other way, I just kept repeating the same prayer.

"God, PLEASE get me away from here," the tears ran harder down my face. "Get me away from here, please. I promise on everything God, I'll endure every hardship you throw at me. I promise I'll deal with family not supporting me, barely having any money, starving and all. Please, I'm begging to leave Altamonte. I don't care what I must go through, just get me away from here.

[Turns around and head to Ronald Reagan].

I continued pleading with God like my life depended on it because to me, it did.

"I promise I'll endure the hardships. I'll deal with losing people close to me. I swear I'll deal with losing it all, just please get me away from here." I repeated these words as I headed back towards Magnolia.

Before I got to Magnolia, I stopped running and sat at the edge of the curb, and just cried my eyes out. I'm crying harder than I did before because I knew I was going to through some storms before I ever see the sunshine again. I may bend, but I'll never break.

"PLEASE DON'T GIVE ON ME GOD!"

I was okay with everybody turning their backs on me and not giving it a second thought. I was okay with not getting the love and the support I truly desired and craved for fulfilment. But I wasn't willing to let God give up on me, not now, not ever. I wanted to make it in life, and I gave God my word that no matter what he threw at me, I will see it through. The strength of my faith will prevail, and I will make it to LSU.

Please don't let leave the hood if I'm not going to make it. That was a legitimate fear of mine. To make it out and have to come back to the hood like I never left. I could see myself my being clowned all over social media. Just the thought of it felt like a thorn in my side.

"How you go all the way out there just to come back?"

"You think you better than everybody else, but you aren't shit just like the rest of them."

"You go be another deadbeat, watch."

Man, I'm not trying to hear none of that bullshit. I was working way too hard to be derailed by other people who didn't have anything going for themselves. Maybe it's me, but I never understood how some people can talk down on someone and they have nothing to show for it.

I can't be around here no more. I have to leave. I'll stay gone if I have too. Take me away from here. Please don't leave me here. I want to be somebody in life. Please don't give up me, God. I promise from the bottom of my heart and soul, if you give me once chance, Imma do right and make it. Don't give up on me God like everybody else. I'll give my last breath if you take me away from here and let me go to LSU.

As I sat on the curb having a pity party, the voice came to me again.

"GET UP! I TOLD YOU I WAS COMING BACK! GET UP!"

I didn't move right away. I was kind puzzled and just frozen for a second.

"GET THE FUCK UP AND I'M NOT SAYING IT AGAIN!

My heart started beating rapidly and I can feel the adrenaline rushing through my veins. My muscles started twitching

BE GREAT TODAY! NO DAYS OFF!

throughout my body, and nothing but excitement fueled me to keep going.

I jumped up quickly and took off running. I was trying to figure out where this voice was coming from before realizing it was me. But it wasn't the current me on *Sanford Ave*. This was the future me, the better me, the stronger me. I knew when he spoke people listened. I was scared and empowered at the same time because I can hear my own greatness.

"KEEP RUNNING!"

I felt my future-self taking over my whole subconscious.

"I am you, dumbass. I'm the best part of you! I am the motivation you need to make it in life! I'm going to show you how to make your mind and body connect! Now, pick up the pace, keep running at this pace the whole time."

I did exactly as instructed.

"YOU WILL GO TO LSU! YOU WILL MAKE IT! YOU'RE GETTING THE FUCK UP OUT OF HERE!"

I felt my future-self having a pep talk with my current-self, and it was well needed. I was reminded that just because I'm struggling right now, does not mean I won't make it. I had to stop stressing about things I couldn't control and focus on the things I can control. All the doubt that grew in me and flourished like flowers blooming in the summertime, I needed to pray harder on it for it to go away. Whenever I feel doubt trying to creep back into my life, I needed to stop and thank God for the things that he has done for me and the things he was going to do.

I discovered that it was hard for me to fight all of the negativity and doubt on a continuous basis because I didn't have reinforcement to tussle through this fight for the long haul. My only goal was to go to LSU, but nothing else. And there lay the dilemma.

"I'm going to set this up all for you."

[Slap the stop sign on Ronald Reagan]

As I head back to Magnolia, I told myself.

"When you get 50 meters out from the stop sign, give it your all. Maintain your form the whole time."

DARNELLE CUYLER

I kept receiving the positive affirmations needed for me.

You will be different from anybody at LSU.

You will show people everywhere that sports aren't the only way out.

What is something we've never seen come out of Altamonte Springs? A Mathematician. That's who you will be and you're going to show little black boys and girls that it's ok and it's amazing that they venture into STEM.

You may be the only black math major in the program, and that's okay because you'll open the doors for the people that look like you to come through. Matter of fact, you probably will be the only black math major to graduate from LSU in your class, your community, and most importantly, your family.

So, you see, you have to make it. It's no longer just about you. It's about the generations to come. It's about the neighborhood you will inspire. It's about your family seeing that the impossible is possible.

THAT'S ON GOD! THAT'S ON THE TRENCHES!

On top of grinding to be a Mathematician, you going to do research with world class researchers. You will touch base on subjects people shy away from because it's 'too hard.' You're going to approach it head on and because of the hard work you put into it, you'll grasp better than your classmates who counted you out.

You do your part and I'll make sure people some respect on your name. Sure, you'll be the hoodest nerd anybody has ever met, but you'll be respected in any territory you may roam. You'll grind with the odds against you and prove to everyone that the impossible will be done!

[Sprint and then slap the sign of Magnolia]

Not only will you strive to bring greatness in academics, but in athletics as well. You'll Train and workout with students that compete in all variety of sports. You gon make them respect this shit too!

You gon show them the true craft of having control of your mental game and how body will continue to perform on an extraordinary scale. Matter of Fact, we running against Olympians to

BE GREAT TODAY! NO DAYS OFF!

let it be known you real! That's Mandatory! You going to have range when it comes to Academics and Athletics.

PICK UP THE PACE [slaps sign of Ronald Reagan].

Everything from phase 1 we going to back to talk to God!

God, please let me grind until I prevail! My success will depend on MY WORK ETHIC! I will put in the work every single day! I won't take a day off from the grind!

I will grind and chase my goals and dreams with relentless effort! I will be tenacious and aggressive behind my goals and dreams! I don't care about what anybody talking 'bout! I was running out here when they were shooting, God, I'll let be known that I'll die behind these dreams! I'll do whatever it take to make it!

Right now, I'm being my own hype-man.

God, I'll endure all the struggles you put me through! I'll fall in love with them! After I graduate, I'll turn around and start a scholarship fund at the schools I graduate from.

"I WILL BE THE REASON SOMEBODY MAKE IT!! I promise I will!"

PICK UP THE PACE [slaps the sign of Magnolia].

At this point I'm just premeditating my life and actions going forward.

I promise myself I'll stay solid on all of my goals and all of my dreams. I promise I won't throw my goals and dreams away just because of adversity I'm experiencing for triumph is at the end of the tunnel. I will never allow myself to take the easy route or to fit in! I promise I'll stick to the game plan!

God, I promise you I'll motivate people to want to do better. I don't want to down and degrade people, every day I'll uplift and motivate people! I'll grind and pave the way for people. I promise I'll do better. I'll give motivational speeches to make them feel empowered and supported.

PICK UP THE PACE [slaps the sign of Ronald Reagan].

God, I'll pray and thank you every day. I'm grateful to meet and be around extraordinary people along this journey. I promise I will enjoy life. I promise I will give my last to the people that love and support me. I promise I won't give up on them nor turn my back on them. To the people I'm going to meet, and they become a

DARNELLE CUYLER

part of my family, I promise I'll give them everything in me and will go to war with anybody for them.

I repeated this that thought until I got to the stop sign.

PICK UP THE PACE [slap the sign of Magnolia].

I promise I'll make sure that every day I make my presence so strong and know that they don't have to stress because I'm here putting in work with them. I'll pick up the slack time and time again. I'll make them laugh harder for every time they cry. Whenever they hungry, I'm coming with Oreos. I'm bringing the Oreos because they my favorite thing to eat, and more than likely I'll still be broke! Haha. Even when I'm broke, I'll still feed the ones that fed me.

I put that on God! I'm not ever switching up!

I promise I won't count my struggles, but I will help those through theirs.

Every day I'll put forth the effort to reach out to them and tell them, "I'm proud of you! I love you! Keep grinding! You Got This!" When I tell them, they're going to know I mean it, whether it's in person, a phone call, through a text, or social media. Imma give them all the love and support that I've always wanted. I'll be their biggest hype man, biggest fan, and source of motivation, especially when it comes to motivational speaking. I'm coming straight from my heart every time! I will cherish the ones who accept me for who I am. I'll keep them smiling!

I know I have a laughing problem, but if they can accept that then we're good for life.

I don't care about race, gender, religion, ethnicity, or any of that other stuff. When it comes to supporting people, showing them how to have faith, how to love others, and most importantly showing them to value themselves, I'll be there to provide guidance every single time.

When I deliver motivational speeches, I promise Imma make them all feel me! They gon know it came from the bottom of my heart because I'm going through the struggle with them. I'll do my best to touch the hearts and souls of not only those in need, but those who need to hear it for it themselves to become a blessing in someone else's life. Every day I'm going to strive to uplift people.

BE GREAT TODAY! NO DAYS OFF!

I'm going to do things different. I'm going to turn out differently than my hood intended me to be.

Instead of killing someone and taking a life, I'm going to save a life one person at a time. I'm going to make sure my words are impactful enough to stop someone from committing suicide, realize that they are valued, and their life is worth living. I'm will show them how to fall in love with the grind and fight through the hard times instead of taking the easy way out or giving up. I will teach them discipline and dedication. I promise I don't care how long it takes. It can take a day, weeks, months, or even years. I will not give up on them.

[To the people still watching me after all these years, I promise I haven't given up on you. I'm still working every day. I promise I'm still proud of you.]

I promise I'll show people that through hard work, they can achieve their goals no matter how many obstacles stand in their way and no longer it takes. Every day I'm going to fight and bring my best to the table.

PICK UP THE PACE [slap sign of Ronald Reagan].

God, even as I struggle and deal with the lack of support, I will find a way to make it. I promise for every night I starve, cry myself to sleep, or both, I will wake up the next morning and grind and smile harder!

Imma stand on that!

God, keep me fighting this fight.

Please don't let me lose my soul trying keep people around that's not meant for me! I promise I'll get back aggressive with the grind before I throw myself away over other people.

PICK UP THE PACE [slaps the sign of Magnolia].

No matter how hard it gets from being broke, starving, or even homeless, I promise to God & *The Trenches* I won't fold and start to selling drugs. I'll stand solid in the slums until I make it out.

God, I know you'll save me every time. I know it'll always be on time and that you'll do everything you can to strengthen my

DARNELLE CUYLER

faith along this journey. Just please don't let me give up on myself before you work your miracle.

I promise to be an inspiration to people.

I'm going to make my goals so big to the point I won't give up. I can't give up. I've noticed that when people give up on themselves or their goals and dreams, they become jealous and envious of other people. I'm going to do everything I can to prevent myself from doing that.

I am going to put in work every day at LSU. Matter of fact, I'm going to put in work even beyond LSU. I didn't get in Florida State the first or the second go round, but I'll find a way to graduate from there too!

And after I'm done with school, I'll get an elite job and buy me a Lambo.

A Black one.

I'm chasing everything I prayed about!

IM NOT GIVING UP ON ME!

PICK UP THE PACE [slap the sign of Ronald Reagan]

I promise on my life I'm going to come across extraordinary people and grind with them. I promise this mindset coming out every time you hit your lowest point!

This mindset gon let it be known, "You're from Altamonte Springs, Florida! You gon make them respect these streets! You the realest thing to come from The Bottom and Grenada!

PICK UP THE PACE [slaps sign of magnolia].

[Stops running and starts walking]

At this point I am depleted and heading home.

The hype is so real right now. I can feel the excitement flowing through my veins and feeling more confident in the pursuit of my goals.

"Every day I'm going to strive to be all that I can be and better others around me along the way."

I'm promise from the bottom of my heart and soul, I ain't gon never stop grinding! I won't ever give up! Every day will be an opportunity to be great!

Every day I'm going to tell people with from the bottom of my heart and soul, "BE GREAT TODAY! NO DAYS OFF!"

BE GREAT TODAY! NO DAYS OFF!

New Beginnings: LSU 2012

The day for me to leave Altamonte finally arrived, and got dammit, I was excited! I had my bags packed, made sure I wasn't forgetting anything important, and was ready to get the hell out of dodge.

And there I was sitting in the backseat staring out the window, lost in a mental abyss. Although I was excited to be leaving the place I fought so desperately to leave, I couldn't help feeling a little guilty. I was leaving my family at a time everyone was going through it. My uncle had cancer and it was so severe, that he had less than a year to live.

On top of that, my grandmother, as active as she was, was starting to move slower. The guardians of time were catching up with her, and the weight of the family drama was weighing her down. I knew she was tired of the family always having issues with another, and to watch my uncle, her son, fade away slowly before her eyes only made it worse.

But I remembered the prayers I said before I embarked on this journey. Accepted the adversity I knew I'd endure. This is what I needed to do, and I needed to see it through.

I saw this as an outlet to bring positivity and hope to what was really going on in my life.

I was the outlet.

BE GREAT TODAY! NO DAYS OFF!

My grandma and uncle were proud. This was my first time ever leaving home and it was a new experience for me.

It was early in the afternoon when I arrived at LSU. I couldn't get settle until I registered for classes and then find an apartment all in the same day.

Now, Mrs. Soula O'Bannon in the math department, was a real one from the start. She was always there for me whenever I needed and was always willing to help wherever she can. Whenever I came to her office, I can hear smooth jazz whistling in the background.

She got me situated with my schedule and after I left her office, I found my first apartment. I lived in a place called *Tiger Plaza*, and it was next to a bunch of clubs in *Tigerland*. It was wild because the first night, we were walking by and seen this guy laid out in front of a store. We figured he was either a drunk or a bum.

The next day I'm sitting at a booth in the McDonalds across the street, knocking down a McGriddle and I heard on one of the television sets, "here live in Baton Rouge, Louisiana a dead man –."

I looked up immediately. Squinting my eyes trying to get a clearer view.

"Damn, that place look familiar," I said to myself. "I think I been there before."

It took me a couple seconds to realize that this was directly across street! That's not even the crazy part. The crazy part was the guy we saw laid out was the same dead man they were reporting on the news.

My first day in Louisiana and I see a dead body.

Welp, this was familiar and to be honest, it didn't even phase me.

My mom and my twin was already heading back home prior to this so I walked back to campus and explored for a while. I was amazed at everything. The buildings, the landscape, the art. All of it was beautiful to me. Hell, Tiger Stadium is one of best places I've ever seen and been in.

After I got everything for school situated, I then started to look forward to my first day.

"I really go to LSU now," I uttered to myself.

DARNELLE CUYLER

I was praying, thanking God for seeing me through, and telling myself it didn't matter what I endure while I'm here.

I'm going to graduate.

Now, I did have a roommate, but I only seen him two or three times during the entire lease. So basically, I lived alone. The first week of school was cool though. I was back at taking 7:30 am classes. I felt like I was in high school again. Thankfully it was only three times a week. Later on that week, I met up with this dude name Bryce. Turns out Bryce & I went to the same school since elementary, and coincidently transferred to LSU. When I met up with Bryce, he introduced me to this dude from Miami name Nestor. Since we all were from Florida, we automatically became family.

Side note, everybody that I met out here that was from Florida, instantly became family. For each other, we were the home away from home. We all had a purpose, and all had things to prove so ultimately, we stuck together and held each other accountable. And also, real recognize real.

After I met Nestor, I met this guy name Curtis. Now Curtis was from Detroit, but he really became a brother to me during my time at LSU.

Now, LSU was a lot of things and boring was not one of them. They really put forth a lot of effort to spread excitement around campus. The hype was real. I couldn't lie to you even if I wanted to. Fall Fest or Housing Fair was always the move. Any event they created that gave out free shirts was nothing short of greatness. It was the real deal. Whenever they were serving free food and drinks, I was in the building because who doesn't love free shit? I love crawfish and they had them by the boat load. The only thing about crawfish that annoyed me was that I'd get tired of picking them long before I was ever full.

Now, class wise, my classes were straight the first semester. You know, nothing too hectic. One of my classes, which was probably my favorite class at LSU, was AAAS 2000. *African and African American History* with Dr. Sullivan.

BE GREAT TODAY! NO DAYS OFF!

On the first day, he said, "Welcome! Now that everyone is seated, I know where everybody is going to sit for the rest of the year. Everyone always has unassigned assigned seats."

Who thinks of that?

However, he wasn't wrong. We all sat in the seats for the rest of the semester.

"Before we get started, all of you will introduce yourselves. I need you to state your name, year, major, and your potential plans after college."

Man, I don't want to do that. I was talking a lot of shit in my head and under my breath. But when I was called on I stood quickly.

"My name Darnelle Cuyler. I'm a transferred sophomore and I'm from Orlando, Florida. I'm also a math major. I just want to say I love all y'all redbones, and when I graduate from here, I'm getting a Lambo."

The whole class laughed immediately, even Dr. Sullivan.

Dr. Sullivan probably thought I was going to be the class clown, but I wasn't. I only spoke when asked too.

After we introduced ourselves, he said, "This class will be based off participation, and no cursing will be permitted in my classroom.

Shit.

I raised my hand.

"We really can't cuss forreal."

"For real. Y'all can state your opinions but you must do it without cursing."

I already knew I was going to fail this class since we can't cuss. Hell, I cussed on the first day. I only had this class on Tuesdays and Thursdays, and every other session it would go from 0-100 really quick.

Dr. Sullivan class always started off cool, calm, and collected, but he never ended class that way. He always took the lead on the topic of the day, then one of my classmates Cimajie would voice her opinion, and it felt like every woman in the class would just follow the leader. Depending on the topic at hand, I would just start laughing whenever I heard a funny take on something. This was also my way of inserting myself into the debate.

DARNELLE CUYLER

"Darnelle," Dr. Sullivan would call me out. "Go ahead. Remember, no cussing."

All the male athletes would laugh before I started talking because they knew I was going to go in and take the class for a spin. During our discussions, in the mist of me laughing and cussing, Dr. Sullivan realized that I be dropping deep knowledge on the topic. One day, our discussion was so great and so informative, that he didn't want to stop the conversation. So, he told me to come by his office during office hours so we can keep it going.

One day my classmates noticed me walking to campus. It was funny to them, but they just didn't get it.

"Bruh why you don't take the bus to campus?"

"Because I would beat the bus to campus every time. Plus, I been walking to school since the 6th grade. I ain't stopping now."

They laughed.

To be honest, I never thought about it. I put on my headphones, listen to Boosie to start my day off right, and then I just start walking. Plus, I don't even think about it.

The only time I caught the bus is if it was raining. Other than that, I was footing it.

One day me and a few of the athletes were leaving Dr. Sullivan class and we had a heart to heart.

"Oh, you're a math major? You're gonna make it. You gotta make it for all of us too. You can't be out here playing and getting caught up. You need to be in the library."

"I go to Middleton literally every single day except game day."

Afterwards, we all parted ways for the day. I was on my way to the Urec to work out and I called Seth. Now, when it came to sports, Seth knew if an athlete was the raw or not.

"Aye, I hang with the starters on the football team all the time, and we got class together. Have you heard of this dude Russell Shepard?"

He said, "hell yeah. He was like the number one recruit coming out of Texas. You moved out to Louisiana, and you hang with D1 athletes now? You're primetime now."

BE GREAT TODAY! NO DAYS OFF!

"Nah, I ain't primetime. I'm just meeting people, hanging with the athletes or Bryce when I'm not studying."

I remembered we went to the National Championship game in January. It was wild game and although we didn't win, with the team we had, I believed we had a chance to make another championship run.

That wasn't the case though.

LSU started catching more L's like it was normal when it wasn't.

I remember someone warning me saying, "When LSU lose a game, it gets real dead out here. Campus will be on suicide watch."

This shit ain't that deep, I thought.

Man, right hand on the bible, when we lost the first game of the season, that following week, campus was so quiet. I didn't see a soul. It was so bad that the whole week my classes felt like graveyard.

All in all, I met a lot of great people, and I learned a lot from that class. My boys Anthony, Russell, and Mickey were on the football team. And my boys Rodney, Aaron, and Rynell were on the track team.

When I was trying to get on the track team, I always talked to them about it. Rodney and Aaron looked out for me when I was trying to get on the track team. But we'll save that for another time. I can't forget about homies Keurvosie, also known as Cookie, Gaby, Alaysia, Tee, and Cimajie. Dr. Sullivan suggested I take a few classes to keep my GPA in good standings. He ended up being one of my mentors at LSU. In fact, he's still my mentor to this day. Throughout the semester I had the same routine. I literally went to class, gym, and the library. I even went to the library on the weekends. I didn't have the money for the books I needed so things were tougher than it needed to be. But I needed to pass no matter what. The first semester had a lot of ups and downs, but I made the most of it.

Campus life brought a lot of excitement into my life. From *Fall Fest* to meeting new people to game day. LSU game was definitely a lifetime experience, to say the least. Now, most schools start tailgating on Friday's. LSU start tailgating on Tuesday's. I know

DARNELLE CUYLER

that sounds untrue, but I'm deadass. I was confused when I saw people in RVs and cars going up and down *Nicholson Drive* on a Tuesday evening.

"What's going on?" I asked this random person driving by.

He shouted, "we're here for the game on Saturday."

Do these people not have jobs? Even if they did, it didn't matter. They were willing to quit if they didn't take a week off for an LSU game. If you knew a lot of people, tailgating on Saturday's would be a blast, but if you didn't, it was straight. One thing I did learn while tailgating on game day was that LSU fans are die-hard fans.

One guy yelled, "you wanna go, bro?"

"You wanna go?" The other screamed back.

What the fuck does that mean, I thought.

Then they started fighting. *You wanna go, bro* means let's run these hands if you about that life. Now, the first half of the semester I didn't tailgate, nor did I go to any of the games because I didn't know anyone. Bryce and Nestor were already turnt up, and I would just watch the game at home.

However, the first game I did go to was live as hell. I went to the *Gold Game* where they played South Carolina. I remember like it was yesterday. It was October 13th, 2012, the same day as my niece's birthday. We were deep. It was me, Bryce, Nestor, Curtis, and a bunch of their friends they met from summer semester. LSU was losing the whole time until the fourth quarter. My first LSU game and they were able to get a dub.

Every game after that was live. Especially in 2014 when we rushed the field after a huge win over Ole Miss. Every game after that I got on the jumbotron, national tv, and won a free shirt. Every Saturday was a shake back from how rough the week was for me. I even remember the day my uncle called me and said he saw me on TV. I was so hyped. I couldn't believe it. Over the next four years, that was the life I was living when I went to the game.

That following week of school, campus was back to life. We went to a party with Nestor friends it was on a Tuesday. It was straight, but that's where I met Meagan. Meagan told me she works at the Urec and I told I was in there every day. But since our

BE GREAT TODAY! NO DAYS OFF!

schedules were different, we never saw each other. One day I went during her schedule and said Hey.

Even though I had quite a few good moments, this semester always felt like the bad out weighted the good.

On a day-to-day basis, I was constantly fighting ongoing stress that I was really out here struggling with no money. I was constantly struggling to make sure I was going to get a good meal that day, or else I was going to starve, and I starve a lot of nights out here.

More nights than anyone would believe.

No one notice, but I was always embarrassed to share that anyway because I was basically out here with the clothes on my back. Every time I called home for money it was always a problem.

Always.

My mom always made it seem like it was a bad thing I left home.

"Why didn't you wait till the spring so I can help you?"

I ignored her. How I saw things, if she wasn't going to help me now, she was never going to help me. She acts like I didn't know what was happening in our family and in the neighborhood. Like we didn't grow in the same place. We were literally watching my uncle waste away in front of us and then there's certain people in our neighborhood that just wanted to sell drugs and shoot people.

What was the point of me staying around all that bullshit?

Nothing.

My brother and sisters were the same way too. It was hard asking them for money or help. Granted, they had they own bills, problems, and had to deal with the same problems as the family too. But they made me feel like it was a burden to help me do better in life. My family was really going through hard times, and in a time, we should've banded together, we were divided. Whenever they did send money to me, it was never from the kindness of their hearts. It came kicking and screaming, so to speak. But I watched them give other people money like it was nothing. This frustrated me the most because I felt like if they can do that, they can certainly help little by little every month. I knew they hated when I called because a couple of times, I can hear them talking shit about me before hanging up the phone.

DARNELLE CUYLER

The worse is when I get off the phone after being torn down by my mom, I would have to call my grandma. It was the worst because I would be trying to talk cool, calm, and collective like everything was good while I'm starving and rent coming due. My grandma and I would talk about the good, the bad, and how everyday I'm working so hard. She would tell my mom to add money with the money she was trying to send.

"I will make a way grandma."

As long as they sent the money by the first so I can pay my rent and not be homeless, I was fine. When things got really bad, I had to swallow my pride even more and call Peanut & Stevan. I ask if they can give me half because I was already getting the other half from my mom and grandma.

I needed a job badly.

This was my life from September through December. I just kept saying, man I need me a job. If I had a job, I wouldn't be struggling like this. I wouldn't have to ask anybody for nothing, and I'll be alright.

September and October weren't the best months for me. It was always something. If it wasn't one thing, it's another. I started failing exams and I was devastated. I just got here. I can't be taking losses like this, this early in the semester. Then we took a devastating loss back home. I couldn't catch a break. I was trying to stay keep it together mentally. I had to work even harder than before if I wanted to make it out here at LSU. I had to endure the *hard grind*. I had to do a lot of late-night grinding in the library. Just to turn back around to get in there first thing the next morning. Walking home super late down Nicholson Drive was always endured by my headphones and good music. I had to tell myself that in order to do what's never been done before, I have to put in the work. In order to be successful, it's going to take some lonely days and some lonely nights. While everybody was out getting drunk or just kicking it, I was putting in the work. People want the success but don't want to put in the work.

I refuse to let up on this dream.

November and December were just terrible months. Jobs were turning me down left & right, and I been living off $20 worth of groceries every two weeks because everything I had went to rent. I've been living like this since I first got to Baton Rouge. I found out this job was hiring in October, I did the interview in November, but I wouldn't be able to start until January.

I couldn't catch a break.

I can say November was a bit better because it was my birthday month and I always enjoy myself on my birthday. I promise myself that if I don't do anything else, I will enjoy my birthday. I did what I do best, went home and enjoyed some Oreos.

Throughout the semester I would write motivational letters too myself to keep my head up.

I kept writing letters and notes to help me stay true to the game plan. I have to keep the prayers and thoughts that were created on Sanford Ave alive. I'm not even going to lie to you, it was hard out here. And it was lonely.

God, I humbly pray to you to send me some friends that I can just laugh with. I did like the few friends I made, but I don't hang with them too often.

I pray you send me some that I can cry laugh with.

I think that's what I needed the most to get through these hard times. I'll give them a collateral to grind and struggle with them. I think the cry laughing will go hand and hand for each of us. I won't be greedy and ask for a lot but send a few real ones. I promise I'll be grateful forever. Bring me friends that'll accept me for who I am. One's that'll laugh with me when I walk through the door or come see them.

I know a lot of people see me and think, "oh here he go with the bullshit. He full of shit."

I mean, I kind of am but I'm also full of Oreos and laughs too. And I'm here to have a good time so, let's do this! We can scrape up money to share food. Hell, we can even wear each other clothes. I don't even care. I'm not embarrassed because all I know is the struggle. I'll take away the embarrassment for them. We're struggling together. I'm sitting here laughing Lord because I know when you send them, they'll be my family. You'll send them all at the right time. Even the few I've already met I can tell we already here for life. I'm trying to keep it as simple as possible, but I don't know what to really ask for. Plus, all that laughing will keep these

DARNELLE CUYLER

abs looking good. Sometimes all I want to do is sit and laugh because it's draining trying to stay motivated and to stay strong every single day.

Sometimes my head hurts.

I'm getting tired of missing meals because roman noodles got the best of me. I'd rather starve then to keep eating them but starving just to eat breakfast in the morning be killing me too sometimes. I think that if I was around good company, I wouldn't be thinking about my struggles as much. I also don't want to be selfish. God, let me benefit and be of value to them as well. I want it to be known I'm here with and for them. I'll stand with them through thick and thin. They don't have to be lonely or struggle by themselves. We are riding that struggle bus together. We can also laugh in important meetings, or loudly in public. I don't want them to second guess the type of person I am. I'm not really good for much else when it comes to natural talent. I pray that you let them know that I'm behind them 100%.

I'm only behind them while I laugh and open up these Oreos from a vending machine. The good thing about it, I'll share because it'll brighten the mood. Plus, we both broke and hungry.

I pray you bless me with friends that will truly understand and value this Louisiana culture. From a person that's not from here it's definitely one to experience. I'm an open-minded person and like new things, so I wouldn't say everyone will accept it.

I really love how it is LSU over everything out here. It's either you down with us or it's fuck you.

It ain't no in-between.

I mean, I wouldn't want there to be, but it's wild that every person really has that mindset out here. I think it's wild that this university produces a lot of the resources for the entire state. I guess being from Florida and we have multiple powerhouse schools I guess I never thought about how one university can make such a huge contribution to a state.

A culture with this environment and amazing food is also wild to me. They argue about what area code has the best food and just act so glorified from it. Some areas are better for seafood while others are better for the meal entirely. All honestly, I think it depend on who cooking it and where did they get the water from to prepare the shit. I kid you not, it's people that's using double filtered water and those that's using that water were straight out the swamp waters of the Mississippi River. All they do is drown the food in salt and pepper to claim that it has flavor.

Nah.

I had jambalaya where you taste nothing but salt and pepper.

"Oh, this taste so good!"

All I taste is salt and high blood pressure, y'all tripping.

It tastes good when you hungry, of course, but on a regular day some people just over do it with the seasoning. All and all the food good everywhere. You just have to be careful about where you get it from because some people think that the more seasoning the better but nah. I also try to figure out the music ratio, which is wild to me. Especially during game day. They literally go from the most backwoods Alabama- Tennessee- Texas ass country music to Set It Off by Boosie. I don't mind the music at all though. I just want to know who taught y'all how to DJ? They making sure everybody has a good time to say the least.

I'll get used to it eventually.

As I sit here and think about the way of life out here, I just pray I have people that will help me enjoy it to the fullest. I can't wait for those people to show up in my life because this life I'm living now ain't it. I know it'll all work out. I just have to keep praying until they come. Until then, I'll continue to practice on staying strong and staying positive.

I would get so lost in my thoughts about the transition out here to the point tears would roll down my face. It was like this every night until I fell asleep. But I would wake up every day stronger and walk down *Nicholson Drive* with pride.

I go to LSU and I will be the first one to make it out.

As the semester was ending, I received an email from the bursar's office.

"If you don't pay for your classes for the upcoming Spring semester, you will be released from the University." ...

Man what?

DARNELLE CUYLER

What the hell is this? I just started going to school here! How can they do this? I started stressing immediately but I quickly told myself to calm down and go talk to someone.

December 2012 really changed me. Rent was due and my family was barely answering, I finally got them to send me some money and God is my witness, they sent the barest minimum. I had to call Peanut and ask for some money again.

"It's hard over here. I don't have that much to give. It's tough over here."

I started begging. "Trust me, I know. But can you please send me money one more time? I'm crying and I don't have anything. I promise you, I'm trying. I finally got a job and I start in January. I promise if you send me money one more time, I'll never ask for money again."

I was passed embarrassed.

Pride? What's that? I just didn't want to be homeless in Baton Rouge, Louisiana for the holidays.

On the last day that campus was open I went to bursar to try to figure out what can be done about my classes. When I got there, I just had to tell them what it really was. I told myself I wasn't going to cry but fuck that.

"Can y'all please help me? I don't have anything to my name, and I came all the way out here from Orlando, Florida. I can't go back. I'll find a way. I'll get scholarships or play sports or something. Just please don't kick me out of school. I finally got a job and I start in January. I will take what I can out of my checks just to show I will make payments. Please help me. I'll graduate from here and start a scholarship for people that struggled just like me. I'll do whatever needed if you help me. Just please don't give up on me."

"You'll be ok," they said. "The payment isn't due until late January and the university does give extensions."

I felt so relieve. I saved a lot of money to get here, and I didn't want to leave. I felt bad for breaking down in front of them. I went home and just ate some Oreos while contemplating life. Christmas was coming up and I didn't have anywhere to go. I sat in my apartment all alone. The only person that called to tell me

BE GREAT TODAY! NO DAYS OFF!

Merry Christmas and talk with me for a while was my grandmother. It was at that moment, I no longer cared for the holidays. My brother did send a gift a couple days later. It was stuck at the post office, but unfortunately, it didn't change how I felt.

Rent was due again, and this time my mom and I got into it until she just sent the whole thing.

During the holidays my mom would always try to go above and beyond to get everyone something for Christmas so nobody will feel left out. She'd work hard to make sure everybody would at least have something. She was definitely a caring person when it came to the holidays.

Out of frustrated, I lashed out at her.

"You always doing stuff for other people that never do the same for you. You can give everybody money, but when it comes to your kids, it's a problem. You're buying everybody and their momma something for Christmas but none of them ever asked if I was straight? Bought your kids and grandkids something for Christmas? Never!"

Needless to say, she didn't like that shit. She sent the rent money and didn't say nothing else. I never cursed my momma out, but I'd damn sure gave my brother an ear full about that. It was hard constantly trying to explain everything to everyone. No one knew this, but I had a prepaid Boost mobile cell phone. I could only talk for so long otherwise I would run out of minutes. I kept the conversations to 2minutes or less otherwise you was getting hung up on. I was really struggling this semester.

I kept my word about not asking Peanut for money anymore. I knew come 2013, I was going to have to work my ass off. I'm done relying on my family and begging all the time.

Now that I have a job, things will get better. Things will be different.

As the new year was approaching, I evaluated the good and the bad of 2012. I knew I had to get my mind right for 2013. I was getting ready to further my Journey at Louisiana State University.

LSU 2013

After the second week of school, I was officially locked into my classes. I would go to the Urec every day after my AAAS 2000 class. Even if I didn't go after class, I would still go to the Urec before the day is over with.

I still remember when I first went to the Urec.

I swiped my card and I walked around the facility. I found out quick that the rec was dead from 11:00 AM to 2:00 PM. Anything after 2:00 PM, you can let it go. I would go there and workout to get back in shape. I made friends with the best athletes on the track team from my year, so I was good on the amount of people who could vouch for me. Even though my papers came late, and I didn't get to try out this season, I would still come to the rec every day and workout so I'm ready for next year. So, I would go to the Urec for about an hour or so to workout. After I work out, I would be in the Urec longer because I would use the computers in the front to do my astronomy homework.

The Urec track was my new *Trenches* that took the place of *Sanford Ave*. I can run on the indoor track for hours because there was no one there during that time frame. There was a day September that I ran 5 miles. I needed to clear my head of what was going on in my life; from family issues to school conflicts to financial hardships. And then I heard about a loss that had just taken place in the hood back home.

It was too much happening all at once.

I stopped running for a second because I saw this dude hop on the track and started doing sprints. So, I started doing sprints as well on the other side of the track.

Everybody out here real, but I'm from Florida so I'm realer. Easy money.

So, I'm watching him run and I'm like, "damn, buddy sliding. He's probably an athlete. He probably run a 4.4 in the 40m dash. He really is sliding. Fuck it, Imma race him."

I started running slower and positioned myself a certain way so we can end up taking off at the same time. I timed it perfectly in my head. I never looked at him, but he knew we was racing. Even after running 5 miles and 6 sprints, not only was I not tired, but I didn't have any plans on losing. My competitive nature wasn't going to let me lose.

Once we finished racing, I was slowly walking off the track. He walked up behind me.

"Aye yo! You ain't have to leave me like that."

Trying to catch my breath, I ask, "did I leave you by a lot?"

"Hell yeah. You were fucking moving."

"My bad bro. You just looked so fast, I just had to race you."

"What's your 40 time? 4.3? It definitely can't be slower than a 4.4."

"I don't know but I am training to get on the track team."

"Bruh, you got that with ease. Do that. My name Carlis bro, take my number. Let me know whenever you plan on doing sprints. I'll be down to run with you."

"Alright, I'll be in here tomorrow. I come every day. No days off."

"Oh, word. I'll be in here tomorrow."

And then the next day we were back at it. We got to talking about a few things involving school, sports, and then he asked if I ever used the sauna before. Of course, I did. After our workout, we sat in the sauna for a bit. In between us doing sprints and decom-

DARNELLE CUYLER

pressing in the sauna, we got to know each other more and gave our life story.

From that day on, Carlis really became one of day one's. He was telling me how he was born & raised in New Orleans and trying to make it out doing what he loved to do as well. What track is for me, wrestling was for him. He was honestly the first person I met on campus I felt comfortable enough to talk about my problems with. We were putting in work every day after that like our lives depended on it, in which it did. I remember telling him "I came here with nothing and I'm going to put in work every day. I'm going to motivate everybody I become friends with. Imma do whatever it takes to make sure we all make it. Imma be everybody biggest hype man and nobody from Louisiana will outwork me." Carlis was already working at the Urec, and grinding was not something that wasn't new to him.

One day, as a gift, he gave me a red g-shock. I still got it and use it to this day to time myself when I run.

A week or so later, I stumbled into the gymnasium on the basketball court and watched this dude shoot around. Man, the way he moved and shot the ball, I just knew he had to be on the basketball team. Everything he shot he made. He made the shit look easy.

"Damn, you be shooting. Are you on the basketball team?"

"Nah," he chuckled. "I practice with the girls basketball team to help them get better. I would practice with the men's basketball team but the way my schedule set up, it's not feasible.

"Damn that's crazy!"

"Yeah, I know. My name Chris by the way, and I work here at the Urec. Obviously, you know I go to school here and work with the basketball team on the side."

"Nice to meet you man. My name is Darnelle. You're the second person I met at the Urec. I met Carlis last week."

He laughed a bit. "Carlis? Oh yeah, that's my boy. Where you from?"

"I'm from Orlando, Florida where you from?"

"New Orleans."

Damn, everybody from New Orleans.

BE GREAT TODAY! NO DAYS OFF!

The next day Chris, Carlis, and I had a workout session. I started telling Chris about my life, everything I was enduring, and surprisingly, he was going through similar issues. From that moment on, we became brothers from different mothers. We were always hitting each other up making sure we were straight.

Now, as we head into October, my life at the Urec started changing. I walked in the rec one night to work out and sit in the sauna afterwards, but life had other plans. I finished a decent workout on the stationary bicycle, and then got some water from the water fountain. This white dude came behind me and was smiling hard as fuck.

In my head I thought buddy tripping, but I decided to be my normal friendly self and overshared more than I needed to. Call it a nervous mechanism.

"Damn bro," I wiped my face. "I see you pushing a lot of weight. I used to lift weights in high school. I was on the weightlifting team and when we were training for the upcoming track season. I should've went to states my senior year, but I got cheated at regionals. I still lift weights from time to time to stay in shape."

He looked shocked. "For real? You ever thought about trying out for our track team?"

"Of course, but I missed the deadline to talk to the track coach about joining the team."

He took a large gulp of water.

"Ah, okay. You think you can swing by our powerlifting practice on Thursday to see how you like it?"

Now, you know I agreed to come to go check them out. I had no reason to not go. This was going to be an opportunity for me to see how they practice and a way for me to introduce myself.

"Yeah, I can be there."

"Alright, cool. My name Kaleb by the way."

"Darnelle." We shook hands.

"Alright Darnelle, nice to meet you. See you Thursday bro."

He was still smiling kind of hard. I kind of laughed with him but I was more or less trying to figure out why he cheesing so hard? I still don't know to this day, but whatever.

DARNELLE CUYLER

When Thursday came, I made my way over to their practice and he introduced me to everyone. He also walked me through their practice and let me watch a few of the guys that was near my weight class. I went to the back and seen this dude sitting in the bench. He was huge and quiet.

"My name Alvin, but everybody calls me Chip." He extended his hand.

"Chip as in Alvin and the chipmunks?" We both laughed.

Their practice was short, but Kaleb wanted to see what I can really lift to see if I can make the Powerlifting team. This would also help him see if I was a compatible to get along with everyone else. I was lifting in front of Zack, Big Travis, Tyler, Malcolm, Chip, Conor, and Ariel. They complimented me a lot and let me know that I was pretty strong. I knew I could do more, but I was a little drained from my workout earlier.

I deadlifted 315 pounds three times for the first time.

"Give me a couple of weeks, I can probably do 405.

Kaleb laughed a little. "That's a huge jump from 315 to 405. No one makes a jump like that, that quickly."

"Ehh, I know how to perform when I'm fresh. I'm very competitive and I'm keeping my legs strong to run track here."

To be honest, the weight wasn't heavy at all.

Chip was quiet the whole time and didn't say much after our initial interaction. But when he heard me mention something about track, he broke his silence.

"Who you know on the track team? I train with the track team every day. I never heard of you."

I knew he was trying to fact check me. He probably thinks I'm a liar or full of shit and that's cool. He doesn't know me, but he's going to respect me above all else.

"I hang with Rodney and Aaron every day. We got class together. I would've talked to the track coach, but my papers came late. So, I had to miss this season.

As we were leaving, we got a chance to chop it up a bit. He was a thrower, so he threw the discus and the shotput. I can feel it in his tone that he was still doubting me. He could've just called them up if it was that serious but never did. Then the following

BE GREAT TODAY! NO DAYS OFF!

Tuesday, he sees me walking through the quad with Rodney and Aaron cracking jokes like we usually do. His tone was different when I showed up to the next practice.

"I seen y'all in the quad. You really do be with them. Respect."

I sat there like damn, he really thought I was out here lying. After that Thursday practice, I joined LSU Powerlifting team. They were really supportive in the weight room, and they really became my homies. I made some new friends as well. Jalynn, Malcolm, Travis, Beau, Jordan, Jessie, Emily, Jessica, Blood, Pat, Ryan, Blake, Picou, Gabe, Trey, Keya, Hollie, and Tyler. Kaleb, Conor, Ariel, Tim, Zack, Kayli, Taylor, and Chip became family or part of my tribe as the years passed.

Chip was a man of a few words, but the weight rack was always talking for him. Chip and I were cool, but it was a little tension because of where we were from. As you know by now, I'm from Florida. He was from New York. It was a silent competition of which state was superior but real recognize real and it was all love at the end of the day. What got us closer was the fact that we were going through similar financial situations as well. The out-of-state fees was killing us. We talked about our lives back home and being that relative to go to college to make it out. The pressures of being a black man in this society and always having to beat the odds. Chip started to look out for me. He would always swipe his student ID card for me for either lunch or dinner at *The 5* or *459*, our dining areas on campus. I didn't peep it at first, but he became my mentor really. I needed it too simply because I was struggling. I had multiple people trying to keep my head on straight since I was dealing with a lot on a day-to-day basis.

We had practice Tuesdays, Thursdays, and Sundays. I was working out twice a day on those days, because I still was going in between classes from 11:00 AM to 2:00 PM.

In between classes on some days, I would go to the *Middleton library* and do my homework on the first floor of *Middleton*. Now, the first floor of *Middleton* was always the best place to be social wise. However, I was so focused that I never paid attention to none of the shenanigans happening. I just did my work and then walked

DARNELLE CUYLER

down *Nicholson Drive* to the crib. There were some nights I went to the library after powerlifting practice.

I remember one night after practice, Chip, Zack, Tim, and I went to the library to get some work done. We walked in and I remember making a smooth left to go to my usual spot on the first floor.

Everyone looked confused.

"Where are you going bro," Zack asked.

"The first floor"

"The first floor? Who the hell sits on the first floor?"

Everybody was laughing.

Now, in my defense, I never walked far enough into the library to figure out how to get to any other floor. He made me feel dumb a little. On top of that, he was laughing way too hard for my liking. You ever been roasted and then the roasting session turns on you? That's my current position.

"Always go to any floor except the first floor to work in peace and quiet."

I snapped a little.

"I tune that shit out, and just do my homework. I never cared for the noise to be real."

After spending so much time grinding together in the weight room and the library getting work done, we all could eat together. After practice on Sunday, Zack invited us to his mom's house to eat dinner.

"Y'all want to go my momma house for dinner?"

It was perfect timing because I was actually planning on starving that night, but eating actual food is a better idea.

Mr. and Mrs. Coleman showed love since day one. We went to dinner at Zack's parents' house just about every Sunday after that. Because of my situation, I knew I was guaranteed a meal on Sundays. I just needed to figure out the rest of the week.

One day at a time man, one day at a time.

A few days later, Chip and I went to go workout at the Urec, and I was able to introduce him to Carlis and Chris. Then we all started pulling up to the sauna like it was the meeting grounds for therapy. We would vent about what's going on in our

BE GREAT TODAY! NO DAYS OFF!

lives, what challenges we were facing, our grind, and even crack some stupid ass jokes. One day we sat in the sauna, and I was pretty much being vulnerable with them by sharing my life and things I was facing every day since I've been here.

"Every day I'm out here struggling to stay afloat. I have to be at certain places at a certain time, or I was going to starve that day. I have to make $20 of groceries work or else I'm ass out. Sometimes, I go almost a whole day without eating and when I'm starving, it's hard for me to sleep when my stomach growling at me."

They had that look on their face like damn,

"This is my life on a week-to-week basis because I just don't have money to eat. Between hunger, studying, and stressing, sleep passes me by. The times I did sleep, I cried myself to sleep every time. I can't call my family because when I do, they always feel like I'm begging. A few weeks ago, we took a major loss in the hood. And it's hard to sit in class and focus on the lecture because there's so much violence going on in the hood. I'm working so hard to do better and make my people proud. I'm trying to be the change so they can see that it is possible to be more. Yet, that's not the case. I'm a burden to my family. I see people in my neighborhood them shouting out everybody in jail but won't say a word to me. They all think that I think I'm better than them because I left for school, but I really just wanted a better life. A better hand at the cards that I was dealt. I can feel hatred and jealousy they have towards me, but I'm still working hard to make them proud. I just want to motivate people to go hard and do better even though I'm struggling. Y'all really all I got. Y'all the only ones who from the hood and know how hard it is to try to make it while feeling alone."

Carlis patted me on the back.

"You the realest bro. Shit, we'll be your family. We'll support you in any way we can."

Chris blurted out, "every time we see each other it's family over everything from now on. We got you."

"Word," Chip said. I told you, he's a man of few words.

Every day I tried my best to not let what was I was struggling with on the inside, show on the outside. I had keep telling myself *I Will Make It. Don't Give Up. No Days Off.*

DARNELLE CUYLER

I remember walking home from campus one and the weather was so nice, it prompted me to call my grandmother. I was telling her that I was doing good in my classes and making new friends. The only thing I needed was a job.

"You'll get a job soon. Just keep the faith and you'll be alright."

Now at this time, we're approaching the end of October, and it seems like the janitors at the Urec changed their schedules or something. I would see these two older black janitors, and one of them definitely had a calm presence about them. One of them would walk by and say, "alright now, young fella," and I would always greet him. He'd always smile and seeing him every day always made my day a little better. I was still going to the Urec to do my Astronomy homework at the same spot every day.

One day he spoke to me and we had a longer conversation than normal.

"Man, I see you in here every day. They need to give you a job here at this point."

I laughed a bit. "I wish! I need a job so damn bad and I would love to work here! I would come to work every day, I promise."

He smiled. "God got you young fella. "I'll keep a look out for you when they start hiring again. They call me Stanford by the way. That's Gail over there. I'll see you around little brother."

"My name Darnelle. I'll being seeing you, Mr. Stanford!"

Mr. Stanford was so cool. His nickname was Smiley cause that's all he do is smile. Every day I would make it my mission to go say hey to Mr. Stanford. I also informed him on what was going on in my personal life and he told me that he was praying for me.

During the last week of October, I saw the hiring sign on the desk. I applied as soon as I could get to a computer. I remember letting Carlis and Chris know about my application, and they said they'd put in a word for me. Not too long after, I saw Carlis and Chris talking to a supervisor on shift, and they introduced me to her when they saw me. Her name was Nicole. They pretty much hyped me up to her and let her know about a few things I was experiencing. Nicole told me she'd only do it if I work every day because some people don't like working and she didn't like working with slackers. I promised her nobody will out work me, and I won't take a day off if she helped me get the job. I'd pick up every shift that hit the trade board no matter the time.

I was still stressed and struggling, but I finally had some good things brewing. November came and the weather and atmosphere was so refreshing. November was always a good month for me. I forgot which week it was in November, but I got an email saying, "Congratulations. We would like to interview for a job at the LSU UREC."

I WAS HYPED! I PRAYED every hour like clockwork that I would be able to do well at this interview and land this job. I was fighting to keep my grades up, enjoying my new friends, football season, and being a part of the LSU Powerlifting Club team.

In the middle of November, I got the details of when the interview would be, and I showed up twenty minutes early. I wasn't nervous at all. I was determined. I sat in the front row and then this girl sat next to me. I realized she was in Dr. Sullivan class with me. She sat in the first row, but she never spoke except the first day of class. However, I missed what she was saying since I was too focused on what I was going to say.

The Interviewers walked in finally.

"Hi, I'm Julie!"

After Julie introduced herself, everyone else introduced themselves. She asked us to submit two forms of identification which was our driver's license and our social security card. I didn't mean to, but the girl next to me, I peeped that her birthday was right by mine.

Then I looked at my ID.

Damn my shit ugly, good Lord.

So, I hurried and put my paper over my license. As we were going through the interview, they asked us about ourselves and why should we hire you. Everyone was pretty much saying the same thing, so I had to make sure I stand out.

"I'm very motivated and determined. I come to the Urec every single day. I come here to do my astronomy homework and I can easily get on the shift afterwards. I've used every machine in the facility, so I'm comfortable with teaching people how whenever necessary. I also know a few people that work here, such as Carlis, Chris, Nicole, and Mr. Stanford. I told them I would come to work every day if they helped me get a job. I promise if you give me a chance, I will make you proud and you won't have any issues out of me. I promise I will give my all and come to work every day. I will bring high energy to the table and motivate everybody every day. I promise I will if you let me work for you."

After I spoke, I can feel my emotions rising inside of me, but I was able to stay calm and collected. I also felt the energy in the room change. It was almost like if everyone wanted Julie to hire me. She smiled and kept it moving. I felt my eyes watering up, so I hurried and wiped them.

Julie finished taking notes.

"Okay, I'll be sending out an email later in the week."

As we were leaving, I spoke to the girl sitting next to me.

"Wait, don't you have Dr. Sullivan class with me?"

She giggled. "Yeah. You be in there acting crazy and going off."

We both laughed.

"Darnelle." I introduced myself.

"Edcharra."

"I peeped yo ID."

She laughed again. "I peeped yours too. We got the best birthday. Good luck. I hope we both get this job."

"You too! We got this!"

We went our separate ways.

I felt super good about the interview, but I needed to go home to pray and get my mind right. I got home and opened up a pack of Oreos so fast. I had to calm my nerves. I started praying and thanking God. I knew it was going to happen. I put in the work for it.

"God, I promise I'll stand on my word if you let me get this job. I promise I'll give them people my all. I'll work every day if I need to. No Days Off. I'll pick up everybody slack. I won't com-plain at all. I'll be able to work and not have to stress my family out about money. I'll keep my promise to Carlis, Chris, and Nicole. Thank you for placing them in my life and helping me even get an interview. Please let me get this job. I pray this prayer in your name, Amen."

I tried not to think about the job so much the rest of the week. So, I just put in more work on my classes and working out. The next week came I got another email.

"Congratulations! We would like to offer you a position for Operations Assistant."

I was so excited!

I finally got a job! I was walking home, called my grandma and told her the good news. When I got home, I reread the email and it said the start date was January 7th, 2013.

Jesus take the wheel.

I can't catch a break. I got to wait two months to start! Then my birthday came, and I didn't do anything, but go to class and devour some Oreos when I got home. This was also the first birthday I experienced where I didn't see my twin. We texted each other happy birthday and that was it. I still enjoyed the day though since we were coming off a win over Ole Miss this past Saturday. Then Thanksgiving came, and I just stayed at the apartment all day. It wasn't much but I was thankful I was going to LSU. As the sweet joy of November was coming to end, December didn't seem like it was going to bring any cheer to my life. As the semester was winding down, I was doing all I can to stay positive and to stay afloat. I finished with 3.0 grade point average. It was a decent GPA but I didn't anticipate it to be that high again if I was going to keep struggling the way I was struggling.

The powerlifting team signed me up for a small meet to qualify for nationals.

"Man, I can lift over 405 on the deadlift."

They really thought I was all talk. They wanted me to hit certain numbers to just qualify. I did do good on bench and squat and I was begging them to let me go in on the deadlift.

"Yo, let's just see if he can really do it," Zack said. "He's just going to keep asking about it."

Tyler and Ariel were not trying hearing it. I was in the back warming up and I couldn't pick up 315lbs because my hands was sweating. I couldn't get a good grip on it.

Big Travis walked by saying, "yeah, you all talk."

DARNELLE CUYLER

They were all was looking at me like I was a scrub. Chip, a man of few words told me to put some chalk on my hands and try again. It was too easy to lift after that. They went from thinking I was all talk to thinking that I can actually do this. They put on 385 pounds, and it was easy money for me. So, they decided ok, get the first lift to secure nationals and then we can go from there. So, they put 405 pounds to secure a spot. Then, 435lbs on the bar for my second try.

"Stop playing with me. Put 500 pounds on the bar. Imma crack it right after I bump this Boosie."

I'm focused and ready to do work. They definitely put on 450 pounds. The whole team was hyped. They were looking at me differently after the meet. They realized I was a monster in the weight room. I was kind of pissed and told Chip that I could've easily did more and I'm going to pull 500 pounds at nationals. Since I wasn't able to run track, Imma just go hard on the power-lifting team but still do my sprints every day. I definitely was striving to bring a different level of energy to the table. They started to re-alize that I talk trash for the hell of it, but I'm able to back it up with my work ethic. My words weren't going to do me justice when it was time to grind, and that's okay. They were witnessing full mind control and motivation when it come to the grind. During the holiday break I was having a lot of personal problems, but I was ready for the new year. I got a new job, new classes, new friends, and people supporting me throughout this journey.

It's 2013 now. LET'S DO THIS!

The first day of school was good. I received another email about my fee bill, and it started to bother me a little. But I told my-self that I had an extension and to just focus on my classes and work right now. I went to the training at work and then we had to work a shift in every position before we could pick up shifts. I saw my friend Edcharra got the job as well and we were hyped for each other. We had to get some shifts together. My first shift was working the front desk with Madisan. When I was getting off, that's when I met the other supervisors coming in for a supervisor meeting. The next shift was the best one. I worked at the EQ desk with Emily Mason. The EQ desk was where all the equipment, rentals, clothes, and other things imaginable were located. She reminded me quick that it's hard to get EQ shifts because the vets love them. We talked about our life, sports, and how we both was from out of state. She the one who made me realize I'd just missed the cut off to get in-state tuition after two years. After this shift Emily and I became close friends for sure.

The next shift was the gym court. This where I met Myron. Myron was like the face of campus rec. He had three jobs. Which was crazy to me. He had his on tv show on campus. Gym shift was my least favorite at first, but it grew on me after doing it for a se-mester. Then I was able to pick up shifts whenever I wanted. Julie didn't know what she did when she hired me. I know she was prob-ably thinking that I'd only work there a semester or two and that was it. Nah, she doesn't know me. I'm a man of my word. Imma work every day until I graduate. Since she gave me my first job here, Imma give them my all. I was picking up every shift that touched the trade board. I needed money so bad. The next week I had max hours for the week.

The best shifts were the EQ desk shifts. Chelsey and Carlis wasn't letting up on those shifts either. I always did what they told me not too. We couldn't change the channel, eat, or do homework. I did all three every single time.

"Now, if Brad catch you, you're going to be in trouble."

Brad literally saw me eating Oreos and watching Tom and Jerry on a shift. I offered him some, he just shook his head and kept going about his business. He probably didn't mind because those mid-morning shifts were super dead. My schedule was literally class, workout, library, and work. I mean every rotation possible I made sure I hit the Urec and library Monday through Sunday. I took no days off. Not one.

At the beginning of the semester, I was in financial aid and bursar every day trying to get my classes cleared. I told them I fi-nally got a job at the Urec, and I can pay on my tuition. It was stressful. The only people that knew this was happening to me was Chip, Carlis, Chris, Curtis, and Myron. I never said a word to no one else about it. Some days they would sit in the lobby and wait for me. I would go to them every day and no luck. Now, this prob-lem took place every semester I was there. Carlis, Chris, Myron,

DARNELLE CUYLER

Curtis, and Chip stood by me every semester as I dealt with this until they graduated. I remember getting released from the university and was still going to class. I had to go to Mrs. O'Bannon office every time to get my classes registered again. I was so embarrassed every time, but she was so proud of me. At the last minute, I would always get my classes registered. I was still dealing with the same struggles of last year, but I was working which made it a little easy for me. Working had its setbacks too. I was working too much, and it took away from my studies, which led me to failing a few classes here and there.

I loved working at the Urec. I was happy to come to work every day. I told myself that I won't be person people want me to be, I'll be the person people need me to be! I'm coming through like Batman haha. I started working squad shifts with Chris and Carlis. I started a tradition that I would call my grandmother every Sunday to tell her how I was doing, update her on my life, and spend time just talking with her.

February was quickly approaching, and I was short on my rent. My grandmother told me she would make my mother send some money and say it was from her. I ain't want to ask her for none, especially since she just sent me some money not too long ago. Then the Sunday before rent was due, when I got off the phone with my grandmother, my mom called me right after. She was cursing at me asking why I didn't wait for her to help me.

I just went off.

"Don't curse on my phone no more! All you do is tear me down! And what do you mean wait till the Spring? It's the Spring now and you barely trying to help. You help me pay rent but it always come with you complaining and trying to argue. If you, Candice, Arthur, and Danielle send me just a little bit consistently and collectively, I'll have enough leftover and I wouldn't be struggling like this. I know how much y'all make and the bills y'all got. There's no way y'all can't be helping me more. I had to call and beg Peanut all last semester cause y'all won't step up. You do the bare minimum of what a parent supposed to do. I want to do better in life and y'all don't help. Y'all sent money twice and swear y'all sent the world. You are mad cause I wanted to leave? You act

BE GREAT TODAY! NO DAYS OFF!

like I want to be in Altamonte while all that drama going on. But you know what? Now that I got a job, soon I won't even have to ask y'all for money no more. I promise to God on everything I stand for, you call and cuss on my phone again, I promise you'll never hear from me or see me again. I don't care what happen. I'll die out here before I ever call on you if you cuss at me again. All I try to do is work hard to make y'all proud and all you do is cuss me out. I don't ever cuss at you but that's all you do to me. I promise to God, cuss on my phone again and it'll be your last!"

I hung up in her face. I didn't give a damn. I'm not having nobody talk to me crazy like that anymore. She just sent the money and let it be. From that day forth, she didn't cuss me out no more, at least not over the phone while I was living in Louisiana.

In the month of February everything went South. I was struggling in my classes, I was going to work every day, but I was dragging a bit, and then I had a death in the family. My uncle passed away from cancer, and it was hard on the entire family. No matter how much we prepared for it, it was still painful. I didn't want to go to the funeral because I'm not a fan of them, but my mom sent me the money for the plane tickets. I didn't want to mention how all of sudden she got money to pay for plane tickets but argue when it was time to send rent money. I flew back into Orlando Friday night for the funeral on Saturday. I haven't been home in seven months. When I came to the funeral everyone was sad and devastated. As the funeral progressed, I sat there thinking about my uncle and some of the things he said to me.

"Every family have somebody that make it. If at least one person makes it, then their family will be alright. You're going to be the one to make it in our family."

I wanted to cry thinking about that, but the solider in me wouldn't allow me to shed a tear. The pastor opened up the floor to anyone who wanted to speak with a two-minute limit per person. I looked at my cousin and asked if he was going to say something.

"Nah, fam. I don't know what to say."

He is tripping.

"Last Call."

I got up. I never gave a motivational speech at funeral before. I might as well let this be my first speech if I want to get good

DARNELLE CUYLER

at it. I came home to uplift my people and that's what I have to do. I kept it brief but I finished it saying, "it's hard at LSU but I will make it. Uncle Hodges said every family have one person that make it. If one of them make, then they all make it. I promise I'm working hard every day through the struggle to make it. Because if I make it, then we all make it." I walked away from the podium. Then everyone was clapping really loud and smiling. I can tell I lifted everyone's spirits for the time being.

After the funeral everyone was asking me when do you go back to Louisiana? I told them tomorrow morning.

"But you just got here last night."

"Okay," I said. "I still need to go to class and work. I have to study. I didn't come here to mourn for too long or kick it."

One thing about me is I didn't know how to grieve about stuff like this. All I knew how to do was acknowledge it and to put in work tomorrow for that person who isn't coming home. After the funeral, I was talking to one of my boys for a little bit.

"Man, everybody around here hating on you dog. Everybody mad that you left and trying to make it."

"What? The last 6 months, I haven't been doing nothing but struggling. I been starving, broke, barely getting any sleep because I'm stressed all the time. And people hating on me? I have to literally beg my momma to send me some money. I don't even have a bed to sleep on. I had an air mattress, and it popped the first week. I've been sleeping on the floor with one cover for six months and you telling me somebody hating on me? That's crazy."

"But you're making it work though. Man if no one tell you anything, I'm proud of you bruh, and that's real. I already know it's hard and you going through it. Don't let up."

I went back to Louisiana the next morning and picked up a closing shift that same night. I was glad to be back at the Urec. The next day Zack actually brought me his spare bed that was at Mrs. Coleman's house. No one was using it. I was so thankful for that. I was able to get better rest instead of tossing and turning on the hard floor. I didn't say nothing to my family for a couple months. I just kept my head down and put in work. My uncle's death hit my momma and grandma the hardest, so I let them be. I just took my

BE GREAT TODAY! NO DAYS OFF!

losses and paid the late fee when it came to rent. Thankfully Carlis helped me out in my time of need. When Spring break and *Mardi Gras* came, I was working. I had a little fun, but not too much. If there was an opportunity to work more hours, I was taking it. I was trying to get as much money as I could at all costs.

From February through April, I was working like a mad man. I was trying to do all I can without asking anyone for help. The fam was still looking out for me every step of the way. I was picking up shifts with Nicole, Chris, and Carlis. They were the top dogs at campus rec. I worked so many shifts that eventually I knew all the procedures from opening to closing, the supervisor's role and responsibilities and all. I was really giving them my all and putting the team on my back.

"Y'all and Myron are all I got. Y'all my family."

So, I came up with the term *UrecFam*. I was still working out between 11:00 AM – 2:00 PM if I didn't have class. I was always hyped walking into the Urec.

Slowly but surely the Urec was becoming a place I call home. I definitely felt like this was my place of peace. It was my own sanctuary to relax and destress myself. I know it sounds ironic because I'm going all out pretty much every time I step in the door. The support and the love growing as the days go by.

One day I got caught slacking. I met this dude name Zach Wood. He was the tallest on the professional staff and a Ph.D. student. He was probably the only person beating me when it came to spending time in the rec. He would play basketball every day. One day I was shooting around with him, and we got to know each other. Then after that every day we would see each other, and our interactions were always funny.

He'd asked, "what's up, brother?"

"Nothing much. Just grinding every day."

"Everyday baby, every day."

"One day at a time," I said. "And ball is life."

He'd laugh. "Ball is definitely life."

We'd say the same thing every day for consistency and accountability. During lunch time, Chris Bullard and Zach would have a few of the staff members playing basketball and we would have to play full court and all. I'm confident enough to know that I would make the team, but I wouldn't be a starter simply because I was not a shooter. I can play defense and pass. Every day when I went to work out at the Urec, it got cut short because I had to play basketball.

Ball Is Life.

Zach admired my drive. He also likes to challenge people to bring out the best in them and I love a challenge. His challenge for me was to always shoot some shots every time I come to the gym so I can get more comfortable shooting. From that day forth I promise, I put up shots every time I worked, worked out, or just stepped foot into LSU Urec. For the rest of my career, even if I worked the 5:30am shift, I would make sure I put up shots and whoever was supervisor with me had to too. I never told no one that I take shots every day because Zach wanted me to get better. He knew I was doing it cause sometimes he would come watch from a distance, or he'd see me taking more shots in the games. I love being around people that want me to do better, and I can motivate them to do better as well.

April came, I was still in grind mode. It was time for Nationals for powerlifting. We all were excited for this, and I just knew was going to set a record for myself by deadlifting 500 pounds. Nationals was held in Killeen, Texas and you know what they say, everything is bigger in Texas. I lifted on the second day. I was encouraging and motivating the team until it was my turn.

The first night there, Kayli, Zack, Chip, and I stayed up super late watching the Boondocks. We started a gang, The Docks. We would say "Dock Life" whenever one of us was about to lift. I did good with my squat and bench lifts, but the goal was to give it my all on deadlift.

"Put 500 on the bar today. I'm not playing." I know I was coming off aggressive and I know some people was feeling a little uneasy around me. I was in full competition mode. I had the black tee on with Boosie bumping.

Kaleb said, "you should calm down, so you won't waste your energy."

BE GREAT TODAY! NO DAYS OFF!

"Nah," Chip intervened. "Let him go. Let him do whatever he needs to do for him to get the lift. If getting hype will help him perform at his best, then let him be."

So, I went out and did my first lift with the lights directly on me. They put 465 pounds on for my second lift and it was easy money. Everybody was getting hyped now. They knew it was on now. All the other lifters, judges, and audience was watching me then.

"Put 500lbs on the fucking bar! Stop fucking playing with me!"

Zack blurted out, "Yeah! Put it on!" He was running around like a mad man just hyped. They put 500 on the bar and everyone got quiet so quickly.

Three, two, one, lift! I exploded the weight off the ground. I got it to my knee and my right hand clipped my inner knee and the thigh area and I dropped the weight.

Fuck!

I was so mad, but everyone in the room was standing up clapping and screaming. I still came in top eight out of 60-70 lifters. I probably would've gotten top five if I would've landed the lift. One of the judges came up to me afterwards.

"That was an impressive lift! But now we have to test you for steroids."

"Test me? I didn't even win. Why me?"

"It's random. You could've bombed out and still possibly gotten tested." I kept cheering the team on after that. They all looked at me differently, especially all the vets and leaders of the team. Now, they respected me more. I sat in the car in silence as we traveled back to Louisiana. I really wanted to put the team on my back and motivate them. I felt like if I would've got the 500-pound deadlift, I would've accomplished those goals. In reality, I didn't need to lift 500 to motivate them, but it would've been nice though. My back and legs were hurting for like three days. I couldn't sleep, and I could barely use the bathroom.

Then one day I was going to the rec, and I saw Ariel. She was telling me about *Summer Powerfest*. *Summer Powerfest* was another weightlifting meet that was held in the summer, and she wanted me to go.

DARNELLE CUYLER

Damn my back hurt and you want me to do another meet?

"Yeah, I'm interested." *My Dumbass.*

"How's your back?"

"It hurts for real."

"Yeah, I know. You haven't been doing the back exercises lately."

How the hell you know I wasn't doing the exercises? She was right though. I hated those workouts.

"Yeah, I've been slacking with them, I was solely relying on my leg strength. I'll pull 500lbs at *Summer Powerfest*, I promise."

I knew not to talk crazy to Ariel. She squatted 600 pounds and did kickboxing as a hobby. In other words, she could kick me in the face and knock my lights out without much effort. That wouldn't be a pretty sight considering I'm already ugly and broke. I can't add too many more Ls to my plate.

I was still struggling at the end of the semester. I came up short on rent and had to call home, which was the last thing I wanted to do. I didn't call Peanut, but I had 3 days to figure it out or I was going to be homeless. But no one helped. In the midst of me stressing, Malcolm said he was moving out and that I can have his room. All I needed to do was pay the rent. I can do that since I had more than enough to pay for rent and buy groceries. The whole summer I just kept thinking to myself, y'all really was going to let me be homeless in *Baton Rouge* and I couldn't forgive that. Now, Big Taylor and I were roommates, and it was cool cause he was always busy. Plus, he cut my hair.

Now that it's summertime and summer semester was about to start.

I was picking up shifts left and right and I was working all the squad shifts. One thing I was glad that was over was the Friday closing court shifts. Chris and I always got stuck working those. I had a few great moments working the court shifts. I also had some weak moments too. Prime example, one day, a couple of the football players was getting into it. Now, both of these guys were about 6'6 feet tall, about 300 pounds each. Now, Ima whole foot shorter and at least half the weight. I called the supervisor to come stop them and help. I'm looking for Micah, our boss, and Chris to come

BE GREAT TODAY! NO DAYS OFF!

because I knew they were in the gym. The supervisor comes in and inquiries about who's fighting. I first mistake was looking upward. I look downward and seen this girl. I look at the athletes and look back at her. The athletes looked at me and then looked at her.

Ashley was the supervisor on shift.

You're the supervisor? What are you going to do? These boys can literally pick you up and slap me with you.

"Where is Chris and Micah? "

She left.

It got worse because now, they were trolling me.

"Oh, he was scared. He called troll. He troll."

Troll? Aw, hell nah. I ain't ever call the police on nobody in my life.

"I'm not a snitch. They just told me to call the supervisor if a fight break out. If it's up to me I'd let y'all go toe to toe and I won't stop it. All y'all from Louisiana swear y'all got hands and I haven't seen shit though."

One dude said, "aye where you from blood?"

"Florida!" They all got quiet after that. They knew what time it was.

When I see Chris and Micah them, I'm definitely cussing them out. They got these dudes calling me the police and then have the audacity to send the smallest supervisor to come stop a fight? Embarrassing. Then Ashley & I exchanged words and It was clear weren't a fan of each other, but as time went on, we became friends eventually.

Then a couple of days later, I had the daytime gym shift, and a fight broke out. I didn't see the initial punch because I thought the dudes was going for the ball. I just heard them say something about fighting.

"Yo," I blurted out. "Y'all can't do that in here. Y'all gotta go outside so y'all won't get banned." Then I called the supervisor. Now, this time Julie and Chris came first. Chris run shit. They all listen to Chris. I'm just here to get this money. As the dudes going outside, Julie asked one of them what happened, and one dude broke it down for her. He was cursing at Julie as he was explaining what happened. I was laughing to myself but as I turned around, they started roasting me again.

DARNELLE CUYLER

"There he go calling troll again"

"He keep that walkie-talkie on him."

Aw, hell nah. I'm done with this. I'm not using this walkie-talkie no more.

"Aye this my gym! Next time y'all get out of line, Imma handle it myself! Tell whoever, next time it's a problem y'all come see me! For y'all that don't know I'm Darnelle, straight out of Orlando, Florida and as of today I run the Urec. I ain't calling nobody. Imma just ban you from the gym myself."

"Wait. You can really do that?" One of the guys asked.

"Try me and see." Then they all knew. After that, we went back to talking about the fight. Julie came and told me I had to give a statement. Bro, what's with all this snitching? I just cussed them out to let them know I'm not a snitch and that I was just doing my job, and now I have to give a statement?

"No one's going to know it was you."

"NO! That's still snitching. You literally know what I know. I didn't see the initial punch because I thought they was going for the ball, and I turned my head. Soon as they started cussing, I called y'all and then y'all showed up. Y'all heard literally everything I heard. All I can tell you is buddy hit buddy."

"Well, that's fine," she said. "You still have to say that."

"Even though you know what I know." She said "yes." After that was over I thought that was going to be the last of the chaos but nah. It was a never-ending story working the gym shifts.

Gym shifts was always hectic. One of my craziest one's was when 2 dudes was playing a game of 21. Now, they're on the other side of the court minding they own business. I turn my head for a split second, I promise a split second, and a dude is running towards me holding his forehead.

"I'M BLEEDING!"

While holding the walkie talkie, I stepped back and said "OH FUCK!...Oh Shit. Supervisor to the courts. Someone is bleeding everywhere!"

Micah came to help. I apologized for saying "oh shit" over the radio.

Julie said, "it's okay."

BE GREAT TODAY! NO DAYS OFF!

"We heard you scream 'oh fuck,' too," Micah blurted out.

We all laughed, and Julie just reminded me not to curse over the radio. I was pretty much tired of Gym shifts. The sad part is, I kept working them. I needed the money.

The shifts in the Summer was lot more hectic than I anticipated. We had people always trying to sneak in the rec without their ID's, the football players acting like they run shit, and the craziest part of it all, people weren't showing up for work. If it ain't one thing it's another. So many times, I'd be working the Ops 1 shift at the front desk and someone would forget their student id.

As Summer school started, I came across some of my old foes. I was struggling with trying to get my classes registered. Carlis, Chris, Myron, Curtis, and Chip was back at financial aid and bursar office with me for the next few weeks until I got it taken care of. Personally, despite few times at the Urec, I loved the summer at LSU. It was calmer, the sun shined harder, and it was the perfect season for sundresses, crop tops, and shorts. The professors were a lot nicer and more lenient. I took calculus 1 and a geography class. This was my first of three attempts at Calculus 1.

Yes, as a math major, I've failed just about half the math classes I took at LSU.

I loved the summer grind the most though. It was class, work, and work out sessions in heavy rotation. I was trying to do numbers in the weight room. A few members on the powerlifting team and I drove to *Summer Powerfest*. I told them I would lift 500 pounds before Kaleb and Conor. They were all laughing so hard, but I was serious though. Zach and I placed a that he'd buy two packs of Oreos if I lifted 500 pounds on deadlift before them. I couldn't resist an easy bet. Kaleb kept putting emphasis on me not being able to make that big of a leap. Conor said if I'd do it, he'd do it. Chip just laughed and shook his head. I wanted them Oreos and I was going to get them. Plus, I needed to make up for Nationals. At the meet I lifted 504 pounds. Then Conor came behind me with 501 pounds. Kaleb didn't touch it. Zach was laughing at him. Kaleb knew I wanted that 5 so he was hyped and proud I got it. He was cheesing harder than me, and I was the one who lifted it. We left *Summer Powerfest* on a good note, but my back was so sore the next few days.

DARNELLE CUYLER

"Good work," Chip said as he walked by. "You still ain't shit though."

I laughed and said, "Bet. We on the bike and in the sauna tomorrow." When we say *you ain't shit* or *I ain't shit*, that just mean we made a power move, but we can do better. We keep each other motivated to want more and to compete more. Every now and then, we had to really tell each other that and mean it in a disrespectful way. But we always end up laughing after we say it.

The campus rec brought in some new hires. I even got them to hire my boy Curtis. Now, we really had squad shifts. Curtis was always trying to get me to go above and beyond to talk to people. He was very social and talkative. Half the time we'd sit there and laugh at the foolishness going on in front of us.

"Yo," Curtis leaned over to me. "You met the new hires yet?"

"Nah, not yet."

"Bro, go talk to the new girl on the court shift."

I looked at him as if he was stupid. "Boy, I can't just leave the ops desk."

"Man, I'll sit up here for you."

We stared at each other for a second and started laughing. I go to the gym shift and start talking to the new hire. Her name was Haley P., and we chatted it up for a good five minutes. We ended up staying on the gym shift longer watching the tournament that was going on. From that day on, Haley became my homie and then became family to me. Over the summer, I picked up a shift and it was Nicole, Haley, and myself. Straight squad shifts with this trio. Then one day it was Edcharra, Haley, and I on another shift. I remember Edcharra and I were talking about life and our summer classes.

"I just want to graduate from Pharmacy school, make six figures, and get a house."

"Don't forget the Lambo."

We both laughed. Every shift I hopped on was a squad shift truth be told. One of the hands down best squads shifts was the day it was, Myron at Ops 1, Carlis at Ops 2, I was at the eq desk, Curtis was on the gym courts, and Chris was supervisor.

BE GREAT TODAY! NO DAYS OFF!

Regardless of what shift I had, I made sure I enjoyed myself. I remember during one of my early shifts, Abby and I would look at all the ladies that came in and stare at their hands to see how big their wedding rings were. One of the best shifts was when we hosted graduations. Those were the best because everyone was dressed up looking nice and everyone was so happy. What I loved the most was the extra hours and overtime hours. Truly the definition of easy money.

During summer school, Chris and Carlis let me in on a secret. We have a mini *French Quarter* in our Student Union. We used to struggle financially but we always made it work. At the *French Quarter* you were able to get a full plate of grits and sausage for $1.50. I promise it was one of the best things on LSU's Campus. We stayed coming in clutch and scraping up money for us to get breakfast in the morning. This was really saving my life. Later in my career at LSU, I had to put the homies on this as well. Then it was Michelle, Seth, Haley, and I use to make moves and come to the French Quarter for breakfast after our shifts.

As summer school was coming to an end, I had to get ready for the Fall. I needed to find a new place to live. Luckily, I found a new place that was affordable. I moved to *Campus Crossing* on *Brightside*. Chip, Taylor, Bryce, and I became roommates. Our apartment number was 1613. Everyone in the apartment weren't from Louisiana. It was never a dull moment with them and I'm glad they were my roommates because every day either one or two things was going to happen. We were going to wild out and get a good laugh in, or we were going to play cards. It was an unspoken rule but if one played cards, we all played cards. This was mandatory.

"Hold on, let me get the Oreos."

From time to time, people from the powerlifting team came over and they played cards. I took a L one night in cards and they still won't let me live it down. We were always wilding. Chip and I used to compete to see who'd get to the next level on *Call of Duty*.

It used to be bad when we used to wake up to Taylor's radio clock going off. It had the original loud buzzing noise. His alarm would be going off for hours and I'll be sitting there like *how the fuck can he sleep through that*. Chip would tap the door and it popped open.

"Yo, He not even here."

DARNELLE CUYLER

"I figured that. Ain't no way you can sleep through that, but then again, he has proved us wrong before." We hit him up and turns out, this man wasn't even in the state. It wasn't our business why he wasn't in the state, nor did we care. We just wanted to sleep peacefully without his chaotic clock going off. Taylor, this man wasn't even in the state. Despite all of that, he did show always show love by giving everyone rides whenever we needed since he was the only one with a car. It was definitely clutch when I needed a ride from to and from the Urec. I was grateful for the rides when I was getting off work and he'd just finished his workout. The timing couldn't get no better.

As we head into the Fall Semester, I struggled with getting my classes registered again for the third time. It was the same thing all over again. Carlis was talking to Chris, Julie and Nicole and he was pissed.

"I don't see why they won't leave him the fuck alone. They let the in-state students come fail out every semester but harass this man every semester. He really out here with just the clothes on his back and he out working everybody on this campus to make it."

By the grace of God, I got reinstated and got my classes registered. I miss the tryouts for the track team this year again because of Title IX. I was back at square one. I stayed on the powerlifting team another year. My classes had gotten so much harder, but I was doing better in my finances. I was paying on my tuition with the money I had left over from paying rent. Working for $7.25 an hour with 20-hour weeks. Since Louisiana had federal and state taxes, my paychecks were very small checks.

I made it work though.

I told the bursar office I would try to get some scholarships to cover some of my tuition balance. I was able to land one and it helped a lot. The first stem scholarship was for minorities and out of state students that was trying to do better. It was the S-STEM program. My first meeting there I met this girl named Amanda and just like me, she was suffering from the out of state fees. She wanted to work for NASA after she graduated. So did I. Amanda and I been great friends from that day forth. We always talked about the struggle, but we always said that we have to make it regardless of the struggles we were dealing with. I was back talking to my family, but I kept it to a minimum. I was trying to focus more on bettering the relationship than getting upset about them sending money. My mom and grandma were helping when they could, but I wasn't putting forth the effort to ask and it didn't faze me if they didn't help. I knew my uncle's passing took a lot from them.

I found myself exhausted more than usual from stress that came from school and work. One day Chip suggested I take a nap throughout the day, and I listened to him. I definitely felt better afterwards. It was still a nonstop grind. I was trying to make the most out of every day and every opportunity that came my way. The temperature started cooling down but every now and then it was too cool. I wasn't really a fan of the cold. Neither was Chip. Chip was wilding for no reason. I remember I was getting ready to go catch the bus, and I yelled out for him to come on so we don't miss it. This man walked out of the room and stuck his hand out the door.

"Nah, not doing that."

When I say we laughed so hard.

"Bruh, you deadass not going to class? Don't you and Kayli got an exam review?"

"Yeah, but Imma pass regardless. I'm not going to endure the cold for a damn review." I shook my head and left.

As November started, life was definitely starting to look up. When my birthday came, the whole Urec fam celebrated my birthday. This was the first year and every year after when the Urec fam made me feel like my birthday was a holiday. One thing that kept me going was the love and support from my Urec family. They kept me going through the thick and thin. I went to a Friendsgiving with my coworkers since half of us couldn't go home for the holidays. I think this year, Chip and I also went to Kaleb's house for Thanksgiving. I was extremely thankful for my Urec fam and the powerlifting team. I was still picking up shifts left and right like it was my first week on the job. This semester was terrible. I failed Calculus 1 again for the second time. This was setting me back with my courses. 2013 was a horrible year for me academically.

As the semester ended, I received another email from Registrar

DARNELLE CUYLER

If you don't make a payment, you will be released from the University.

I just wish they'd leave me alone. I've been here a well over a year now, and I'm still dealing with this issue. I've been here this long. I might as well stay and finish. And I don't care what the price is, I refuse to throw my dreams away due to financial instability. I'll work harder next year and find a way to deal with this. I finally got some real friends and I'm finally getting my life together. I be damned if I'm throwing it all away now. Thankfully, I had supportive roommates and friends during these hard times. I have to step my game up because I intend on making 2014 a great year.

LSU 2014

At very beginning of 2014, I was sitting on the floor in my apartment trying to figure it all out. I've been here at LSU now two years, and they're still hassling me. I don't know why they just won't let me be, but Imma sit here and get my mind right.

I will take over the Urec fully by being more tenacious and uplifting.

I will get more scholarships.

I will join LSU Track team.

I will do research with other scientists on campus. I will improve my motivation skills and be a better speaker.

I won't need to rely on my family anymore because I know I will make enough money to pay my bills and get by. I will take all the help I can get while I'm out here. I have to switch my mindset up because in order to be great, I must believe I am first. I will celebrate the big wins as well as the little wins with my Urec family. I will make them proud of me for sure, but I will also bring positive vibes to their lives. I will bring more dedication and passion to the table, each and every day. All the nights I starve, I'm telling myself "We're fasting tonight" to remain positive and humble. Every time I step in the weight room, whether I'm lifting with the powerlifting team or by myself, I will work hard every time and do numbers. I will keep practicing in the gym and bettering my shots every day to keep my word to Zach. I will do the bicycle every day and finish my workouts in the sauna.

DARNELLE CUYLER

For so long, I was so angry with my family for the lack of support, that I completely forgot that I prayed for this opportunity. I forgot praying to God that I didn't care about whatever I had to go through, I will endure all of the trials and tribulations and still make it through. I will trust him no matter what because I know he hasn't forsaken me nor ignored the prayers I said on *Sanford Avenue*.

I'm still here blessed.

I'm still standing in abundance.

My strength and my will still prevailed.

As I sat there my mind began to change and my attitude towards things got better.

I felt stronger than ever before.

As soon as campus opens back up, I'm coming for everything they said I couldn't have and so much more.

I used to stress about it so much. One day I just said fuck it. I'll take whatever help that come my way. I will stop seeing them as people who were not my blood family and I've only known them for less than a year. Hell, they won't even be labeled as these people anymore. They'll be my people. Some of them will be my family. Some of them already became my family. A few of them want to see me doing better than my own family any way. I started going even harder for them. I was doing whatever it took to take the stress off them and show them they can make it too. I was constantly supporting them and grinding with them too. I was putting in so much work behind them.

Walking down Nicholson, I had to realize that there are people that want to see me do better regardless of my skin tone, my background, or anything else about me. I know in my heart, that I feel the same about them as well. I came to understand that you shouldn't push away the love and support that you want and need because it's not coming from the people you're accustomed too.

Just because a person or people don't look or talk like you, or from your hometown doesn't mean they don't or can't love you. It makes me want to cry because even though I said all these things on Sanford Ave., it's happening to me in real life. Every single day I'm constantly fighting adversity. Every single day I'm being shown that I don't belong here. But every single day people from the LSU

BE GREAT TODAY! NO DAYS OFF!

Urec showing me that I do belong here and that they have unconditional love and support for me.

Every single day I walk into the Urec I feel like I need to go in beast mode to show my appreciation and that I'm grateful for them. To show them that I love them. Going Hard and being everybody hype man is like the only way I know how to express myself fully because words can't justify my feelings. Most of them don't have a clue in the world of really go on in my life on a day-to-day basis. Yet, they don't know how much joy they really bring to me. For a while I was very lonely, and God answered my prayers.

As I got closer to the Urec I felt my heart come down to be at peace, and then my heartrate rose in excitement because I made it to another year of being at the LSU Urec.

The Urec opened back up a week before school and I hit the ground running. I very driven about everything, and I knew my work ethic increased because I was picking up shifts left and right without hesitation, without thinking, and without remorse. I made sure to challenge myself like I promised Curtis and meet new people. I had to keep in mind that if I wanted to be a motivational speaker and help others get better or to the next level, I had to put in the work and network.

Now school started, and like clockwork, the adversity arrived shortly after. I was going back & forth with financial aid and bursar office because even in the midst of things being chaotic, I was still trying to figure out what I needed to do to get things resolved. Per usual, time was of the essence and like a jury reviewing the case of a guilty defendant, time was not on my side. During the last couple of days more stressed and exhausted because the deadline was approaching, and this matter was still ongoing.

I walked into the financial aid office, and I sat there for a few hours just waiting to be assisted.

Waiting, and waiting, and waiting.

The lady at the front desk finally got to me.

"How can I help you, she asked."

Here we go.

I explained to her the situation and told her that I needed money to stay in school. I made it this far and I needed to see it through no matter.

DARNELLE CUYLER

"Oh." The look on her face was not assuring at all. "We don't have any more financial aid at this time."

I stood there dumbfounded. *How?*

"I'm sorry, maybe I heard you wrong. You said the institution does not have any more aid to give students?"

"That is correct."

"Ma'am, I'm not trying to be annoying or aggravating, but I'm sure you can call someone, and we can figure something out."

She came off sweet, but you can tell in her body language that she didn't want to help, or just simply didn't know how. But I already felt she didn't want to help me because she seen me sitting there waiting forever before she decided to help me. She pretended to act like she was the phone to reach someone to help and told me no one answered.

I wasn't trying to be rude, but my energy changed right in front of her, and she went right to back. And what was starting to really pissed me off, she was back there for a long ass time. I guess she thought I was going to get tired of waiting on her and leave eventually.

Nope.

What she didn't know was that I had nothing but time at this point. Shit, I don't even go to school technically right now. So, I'm here.

She finally came out of the back and of course she didn't bring me any good news.

"They're all out to lunch and we're out of financial aid."

Fuck you and get the fuck out of my face, is all I heard.

"Alright, cool. I'll wait."

I know she's probably having a rough day and I knew she didn't want to deal with me. I feel like I could easily make it worse because of how I'm feeling, but you know what, I'm not going to cause a scene.

I'm going to leave for now.

I ended up making my way over to the bursar and let them know that financial aid said they didn't have any more financial aid to give. They told me that doesn't sound right. I left and told my Urec family what was happening, and they said the same thing.

BE GREAT TODAY! NO DAYS OFF!

Same shit I said.

Imma go back tomorrow. Shit, at this point, I don't have anything to lose. The next day, I went back to financial aid, the lady I saw yesterday wasn't there today. They were a lot easier to deal with during my time there. They told me that I would be assisted shortly. Not too long after a man came out of the back and called me.

"Darnelle? Darnelle Cuyler?"

"That's me."

"You can head this way. I'd be glad to assist you."

This man actually said my last name right the first. Oh, yeah this about to be productive as hell. I sat down in the chair, and he let me give him all of the details about the situation. By the time I was done, he knew all of my problems, my goals, intentions, basically my whole life story in under five minutes.

"Aw, no worries man, I can put aid on your account right now and it'll be processed by tomorrow."

"Man don't bullshit me right now." I had the biggest smile on my face.

He laughed as he typed away on his computer.

"You're all set."

"Thank you so much." I almost had tears rolling down my face.

"Good luck with your journey. I can't wait to see you become an LSU Alumni."

I walked out of his office and the ray of the sun was hitting my face. God came through again in the nick of time. He won't regret it. The first thing I did was do a happy dance and go straight to the weight room. I already knew this was another chance for me to put in the work and get better. I wasn't going to squander it away,

Let's Do This!

I was really doing the best I can all of January training and preparing for any new opportunities. I heard about the indoor track happening in February and that I was able to run unattached as an individual. I signed up immediately. I ran the 60 meter dash because I knew my conditioning wasn't where it needed to be to do anything else. I kept working on my take off the whole week because that if your take off is bad the race will be over before you can blink. The day of the meet I seen my track friends and we were all hyped to see each other.

Chip, Carlis, and Chris was there. I didn't win the race but at least my take off was good. It was amazing feeling for me because it was one of my goals to run at a track meet for LSU. While it wasn't for LSU, I was able to still run at LSU. What made it even better was I had the opportunity to race against an Olympian. I thought that was something I can check off my bucket list of trying to do great things at LSU. That experience alone made me grind harder the next day because for myself, I needed to get my conditioning together to run again when the opportunity presented itself.

When March came, I was doing everything I needed to do and more for school and getting ready for nationals for powerlifting. I was the heart and soul for my team, but I was starting to burn out and become overwhelmed because of my classes. Adversity was only doing what it does best and beating me down in every aspect of my life. I was even having negative thoughts about my performance at the track meet a month ago and I didn't know why because I did a damn good job!

When April came, I told myself I needed to pick it up, improve, and do better. One day I was walking out of *Lockett* to head down to *Middleton*, I was feeling down, lost in my thoughts, and overall, having a man to man talk with myself.

"Damn bro you need to do better. You need to have more positive energy & thoughts about yourself and be high spirited like Alex."

Alex was the only coworker I knew that never have a bad attitude about anything. I'm not saying my other coworkers had bad attitudes, but she was just always laughing, making others laugh when I saw her, and just always in a great mood. Even if she was having a bad day, you would never know because she didn't wear her problems on her sleeves.

I'm going to challenge myself to outdo her with having positive energy and uplifting. I know I can't come up with jokes on the fly like her, but my presence can hold the same weight. The crazy thing is I after I left Middleton and went to the Urec, I saw her getting ready to leave.

"Ayo! I was just thinking about you and how you're always so positive & uplifting. I need to be more like you for real."

"Who, me? Shoot, I'm trying to be like you. You always motivating people to go harder and stay having everyone smiling."

"That's crazy because I thought the same thing about you too."

"I was wondering if you were in the library because I know the gang like to be in there, and honestly, I don't feel like being alone in there."

I told her that I'd be there tomorrow so she doesn't have to be alone, and we can study and get some work done. When it came to the grind and studying, we didn't play any games. We literally stayed in *Middleton Library* like we lived there. We would always text the gang to see who was in the library whenever we were pulling up. It would be me, Chris, Carlis, Meagan, Lois, Catarina, Haley, and Ally together studying at our spot on either the second or fourth floor. If we weren't in the library, we were in the Urec. When we weren't in the Urec, we were in the library. We were there so much you'd think we worked there too. It was nothing to us.

7:00 AM to start the day, we were either putting in work or opening at the Urec. The grind never stopped.

The next day Alex and I met in Middleton. We started talking about how we were struggling in a few classes and the stress to pay out-of-state fees. Then she told me she was from Colorado.

"Oh, so you be out there with Wolves. I love wolves. They're literally the best animal in my opinion. They can survive on their own but they're stronger in a pack. I try to view my life like that."

She laughed. I know it was random but hey, it's true.

Then we both started talking about our families and things in our personal life that we were dealing with.

"I'm the youngest out of all of my siblings and there isn't anything excited about Orlando. At you least you live somewhere that got wolves!"

We laughed together.

She sighed. "It does get lonely when you don't go to see the family sometimes for birthdays or during the holidays."

I knew exactly what that feels like.

"Starting today, we can be family in our own wolf pack. We gon' always support each other, keep it real with one another, and keep each other smiling. Even though we're struggling with these out-of-state fees and life in general, we got each other to uplift, challenge each other, be there for one another every day. We'll push each other to do better every day."

"I'd love that!"

"I love Oreos, too."

"OMG! Me too!"

"See we was meant to be family."

We been a wolfpack ever since.

We left *Middleton Library* that day feeling a lot better about life. We would challenge each other at everything no matter how childish it was. I remember one time we were trying to see who could have more telepathy moments between Carlis and I versus her and Haley. After about a week of being annoying as hell, Carlis and Haley had a telepathy moment and told us to haul ass. They weren't having it. It didn't stop there though. We were trying to see who can sneak up on a person the best and scare them. I remember one day we were in the quad, and we saw Carlis chilling with few athletes.

Alex and I gave each other a sinister look.

Before we could do anything Carlis peeped without even looking. His facial expression told it all.

"Don't come out here with that bullshit, or I'll beat both y'all ass right now. Keep that shit at the Urec."

We looked at each other like 'damn,' and burst out laughing. We backed away and went in the opposite direction because Carlis would've definitely beat both of our asses. It wasn't worth pushing it! Alex and I shared some really great times together, but that we definitely had some hard times as well. There was a time where I went to class to take a big exam, and everything was on the line for this exam. I studied my ass off because I needed to do well so I can pass the class. I took the exam, and I didn't have a confident bone in my body with any of my answers. As I was leaving, I just went to the library, and I knew I failed the class. I was sitting there beating myself, and Alex pulled up next to me in the nick of time.

"What's wrong?"

"I failed my exam and I more than likely failed that class too."

My eyes started watering up, and I was doing my hardest not to breakdown and cry in front her. *Stupid ass emotions.*

She laughed. "Shit, me too."

I thought she was playing with me and trying to turn it into a joke. It wasn't the place nor time to be playful.

"No seriously, I failed the exam too!" As she showed me her exam score.

We both started laughing and then the laughs turned into tears. The hurt from not passing eventually trickled out and we felt it. It was a real intimate moment we had together. In the midst of the tears and feeling like things were stacked against us, we were motivating each other to study better, harder, and we were going to graduate from LSU on time.

April was getting harder for me because I was putting more pressure on myself to break my own personal records at nationals. I was planning to bring my best version of myself to help the people achieve their goals. This was one of our last few practices and shit got real. I was on the squat rack with about 485 pounds on the bar. I got myself mentally ready and my feet up under me. Spotters and watchers were all around with Chip in the back spot. I got the weight off the rack and felt the slightest move off my left shoulder.

"YO! IT'S FALLING! IT'S FALLING!"

I dropped 485 pounds on Chip wrist by accident. I felt so shitty. I apologized like three times. Thankfully he wasn't seriously injured. He lowkey was but he wasn't going to say it. He just Iced it once practice was over.

Not all practices were painful, some were a stepping-stone to greatness.

There was one night that powerlifting practice was wrapping up, and Conor randomly mentioned he never benched 315

DARNELLE CUYLER

pounds. I disregarded everything I was doing and started putting weight on the bar.

"Well, you going to do it now!"

"Nah, I'm good bro."

"Man, bring yo ass. You go lift this weight today. Let's get it." I tapped the bar a few times.

I wasn't taking no for an answer. Chip, Coleman, and I were hyping him up as I spotted him. He did it three times. I couldn't tell you how proud I was of him, and we were all hype together. It felt so good helping someone achieve their goal, especially a goal they didn't even expect to achieve themselves. Since nationals this year was in Orlando, I definitely had to outdo myself and put on for my hometown in my hometown. Despite the weight of it, I actually enjoyed myself and did pretty well. After the competition, I swung by the old stomping grounds and was able to meet A'laya, my niece who was born a few weeks prior.

Now that nationals are over, it's time to focus more on my classes and my final exams.

I was going through some more personal problems that I never spoke about and one of them was the Urec. I couldn't tell at first, but I was getting a bit more emotional day after day because the end of the semester was approaching quickly. My closest that I've bonded with, that became my family, were graduating. Their shifts were changing so I wasn't working or spending time with them like I regularly could. It was hard to see when I did knowing that I wouldn't see them for a very long time. I had to step up; no, I needed to step up because I couldn't dwell on it, I couldn't stop it, and I couldn't slow it down. Instead, I was happy for them for making it out and seeing it through to the end.

Finals started as May began. Nothing changed in those last two weeks. We were still in rotation with going to *Middleton*, grinding, and trying to get as much work done as humanly possible. I was still going to the Urec shooting shots, Carlis & I were still doing sprints to stay in shape, and I was still self-evaluating myself on things I can do to be better. I was sitting in the sauna with Carlis, Chip, and Chris doing our usual post workout routine, and another gentleman joined us.

BE GREAT TODAY! NO DAYS OFF!

"Man, it's hot as fuck today," Carlis said.

I laughed.

We all talked about how we'd cover up the thermostat for it to get hotter and other things. This man started talking about the science behind it and I laughed. He kept talking and one thing led to another I mentioned that I was STEM major and I majored in math.

"I'm working on a research project and if you're interested, you can come look at the math and see if it makes sense."

This sounds interesting.

"I have physics students and while I like them, sometimes it's good to have a different major's perspective on the topic. It'll be nice to have a math major to help with this. I can probably get you a stipend and an internship. Anyway, good luck with your finals. Come find me after and let's see what we can work on over the summer."

I sat there dumbfounded as he left the sauna. This sauna is special. I stay meeting great people here, but I never met someone that can do something like this. His name was Professor Jon Dowling, and he was a physics professor in the STEM department.

"Bro, that's crazy," I said.

Chris said, "You're making power moves!"

"Run it," Carlis chimed in.

Chip nodded his head and said, "Word."

I looked up Professor Dowling as soon as I got home from the sauna and he was a big fucking deal in the physics department. Dr. Jon Dowling, a world class researcher, and the most cited professor in the entire world. I told my other roommates immediately and they were all excited for me. Over the summer, I did an abstract research project on quantum physics. We spent a lot time together and I was able to share my background with him. He felt my pain, but he also felt my strong will to preserve past it. He got me a stipend with the U.S. Army Educational Outreach Program and with the Undergrad Research Apprenticeship Program. I was part of this research team for the summer in 2014 and 2015. I was also in the LSU S-Stem program from 2013 to 2016. I was trying to elevate to from where I was academically besides taking classes at LSU.

DARNELLE CUYLER

After I was done with all of my finals, I felt I needed to go home before summer school, research program, and work started back up. I went home for a week, but I didn't have any intentions on relaxing or chilling. I went right back to *The Trenches* and put in work. I needed to keep pushing myself, to keep reevaluating myself. I needed to keep strengthening myself, my goals, and most importantly, my faith in God. Even though I was going to the *Rose Church* with Big Taylor in *Baton Rouge*, I best connection I had with God is when I come to him on my own. The day after I got home, I signed up for a track meet in Clermont, Florida. I still had goals of joining LSU's track team, and it was the only one I haven't achieved yet. So, I needed to go to a track meet and run good times to have a shot.

I needed somewhere to train and have people around me that understood me. So, I hit up the old clique. I met up with my boys at our old stomping grounds, Lyman High School, and we chopped it up a bit. After a few minutes, we got to work. Besides me, it was Anthony also known as A-Rod, and my cousin Isaiah we call Zig. I been rocking with A-Rod since *Milwee Middle School*. I shared the obstacles I was going through in Louisiana, but how I was getting through it as well. I told them about how all these opportunities were happening for me and how it pushed me to be better. A-Rod out the blues asks me,

"Have you kept in touch with the people from here since you've been gone?" A-Rod asked randomly. "Has anybody reached out to you?"

"In all honestly, not that much. Besides y'all two, only D.-Bell, Ed, Seth, Matt, Marlon, and Dijon reached out and that's once in every blue moon though. But I don't focus on stuff like that because I know people have their own life. Real recognize real."

We talked about how we were putting in work every day during the summer of 2011. We had Mr. Forbes, Lyman's swim coach, to thank for that.

Rest in peace, Mr. Forbes.

He was the embodiment of dedication and astound work ethic. He understood that we needed to be in the weight room to stay disciplined to the grind. We walked to the track and spotted

BE GREAT TODAY! NO DAYS OFF!

Coach Cashman on the infield. He became Lyman's sprint coach, and he was obsessed with proper technique and work ethic. I already knew, it was going to be a long week. A-Rod was coaching me and recording my times, Zig was the support system, and Coach Cashman was there to correct my form that would improve my performance. We put in the work every day leading up to the track meet on Saturday. I signed up for the 200 & 400 meter dash. This would allow me to show my speed and strength. This would also help see what I needed to work on.

We drove down to Clermont, and I was getting my mind right for my upcoming races. get ready for my races. This track meet was practically in the middle of nowhere. We were walking around looking for the entrance and a place to sit. As I was warming up on the infield, I spotted some familiar faces, but before I could remember who they were, I heard the announcer announce it was time for me to run the 400.

The official took his stance.

"Runners take you mark," he said emotionless. "Set." The gun went off.

I took off and I was doing well on the first 200 meters, but I felt the lag coming as I was approaching the 300 meters. I just remember Seth dad saying, "that bear keep jumping on your back."

I tried to push past my limit and go to another level, but something was wrong with my left leg. *Fuck*, I thought. I was clutching my leg and even though I couldn't run as quickly as I could, I made sure I finished the race. I didn't have a good time but at least I finished. I didn't dwell on it because I still had a chance to redeem myself during the 200-meter dash.

The announcer came on the speakers. "Runners, make sure you're staying hydrated."

I felt a little embarrassed until I saw other runners looking just like me. More athletes doing the same thing. I guess I was so focused, I didn't realize how hot it actually was. The crazy thing is I didn't feel hot that much. but my shirt was soaked. I was completely depleted, and I needed more fluids. My cousin got me a Gatorade, and as I was relaxing trying to cool off, I started to look at some of the athletes on the field. It finally hit me. There were A LOT of Olympic and pro Track & Field athletes here. I thought

DARNELLE CUYLER

this was a regular track meet for runners trying to improve their time, but this was *Prime Time*. I was racing against Olympians during the 400 meters. I didn't think bad about myself nor my performance because I knew with a little more conditioning training, I can keep up with them easily.

As I was warming, a few of the LSU runners approached me. We never spoke before, but we were about to get really acquainted today. Ironically enough, we were all wearing gear that represented LSU.

"Don't we know you?"

"Nah, but I do go to LSU too. I see y'all running at the track meets sometimes whenever I go. Hopefully after a little more conditioning, I can be a walk on for the upcoming season."

"That's what's up bro."

"But I have to get ready for the 200 meters," I said.

"You're crazy! The 4 and the 2? Good luck!" They all smiled.

We all family now because once a Tiger always a Tiger. I was chopping it up with one of the runners and he was really dropping knowledge and wisdom.

"It doesn't matter if you make LSU track team or not," he said. "You don't have to be on a team at all. You have passion and drive. Don't ever let that go. People need to keep seeing that. Good luck, my boy."

His name was Richard Thompson. Richard Thompson was an Olympian and the fastest athlete to ever wear an LSU uniform. I felt so strong and confident after that. I said a quick prayer and started back focusing on the 200-meter dash. The weather began to get ugly and because it got that bad, I never got a chance to run the 200. It was all good because I was able to get a picture with Tyson Gay, formerly known as the fastest American Athlete.

I left the meet that day with nothing but leg cramps and motivation.

Sunday came and it was time for me to head back to LSU. I knew things were going to be different when I got back to the Bayou. When I got back in town that day, I started getting my mind right. I knew I needed to be stronger and bring more leadership to the Urec. With my heart and soul, I needed to be a great example to motivate Lois, Ally, Michelle, Haley, Chris, Alex, and a few others. Since the OG's were leaving, it was time for the new people to step up and really grind.

When summer school started, I was in a fight once more with my arch nemesis, financial aid and the bursar's office. I approached them head on because this time, I didn't need to stall. I was able to show them that I had more money coming in instead of just the checks from working at the Urec. I was getting better at overcoming adversity confidently, and it showed. This was my third time taking Calculus 1, and I had Dr. Sullivan again. I took another one of his upper-level courses and by the grace of God, his course helped boost my GPA. The workload was easy for me to understand and navigate through, and it allowed me to focus on Calculus 1. I was going to pass this class.

Now, at this time, I was a full-time student during the summer semester, working max hours, doing research with a world class researcher, and I raced Olympians. I had money to cover my bills and had enough money left over that I didn't have to inconvenience or burden my family. I was literally at my best at this point in life and it wasn't even my final form. I was achieving all the things I said I was going to achieve, working harder than ever before, and I wasn't even close to being finished. This summer was a non-stop grind. Haley & I would wake up at 5:00 AM every day so we can work out at the Urec before going to work. On top of that, I had to still train with Carlis, do research with Dr. Dowling, and still stay on top of my summer classes. I was doing more conditioning training so I can be ready to walk onto LSU's track team when it's time to sign up.

I hated the pool workouts because the cramps, whether in my calves or hamstrings, showed me no mercy. Two to three days out of the week, Josh, Abby, Folse, Carlis, and I would do sprints on the campus recreational fields behind the gym. We would run until we were spiritually waving white flags since we couldn't physically do it. We ran at our own pace, but more importantly, we made sure we finished the race. No matter how tired I was, no matter how much I loved them, I had to beat all of them. I was having a mental talk with myself briefly.

DARNELLE CUYLER

How can you inspire them to keep going if you give up? How can you motivate them if you can't push through it? You have to keep going. I am the heart and soul of my people.

Thank God we always agreed to stop whenever the first-person taps out because I always start struggling in the end. We called it the *Dog Days* of Summer because it was always so damn hot. The humidity was unreal, but I was always grateful that they were willing to put in the work with me and helping me chase my goals and dreams. The fam and I had some fun as well. We celebrated more when it came to birthdays, or whenever we chose a day as a relief from a hard week's worth of work. I celebrated more with my loved ones and pushed them to do better. Being around my Urec fam always gave me peace of mind and it was constant motivation to keep pushing forward. I was working out two to three times a day, doing well in school, and motivating everyone around me.

I talked to Dr. Sullivan and Mrs. O'Bannon about everything, and they were so proud. This summer was probably the best one of my life thus far. Even though it was a day-in and day-out process I always had to prepare for it. I had to practice being positive, being motivated, and being motivational. I had to practice praying and thanking God for always providing for me and surrounding me with extraordinary people. I was still walking home throughout the day and on the weekends when I wasn't with Haley.

I always try to unwind at the end of the day by listening to music. Music is definitely a big part of my life because it helps me stay calm and it also hypes me up whenever I need it. It also makes walking back to the apartment a lot easier and quicker. I still remember the day I lost my iPod. I slipped out of the side of my bag and I'm not going to lie to you, I was down bad. I was up and down *Nicholson Drive* trying to find a needle in a haystack. I NEED my music. I needed my R&B slow jams. I needed to listen to *My Everything* by Mary J. Blige every day to slow things down for me. I needed to listen to Boosie and Kevin Gates to get hyped every single day. I needed to listen to my wide range of music from different genres and backgrounds. I even need the random white people songs that come on at the Urec every day that keep getting stuck in my damn head! I was walking around campus for about a week looking dusted and disgusted. And then one day, Catarina gave me her iPod. Man, when I tell you my eyes started watering. I had to wait till I go all the way home to add music to it.

I just listened to the music she had. Thankfully, I was able to listen to some hip-hop and throwbacks to hold me over until I got back to Orlando. She was real for that. The walks up and down *Nicholson* would end my life if I didn't have music.

As Summer came to an end, things were looking up. I passed both of my summer classes. I put in so much work this summer. I was on track with my degree audit, I had the STEM programs and stipends under my belt, I raced Olympians, and brought joy to the Urec. I was ready to carry that momentum into the fall semester. One day I was sitting on the couch in my apartment thinking about any and everything going on around me. Having tough conversations with yourself is always hard but it's always necessary.

I've overcome adversity time and time again. I knew that things were looking up for me, but I had to capitalize on everything to solidify it. I had to stand on my word and do everything that I dreamed of. I been going and against the odds for a long time, but I stayed disciplined and dedicated to the grind. I stayed motivated when failure kept trying to derail me. I stayed consistent even when I couldn't see the results. Even though I kept getting knocked down at one point, I kept getting up to finish the fight with adversity. Staying motivated over the last two years was not an easy fate. I had to constantly keep telling myself that one day I will be an inspiration for someone who is battling with adversity.

I will do so many amazing things for my community and pave the way for others to be successful too. I can achieve anything that I desire; I just had to put in the work first. All the hardships that I encountered only made me stronger. I developed a stronger mindset and a more positive attitude because I've been through the worse and I beat that shit. I bring so much passion to the table because I'm constantly fighting adversity, and adversity hates passion. I don't compare my struggles to others because the struggle is the struggle. I strive to help them get through theirs as I'm getting through mine. Being able to find strength during hard times is tough to do but I will constantly put forth the effort to do so.

I remember speaking at my uncle's funeral, despite how hard it was, it taught me to stay strong and uplift others even when I feel weak. To lift others up when they're at their worst. Why me, you ask? Because I'm built for it. Because my uncle told me that I'd be the one to make it. One thing that I realized is that you don't really make it in life until you're able to help others. I'm doing everything in my power to help others feel loved and valued, even when I'm not the person they want to help them feel this way. I will continue to step up and give an honest effort at everything I do regardless of if I'm accepted by others or not. I will continue to stay relentless and tenacious when it comes to my goals. I will be aggressive when it comes to staying on top of my friends, making sure they're grinding and getting things done. I'm ready to go into Fall 2014 like a well-oiled machine.

As the new semester slowly approaches, we had another operations meeting at the Urec. They shared with us the goals and expectations for the upcoming school year, and we prepared ourselves during the last couple of weeks until the school started. I had a lot on my mind. We lost some of the OG's from the past graduation, and we were losing more in the fall semester.

I went home and devoured a pack of Oreos to decompress. I sat on the couch by myself thinking about the Urec and I would laugh at random memories with the Urec crew. The operation's meetings will never be the same moving forward and I had to accept that. We would no longer see each other on a regular basis for the most part because our schedules were all different now. The ops meetings were the best meetings because everyone working would attend. Micah was always starting problems with Carlis, Allena would throw her two cents in unprovoked, Curtis would just talking about nothing, and everyone else would be having a random conversation. Then there was me, the worst of the worst. I didn't say a word. All I did was just laugh.

During our last operation's meeting with the entire squad. We all sat there in silence. Everyone knew what time it was. It was time to say goodbye and we weren't ready for that yet. They wanted to play the blame game of who always starting it and prolonging the meetings. Someone tried to blame me and I nipped that shit in the bud real fast.

"Bruh, don't blame that on me. All I do is laugh. I never say a word, yet you say I start it. We know exactly who start all the commotion every time. Stop playing." Micah came at Carlis, and it was down the drain from there. However, I did throw a propane tank on the fire to keep it going. I remember one meeting, we weren't allowed to talk at all. The meeting was almost the same, but worse. We couldn't talk like we were supposed to because of the foolishness. Julie was talking and then all of a sudden, it got quiet. The only thing we could hear is the vibrations coming from several phones. All we hear is vibrating. I felt my phone going off so I checked all of the notifications. I was laughing out loud so loud. Everyone was trying to hide their smile and using their phones to distract them. Julie didn't care about the phones at first, she just didn't want the extra talking going on.

Then Carlis and Allena exchange words and Julie says, "no phones!"

Now, the whole time I'm laughing hysterically, Julie is staring right at me.

"Juulliiee, I'm sorry," I was trying not to laugh. "Please don't fire me. I love this job. I just can't stop laughing."

She laughed.

We were able to get through the meeting without me getting fire and all shifts were taken.

Micah always meant well, even when it didn't seem that way. I remember a serious conversation we had, and it was the first time I ever seen Micah be this serious.

"I need you to do better and be a little more professional," Micah said. "The reason we won't give you a chance at supervisor because you don't showcase it. Just because you work a lot doesn't mean anything. You need to be able to lead. Jules wants to see you do better. She cares about you more than anyone that work here. That's why I'm telling you this. I'm not trying to be hard on you or tell you for my health. I'm telling you to do better for others."

I wasn't hearing it.

DARNELLE CUYLER

Micah didn't understand me at the time because he didn't know the hardships I was facing. He thought I just acted this way because I thought it was acceptable. I never thought it was acceptable, and I didn't feel the need to tell him why I don't want to be a supervisor for them. There were a number of reasons why I didn't want to be a supervisor and I was never going to apply to be one. One day I saw my supervisor, Nicole, got cussed out while working a shift. It was too the point where she just left and had to regroup. I'd be damned if someone from Louisiana going to talk to me any kind of way. I was already going through enough hardships on the day-to-day basis. These people can catch the hands. Another reason was the pay. As a supervisor, we couldn't work as many hours and then we can only pickup ops shifts at a very, very last resort. I did the math on the number of hours they work times the pay rate. Nah, I'd be losing money. I'm just now able to pay rent on my own and my tuition without any additional help. The most important reason was because I know my role. I know my part in the campus rec. Being a supervisor don't make you a leader. I knew plenty people that were supervisors and wasn't respected as a leader.

It wasn't my place to lead them.

My job was to uplift them and be the heart and soul of this organization. Staying at Urec allowed me to fulfill the promise I made to Julie, Chris, Carlis, and Nicole. I told them no one will outwork me. I will pick up everybody slack. I will do whatever it takes to ease everyone stress if they gave me a job. Instead of Julie constantly having to mass hire every semester, I'll work the nasty closes, the opens, and on the weekends.

Especially the Friday and Saturday closes that everyone ran from. I knew how to open and close the building because I was taught by the OG's. I'll pick up the slack of supervisors who only wanted the title but wasn't good at their job. I will make sure everyone felt safe and know that they have someone they can always depend on. I was the go-to when the gym shifts get out of hand. I know the game and I told all of them, "any problems come find me." I worked so many shifts at the Urec, you'd think I slept there. I'll be the foundation, the support system, the heart of my people until the day I graduate. I was fueled by wanting to be there when my coworkers were in need, because I know the feeling of not having no one to support you. I definitely wanted to carry myself accordingly regardless of who's on shift or what's going on, they didn't have to stress because I was there. Later down the road Micah will figure that out. For now, I'm an untamed workaholic, and it's going to stay that way.

I was trying to get my mind together before I started getting ready for class. Today was also the day I was going to try to get on the track team. One day Chip and I were at the crib chilling, and we realized we needed to go to Walmart.

"You going to have to stop eating Oreos too," he said.

The disrespect.

"Wait what," I responded. "You deadass? Bro, Oreos are my life, you know that. You are tripping."

"Nah, dog. Are you not trying to be elite? You have to kill all that. You gotta get on the team. I know the shit suck, but if you're trying to make a move like that, that's what you have to do."

"Bro," I was in disbelief. "You're wilding right now. I see people in the Olympics getting paid to be sponsored by Oreo. I can do that easy."

"Yeah, look where they at, and look where you at. You're trying to get to their level. You gotta get in the door. I know you got a lot on your plate right now, but we need you to get in the door. Make moves so they can help you with your school shit."

He wasn't wrong at all.

"Yeah, you're right. But bro, I really gotta stop eating Oreos period? Even if I work harder and do more core work? I mean I guess I can go without them a little while. When I get on the team, I'm slaving a pack the same night. I don't care!

"Word!"

That was a tough day for me because anybody that knows me, knows that Oreos are my life. I have to sleeve a pack or two a week, but I knew sacrifices had to be made so I did what was best. I laughed because Carlis, Catarina, or Lois, and sometimes Ally would randomly pull up when we were struggling, and we'd go in on some Oreos just to feel better. I just told myself whenever I felt the need to get some Oreos, I would just do a core workout. And yes, I was doing core work every day trying to fight the urges.

DARNELLE CUYLER

The semester started and I was entering the fall semester with the same redundant problems. I was fighting to get my classes registered and I had a pretty intense schedule. I had six classes under my belt, with four of them being math classes. This began the everlasting grind of taking mostly math classes to graduate for the next 3 semesters.

My ultimate goal was to get on LSU's Track team this season. I finally had my paperwork, title IX wasn't a problem, and I had over a 2.0 GPA. I finally had my life in order. I finally started making progression towards it and trying to get registered was constantly on the back of my mind, but I knew what was on my mind more. I finally talked to the head coach and the sprints coach, coach Shaver and coach Brazell. I finally was able to officially practice with the team. I already knew some of the athletes, so it was all positive vibes from the start. I remember the first practice I had caught a huge cramp in my legs and lower back and got left behind. No one knew what happened. I told them I felt fine and then the next thing I knew, I was on the ground laying there for ten minutes trying to relax my muscles.

They laughed at me.

I finished the workout though and Coach Shaver emphasized to the team on how important it to stay hydrated. I didn't have that problem anymore because I had my Urec water bottle, and I was filling it up at the union between every class. I couldn't get caught slacking again. The practices were tough because it was so hot late August to early September. Every day felt like it was a fight for survival. Between class, work, internship, and track practice, I was trying to be all I can be.

I was finally manifesting in my dreams. Every day I would try to update bursar for an extension.

"I'm trying out for the track team. I know y'all give athletes more support, and if I make the team, I'd get more help." They were trying to cut me a little slack because they saw the effort that I was trying my best. My work schedule switched up, so I wasn't seeing the fam at all anymore. I was working random shifts and on the weekends. I would literally go to *Middleton*, class, track practice, and work either 11:00 AM to 2:00 PM, or a random close shift. I still needed to max hours so I can pay rent and put down on my tuition. That first week after practice, I would literally just go home and sleep. I wasn't trying to kick it, go to the Urec, or nothing.

After a few days, Carlis showed up to my house. He was sitting on the couch and Chip was sitting at the table on his laptop.

"Dog, where have you been," Carlis asked. "We ain't seen or heard from you in days. The whole Urec asking about you. I said he trying to get on the track team. We all proud but damn. You get on the squad and forget your people?"

I sat on the floor and started stretching.

"Nah. I come home to take a nap before I get back to studying. I have 4 math classes this semester, my internship, work, and track practice."

Carlis laughed. "My dog out here making moves. But on the real, how is it?"

I looked him dead in his eyes. "Man, this shit real. But you know how I'm coming. Every day I'm doing better, and they all can see it."

"Word."

Then I started to do an ab workout because I started thinking about getting Oreos. As we were chilling, my other roommate Taylor had come home.

"Man somebody parked in my spot," he was pissed. "I paid for that spot. I put a nice note on their car. If they park in my spot again, I'm having their shit towed."

I laughed. "Damn Taylor, don't do it to them tonight."

Chip just sat there chilling. Carlis chilled for a few more minutes and then got up to leave.

"Word. I just had to come by and make sure you were straight."

He left. Two minutes later we hear a banging on the door. I open it, it was Carlis.

"Damn Taylor, so you was gon tow my shit? You wrote this note?"

Chip and I laughed so hard.

"Taylor, you wild," I said holding back tears from laughing so hard!

DARNELLE CUYLER

Carlis sucked his teeth. "Man, 1613 don't care about nobody. Y'all got it."

I was damn near rolling on the floor. Chip said, "We keep telling you, we ain't from here and we don't care."

"I'm towing whoever park in my spot," Taylor was laughing but he was dead ass serious too.

"Man, I'll holler at y'all tomorrow."

Even though Carlis for real this time, I was still on the floor crying laughing. I didn't know if I was crying because of the painful soreness I was feeling after my after my ab-workout, or if I was laughing too hard at Carlis. Chip and Taylor were laughing harder cause I was on the floor dying with the note in my hand. I'm always taking it further than it needs to be. Taylor sat down and tapped the table.

"Alright, we can get on these cards now."

We've kept the card game tradition going since day one. After we played cards, I just went to bed to so I can be rested and rejuvenated for the next day.

I was putting in more work the following week than I was the week prior, and I can confidently say, I was getting better. *It never gets easier; you just get better.* My performance was exceeding my own expectations and I was progressively getting better day after day. I could tell I was exceeding others' expectations as well because the coaches' facial expressions showed how excited they were. The team was coming together nicely. Despite how long I waited to get on the team, I never spoke that much while we were practicing and putting in work. Whenever we start stretching at the beginning at the beginning of practice, they go around asking each person a question.

"You have anything for the team DC?"

I always kept it short, sweet, and simple because I was too focused on the workout ahead.

"I'm just here to put in work and help everyone around me get better."

After going through hell in one of our practices, one of my teammates Rod came over to talk to me really quick. I remember after one of the practices I saw Rod and he was saying,

BE GREAT TODAY! NO DAYS OFF!

"Aye DC let me talk to you for a second," he said as he started walking with me. "Aye man, you're doing really good out here, keep working. I can't say much but all I'm going to say is keep working." I read between the lines and took it as everyone was noticing how I hard I'm working and that I needed to apply more pressure. There was so much on the line, so much going for me, I couldn't let up now.

It sounded good.

I was living in a time where everything I prayed for years ago, everything that I just prayed for last week, was now coming to past and I'm here for it. My boy Nethaneel always looked out for me and made sure I had a ride to and from practice. He made sure that anything I needed that he could provide himself, he gave it. I remember meeting him in 2013 through Rynell, who was in Dr. Sullivan class with me, Aaron, and Rodney. I didn't know why but we called him Blake for short, until I realized it was his last name. He was another person that became like family to me because we shared the same values, and he was really about that grind life. I remember after one practice as we were walking towards the training room, he put his arm around me and the towel over his face.

"Keep working, my boy. Don't give them a reason to doubt you. Never, and I mean never let them see you sweat. They're watching you so hard right now, and they see you getting better day after day. Don't let up, keep fighting."

And then he walked away. I kept walking towards the training room, and he turned around. I can feel the heat coming off my body, but I knew I wanted more. I caught up to Quincy, who we all call Q, and chopped it up with him outside of the training facilities for a good 10 minutes. We talked about our track times, events coming up, how we do the hurdles, and so much more.

"Bro, to be real and this may sound crazy, they don't even have to give me a scholarship. I want to get on this team so bad that I'm willing to run any event. I will take us to the national championship. I know it sound crazy, but I will put in the work if I'm given the chance."

"It doesn't sound crazy at all. Just keep putting in work. Everybody can see that you want it because you're looking way better than your first day and you're progressing rather quickly."

DARNELLE CUYLER

After our conversation, I went to the Urec because all this week I was working the evening shifts since I wasn't working my normal shift from 11:00 AM to 2:00 PM. As I was progressing in life, goals being accomplished, and my dreams starting to be fulfilled, I still had some issues brewing in the background. I love training with the track team, surrounded by people with similar goals and aspirations. Every day that I walked to the gates of the track, I would see the Olympians wrapping up their workouts or packing up. Then I would take a moment and stare at the track. I finally felt like I was where I belonged.

I was home.

And speaking of home, my family back home wasn't doing well at this time in my life.

I was a keeping a secret from everybody, and it wasn't one I was ready to share just yet. I didn't tell my Urec fam nor my track teammates because things were going so well that I didn't want to bring any negativity to anybody. No one knew, but my grandmother was dying. I was so focused on my goals and was trying everything in my power to get to a better place that I never noticed this happening. When I did, I spoke to God and pleaded as much as I could.

"Hey God, it's me again. I know you know what's going on with my grandmother and she's on her way to you soon. To be real with you God, I don't want my grandmother to die. She's been the glue that's held this family together, and she's been here for me in more ways than I can count. But if it is in your will Lord that take back your child, your good and faithful servant, I asked that you hold off until she sees me make the track team. I want her to see that her baby boy made it."

I haven't talked to her in a few weeks, and I told my family to call me every time they went to see her. I didn't care what I was doing, whether I was working, in class, training, or practicing, I needed them to call me so I can talk to her. Did they listen? Hell no, but they called me one day and it was the last time I got to speak with her.

"You doing okay, grandma?" I asked even though I already knew the circumstances.

"Yeah, I'm doing fine baby," she sounded so chipper. "I get to go home in a day or so." Her voice sounded strongly, and it was so lively that I didn't think much of it since she sounded like she was in good health. I told her I was making a lot of friends, work was going well, and that I was trying out for LSU track team once semester started again. Everything that we talked about, everything that we prayed for, was coming to past. I remember her telling me that I just had to keep the faith, and I did.

It was finally the weekend and I just made it through a long week of the grind. I was sitting at a desk at the Urec working the night shift that Sunday, and my phone kept going off. My brother was blowing me up, and I didn't know why, and although I should've answered, I didn't since I was caught up in work.

He probably just want to how I'm doing, I thought. They haven't said a word to me in weeks. *What if it's about Mema*, I thought. He probably wanted to talk about her condition, and I wasn't in the mood for any negative energy right now. And besides, it couldn't be that since she sounded fine last time I spoke with her, and they were releasing her from the hospital the very next day. I had just got off work and went to the basketball court to shoot around. I was dribbling the ball and my phone started ringing again.

I finally answered my brother.

"Hello?"

"Where you at? You need to hurry up and get home. Make sure you're by yourself and then call me back."

We hung up. My mind started racing and as usual negative thoughts started pouring in. It couldn't be about Mema going back to the hospital because they just release her. Nah, it's probably some more drama with my momma or somebody got shot in the hood. I got back to my apartment and I hit him back up.

"What up? I'm at the crib now."

"Mema died."

"Wait what you mean? Y'all just said last week everything was straight. Y'all Just said she was going home! What are you talking about?"

"She's gone bro. She's gone."

I was livid, and the pain I felt in that moment was uncontrollable, uncontainable, and unwavering.

DARNELLE CUYLER

"I FUCKING TOLD Y'ALL TO CALL ME EVERY-TIME Y'ALL WENT TO THE FUCKING HOSPITAL! I TOLD Y'ALL!"

I can hear them crying in the background. My sister tried to talk to me but I was trying to hear her.

"You gotta come home," she was whimpering.

"MAN, GET THE FUCK OUTTA HERE! I TOLD Y'ALL TO CALL ME!"

I hung on them, tossed my phone across the room, and broke down crying. I cried harder than I ever cried before. I cried for hours non-stop, with no signs of letting up. I was laying on my floor and through my heavy and blurry eyes, all I could see is my reflection in the mirror until it got too dark for me to see. looking in the mirror. I cried easily for another four to five hours straight. When the tears no longer rolling down my face and I had enough strength to push against the agony I was feeling, I got up and walked to the living room. Chip was sitting at the table.

"You heard me crying huh," I asked. My eyes were red and still a bit watery.

He nodded his head. "Word. You were loud as fuck. I fig-ured something was wrong and you needed to cry it out before talking with you. So, I waited here until you came out."

I had the sniffles. I was trying to maintain my masculinity and seem macho, but it was an epic fail.

"My grandma died today," a tear rolled down my face. "My family ain't nothing but some liars. I told them to call me every time they went to see her. They said she was sick, but that shit doesn't add up. I'm the one who was taking her to her doctor ap-pointments before I left in the Summer. They told me everything was fine. I read the documents saying that she was fine and signed off for her. I don't know what went wrong."

Chip sat there quietly and understanding.

He broke his silence, "I feel you, but you know what you need to do. Try to keep your head up, till test day. Let me know if you need anything."

He was trying to change the subject to get my mind right. I was grateful for that.

BE GREAT TODAY! NO DAYS OFF!

Eventually I went back to my room, and I cried all night long. I tried my hardest to cover my face so Chip couldn't hear me, but it felt like I was attempting suicide because I couldn't breathe.

I was drowning in my own tears.

Life was starting to kick my ass and it showed no desire to let up. I needed a break, and I wasn't going to get one. The next day we had an extremely hard practice, and I was struggling so bad. I didn't seem like myself, I didn't perform like I usually would, and I knew why, but they didn't. So, I spoke up.

"Hey y'all," I did my best to hold back to hold back the tears and stay in control of my emotions. "I'm sorry I'm struggling today. My grandma passed away last night and I'm taking it really hard right now. But I promise y'all I'm going to bounce back and be better tomorrow."

I picked up the slack after I told them, but I was still struggling internally. However, everyone was struggling because the workout was hard as fuck. I don't know what the coaches were on today, but it went from 0 to 100 real quick.

Cyril pulled me to the side, asked if I was alright, and gave me some words of encouragement. I appreciated it for sure. It didn't subside the pain I was feeling but it helped me deal with it a little bit better. I never experienced pain like this before in my life. My Urec fam and my powerlifting teammates were trying to help me, and for the most part, they did. But I was still grieving.

Every day that week I had to hurry up and get home because around 8:00 PM, I would just start crying uncontrollably for the rest of the night. There was one more week for tryouts and I still needed to register for my classes. At this point, I think I had a spot secured on the track team since I was stepping it up a notch like crazy.

Blake tapped me on my shoulder. "Aye, get through next Monday, or so, and you're good." I was fired up.

Make the track team and Mema would be proud, is all I kept telling myself.

I got a call from my brother, and he let me know that my grandmother's funeral was going to take place this upcoming weekend. I was so pissed because I had to go home, and I had so much to do here. Truthfully, I didn't know if I could see her like this.

It was a Friday night, and I was running behind. Carlis did me a solid by dropping me off to the airport in New Orleans. I was checking in and the lady registering me said the door has closed and they couldn't hold the plane for me.

"Ma'am, I have a funeral tomorrow morning for my grandmother. I cannot miss this funeral. Please help me. My family will kill me if I do."

She said, "It's ok. I can get you on a flight going out at 5:00 AM so you can make it to the funeral.

Man, what the fuck!

The number of times I sat on a plane and had to wait on people who were stuck at the gate and y'all didn't couldn't wait five minutes for me? I could've easily made it to the plane if they had given me five minutes.

It's because I'm black huh, I thought.

Carlis and I had to drive all the way back to Baton Rouge to come back to New Orleans for the flight at 5:00 AM. I be damned if I missed this funeral. Carlis was trying to give me some words of encouragement, motivation, and that I needed there for my people to uplift them. I tried going to sleep but I cried all night long and I had a mean ass headache. We got up again and headed to the airport. All the tears were gone and I just couldn't think anymore. I was moving without much effort.

"Be strong bro." That was the last thing Carlis said to me before I got on the plane and flew back to Orlando.

Trent picked me up and we were stuck in traffic on highway 436. Anyone that's ever been to Orlando, or just Florida period, knows that the traffic is just horrible. My phone started going off and as soon as I answered, my sister started cussing me out immediately.

"Where the hell you at? You're late!"

Once I arrived, everything calmed down, but emotions were still high. The funeral was at New Bethel Missionary Baptist Church on *Marker Street*. I got out and walked to the door. I tried to open it, but it was locked. A tall lady opened the door. She looked at me and knew who I was.

"You must be one of the grandsons." Now mind you, I haven't seen my entire family since my uncle's funeral in 2013. The two times I did come home, no one saw me except my household, and even then, I was always in and out. When I walked through the doors everyone got quiet. The preacher acknowledged me and continued on with the service. My oldest sister came up to me crying and hugged me. My momma and my uncle grabbed her off me. I was still numb to anything so there were no emotions behind it. People I haven't seen in years were watching me as I strolled forward to take my seat. They knew I was the closest person to my grandma, and I know everyone was looking for me that week, but I was at school. I sat at the edge of my seat with my hands locked.

Say something uplifting to your people like you did for Uncle Hodges, I thought to myself." And I was going to do it and then I felt my phone buzz. It was an email from the university informing that I was released from the university.

I really lost everything in the span of a week.

Nah, don't uplift them. Cuss everybody ass out. You lost everything.

I heard the pastor say, "now, we will have a brief word from Darnelle Cuyler. Keep it short."

Bet.

I walked to the podium and began talking. It started off sweet, thoughtful, and genuine. And then I switched up.

"Y'all never came to the house," I had no remorse in my voice. "Y'all didn't do shit for her."

People were uttering to one another and advocating for someone to get me away from the podium. The right side of the room was my grandmother's family. The left side was her family from Monticello, Florida, and anyone else that wasn't directly related to her. I was about to cuss them out too, but my uncle got to me before I could and ushered me away from the podium. I went outside possibly cool, and my brother followed me to make sure I was okay. He had my niece in his arms. Her smile calmed me down and I was able to focus a little bit.

"What's going on with you? You straight?"

DARNELLE CUYLER

I told my brother about the email I got. I was no longer a student at Louisiana State University. This was the worst day of my life. I got to bury my grandmother and I'm no longer a student at the place I've been working so hard to graduate from. This shit hurt. We walk back in the church so we can finish the rest of the service and then the pastor started talking reckless.

"It doesn't matter what school you go to, you still going to hell. Now I don't know Ms. Katherine or the type of life she lived, but if she didn't live a good life, she still could be going to hell."

First off, did anybody catch that this man just told me that I'm going to hell? I should've ran up to the podium and body slammed him in front of the whole church. This man was disrespectful the whole time I was there. For the record, my grandma not in Hell. She lived a great life of abundance, and she left this earth with her legacy intact.

We left the church and went to say our final goodbyes at the burial site. Everyone was asking when do I leave and I told them Monday. I wanted to leave sooner but with everything happening with my grandmother, and school, even I knew I needed a break from everything. I was at my momma house and Seth came by. We sat outside to talk for a bit.

"My momma and my grandma were talking about you. My grandma said your buddy was cutting up. He was up there going off!"

I laughed. "I was cussing their asses out. The whole church was about to feel me, and I didn't like the funeral at all. When Mema was here none of them came by the house to check on her. Everyone acted so sad for her passing like they weren't disrespecting Mema all the time. I ain't saying she was the holier than thou or a saint, but don't come to her funeral fake crying and shit. And then I got an email saying I was released from the university."

"Man, you're going through it. But you gon' be straight though."

That night I went to Peanut house, and They were always happy to see me. I told them what was going on and all that had happened. After I left there, I went back to my momma house, and it was tough. We were all grieving in our own way and did our best to stay out of each other's way. When it got really dark out, I went to the *Trenches*. I had to go talk to God and get back right. I walked to the Sanford Avenue and was crying along the way. It was just me and the streetlights. I didn't answer any phone calls or texts. I needed some time alone to get back right. It was okay to cry because no one saw me, and I had a lot on my plate. As I started running, the tears were coming down hard.

"God why did you do this to me?"

I touched the stop sign of Magnolia and then start pouring everything out.

"God, why did you do this to me! I lost everything. My grandma died and I can't even go to school anymore! I lost everything!"

Here's what I mean when I say I lost everything. This is called the domino effect. When one fall, it leads to more things falling. My grandma died, that affected me deeply because I forgot to go to the bursar's office to request an extension, and therefore, I am no longer a student at LSU. Since I'm no longer a student, I was no longer eligible to join the track team. That I also means I lost my job, and my internships, which means I can no longer afford to pay my rent. Therefore, I'm homeless. I lost everything. This week has, hands down, been the worst week of my entire life. And here we are, back the *Trenches*.

"God, I did everything you told me to do. I've endured everything you can possibly throw at me. I starved, I slept on the floor for months, I was basically homeless if it wasn't for Taylor. I uplifted people when they were at their worst. I did everything I can think of and now this? What did I do wrong for you to do this to me? I gave everything I have to the Urec. I stayed focused and disciplined. Why did you do this to me? God, can you please give me my dreams back? I will do anything. I put it on my life I will do anything to get my dreams back. I'll go to hell to fight the devil if I have too. I promise there isn't anything I won't do to get that back."

I cried and cried on the side of the road. My chest was hurting so bad because it felt like it was going to crack, like something was stabbing me in the heart repeatedly. My heart was hurting so bad. Then something told me to get up and go home. God

DARNELLE CUYLER

heard you. So, I got up and went home. The house was full of sadness and silence.

I went back to Louisiana Monday night. Tuesday I went to class, then I went to track practice. The coaches were asking me what happened yesterday, and where I was. I told them I was still in Florida due to the funeral. I told them I show them the tickets to prove it, but it was nothing I can do. Since I missed the test date, I couldn't join the track team. The other sprinters were advocating for me but there wasn't anything they can do. They told me to try out next, but I couldn't because I was graduating next year. I started walking away and something told me to stay calm, hold my composure, and try to get reinstated for school.

So, I did.

While I walked to the bursar office, I just told myself to stay strong and to stay proud. I was glad to train with some of the greats and future Olympians. They all was homies and I was glad to meet some new people on the team. I was grateful and was excited to see what they were going to do the upcoming season. I was glad to grind with Blake, Aaron, Rodney, Quincy, Jordan, Mo, Fitz, Vernon, Acy, Cyril, and Josh.

I cried so hard that night because the opportunity I had was taken from me over something that was out of my control. If I knew was going to happen, I probably would've skipped the funeral and dealt with the consequences later. But everyone was telling me to go home. That semester was so hard. I felt so broken, empty, and alone. The powerlifting team was trying to get me to join the team, but I declined. I needed to focus on school and pass these math classes. They were kicking my ass. For weeks, I would just go home and cry.

In October I started going back to the Urec regularly. I remember going to the courts on of my shifts and I saw this dude playing basketball. This dude was none other than Basem. He had on an Orlando Magic shirt. I already knew that 9 times out of 10 if you're wearing an Orlando Magic shirt, you're from Florida because not a lot of people like them outside of Florida.

"Oh, you like the Magic? You must be from Orlando."

"Yeah, I went to *Apopka High School*. You from Orlando?"

BE GREAT TODAY! NO DAYS OFF!

"Yeah, I'm from Altamonte and I went to Lyman."

"I be in Altamonte all the time. And you went to BUM ASS LYMAN! Y'ALL ARE TRASH."

I'll beat his ass right now and he don't even know it.

"Nah, y'all fucking trash." From then on, we somewhat became friends. He was always selling out whenever I seen him. I remember one day I was walking home, and this man drove by shot me the middle finger and screamed, "Fuck You and Bum Ass Lyman." I just saw red and started chasing his car. I don't know why I was chasing it. I was looking like a fucking idiot. I thought that if I caught him, I would've punched him in the face. At the time the only good thing about Basem was that he could pronounce Altamonte, correctly. I always had a problem with people pronouncing my city incorrectly. The only one who would still say it wrong on purpose was Carlis, but he would pull that card when he was already running around the corner.

I started meeting new people again and working my mid-day shift at the Urec. I remember I was working a mid-day shift at the Urec, and Josh was the supervisor. We went walking around the Urec making sure everything was straight.

"Hey, did you meet the new life-guard yet?"

"No."

He nodded his head.

"Bro, you know everybody!"

He laughed. "I'm the supervisor, it's my job to know everybody."

He was right but I never seen none of the supervisors say a word to the aquatics staff. We walked up and introduced me to Renee.

"Do you know Sarah, the short life-guard? That's my best friend. We be thugging it on the gym shifts."

She laughed a little. "Yeah, she's so nice and helpful."

"You literally work the deadest shift. Rarely does any come to swim during the 11-2 shift. I work and workout at this time, so I know how dead it get in here. I bet you be bored as fuck",

"Yeah, it does get pretty boring."

DARNELLE CUYLER

"I already know, because y'all can't have y'all phone out either. Every time I come in here during this time. I'll be your friend and talk to you, so you won't be lonely or bored in here."

She laughed and said thank you.

Josh and I headed back to the front of the Urec where I was assigned to be.

"You're a good friend. It be too boring on this side."

I did everything I could to fill that void and pain. I went back to eating Oreos and trying to enjoy college football. I remember when LSU beat Ole Miss, and Keya and I rushed the field. That was a great ass game! It was so exciting that a man had a heart attack in the stadium and passed away. Rest in peace to him though. Despite all of the excitement, I was still going home crying myself to sleep.

I told myself I needed to better especially since November was coming. November came and although I stopped crying, the pain was still there. I was failing my classes. My coworkers were all supportive and loving towards me. I started really grinding hard instead of going through the motions. My Urec fam went out to *Pluckers*, and we had dinner as a family. They bought me all types of stuff since they knew I didn't have much. They always made my birthday feel like a holiday. I was so grateful for all of them. Since day one they always showed love and supported me. I had so much joy being around them. I was at the courts shooting alone and I was thanking God for all my people. I definitely want to shout out Carlis, Chris, Curtis, Myron, Nicole, Alex, Eddy, Cash, Meagan, Lois, Ally, Allena, Abby, Allison, Allison, David, DJ, Michelle, Taylor B., Taylor, Haley P., Torrey, Haley, Sophie, Catarina, Ashley F., Kat G., Diana, Kayla, Katelyn, Emily, Chelsey, Jen, Madi, Judy, Stacee, Josh, Jorge, and Zack Wood. And also my aquatic fam Renee, Sarah M., Seth, Shelby, and Tina for always showing love. I'm definitely grateful for Julie and Micah especially knowing I would still need and rely on them after I left the Urec.

The Urec professional staff were all uplifting and supportive people. I definitely want to shout out Laurie, Brad, Kelly, Chandra, Courtney, Megan, Stanford, Gail, Jen, and the rest of the staff for all the support. I was extremely grateful and blessed to

BE GREAT TODAY! NO DAYS OFF!

have them in my life. Looking back over the last couple of years at this job, this was probably the best thing to ever happen to me. Every day, I was able put forth the effort and bring my best to the table. Every day I can be myself and grind with the people I care about. You were guaranteed a good laugh every day. Every day we were knocking down Oreos or Grandma cookies from the vending machine. Every day we were making gains in the weight room.

I can work every single day and enjoy every minute of it. I fell in love with these people and the facility. They can't fix the problems that I go through but some of them put forth everything they have to help me get through it. I give my heart and soul to this facility every day without thinking twice about it. God really did fulfill my prayers and blessed me to be around extraordinary people. I have so much passion and love for this place that I want it named after me. Haha. One day I want to provide extra funding for it. I'll be better about it too. I won't just flaunt my money. I'll set it up for the students to continue to get paid during hard times. I will let the funding go into tutoring to help others as well. I know all too well about the struggle and failing classes. I know what it's like to be out here getting my ass beat academically daily. It felt like my class work was stomping me out like I'm getting jumped by a few people.

But I'm eternally and forever grateful for everything.

I knew going into December I had to dig myself out of a hole. I studied my ass off for my final exams, and I still ended up failing one of my math classes. Adversity is something that I've dealt with time and time again. This new pain and hardships gave me strength I needed to press on. I knew that I couldn't uplift people if I was dealing with these types of situations. The reason my grandmother's death was so painful compared to my uncle's death was preparation. I knew my uncle was running out of time. I had time to mentally prepare for his death to come, whereas my grandma's death was completely unexpected, and I lost more than just her. I discovered that it's not about losing the person that hurts the most, it's the impact they had on you that is no longer there.

I knew going into 2015 I had to do better and continue to fight through it. I know what I desire more than anything and that's to graduate from Louisiana State University.

DARNELLE CUYLER

LSU 2015-2016

I came into 2015 with one ultimate goal and that was to graduate. I took more math classes. I even retook Calculus 3 for the second time. I still had my ongoing fight with the financial aid and the bursar's office for a few weeks, but eventually, I was able to register for my classes officially. You'd think after three years of seeing me every single semester they'd just help a brother out and let me be, but that seems too reasonable.

I signed up for another indoor track meet for February. Even though I wasn't on the track team, the sprint squad and Rod and the other throwers were still happy and hype to know I was still putting in work. I know things didn't work out like I intended them too, but I couldn't let the passion die. I was working hard in my classes as well as doing everything in my power to step up at the Urec. I was trying to celebrate and motivate people as much as possible since I knew this spring, a lot of people were leaving. I'm not going to lie, February and March were really hard months. April came and we had our Annual LSU Campus Rec Employee Appreciation Picnic. I loved it. I won just about every award possible including Employee of the Year. That really meant a lot to me because I was trying my best every day to do better and help others regardless of my hardships and struggles. I was trying to be more like Alex since she won it the year before. I was nominated last year, but I lost to her. She deserved it for sure. I just knew I had to step my game up in order to be the undoubted winner the following year.

DARNELLE CUYLER

This semester was hard because despite taking a bunch of math classes, they were all more intense. I was still dealing with a lot of adversity from my hometown, but that didn't matter in this moment. I knew the goal had to be achieved one way or another. Despite my hard work, I still ended up failing two of my math classes at the end of the semester. Thank God I had a backup plan. I took a Spring intersession course that was an easy A, and it definitely helped my GPA. It was a three-week course that I could maneuver without much effort. This is also where I met the homie, Leonard Fournette.

"Dog, this season I'm not letting up," Leonard said. "They're all going to feel me. Imma put in so much work this summer because when the fall come, I'm giving everything I got."

I patted on the shoulder. "Yeah, do that G. I believe in you. I'm definitely doing all I can to graduate this year. Fall 2015 is our season. We'll grind hard all summer and shine in the Fall."

"Straight up!"

I knew what I had to do when the summer came. I registered for three more classes. Two of them were math classes and the other was an English class. After that, I really only had five classes left in the fall to graduate. Five upper-level math classes at that. In total, I had eight classes standing in the way of me and graduation, and this was a battle I was going to win at all costs. However, I needed a break before I embarked on this nonstop grind until the end of the year. I knew I was going to be gone until I graduated, so this was a good time to go home to Orlando, take a moment to breathe, and get rejuvenated for this journey. I told my family I was graduating in the fall, so they knew well in advance to plan to attend.

I didn't want to hear any excuses on why they couldn't make it.

I went home and ran at another track meet.

The grind doesn't stop.

I saw Aaron and Quincy there as well.

"I'm running the 400-meter hurdles today," I said laughing. "I'm about to die out here today since this is my first time doing

BE GREAT TODAY! NO DAYS OFF!

this. I did the 300 meter hurdles in high school, but I know that extra 100 meters gon hurt."

Aaron laughed. "We're all about to die out here."

"Just finish the race," Quincy chimed in. "The only thing we need to do today is finish the race."

Even though our events were different, they were right after one another. So, we warmed up together. The warmups we did had me feeling right. I just knew it'll all that stretching would help me on the track today. I couldn't have been more wrong. Man, I kid you not, I DIED! After running and jumping 200 meters, I was dead. The fatigue was real. They were congratulating me on finishing. My hamstrings were hurting for days. I ran on *Sanford Ave* before I went back to Louisiana, and I felt more focused, calm, and strong.

I was retaking Calculus 3 again for the third time because I refuse to give up on passing this class. I was also taking probability and an English course with my boy Nethaneel. The grind that summer was real, and I can honestly say, it was one I'll never forget. I was keeping Dr. Sullivan, Mrs. O'Bannon, and Dr. Shipman up to date with everything. All my mentors, and all of my advisors were proud of me. I was putting in work all summer long and all that hard work paid off.

I passed all my summer classes!

Everything became surreal in this moment. I was literally five classes away from graduating.

The Summer grind was still the same at the Urec. The ones that were there knew the deal. We are here all summer long and I was going to be make the best of it because I knew my time here was coming to an end.

As the fall semester approached, Chip and I were no longer roommates. I moved in with Pat who stayed closer to campus. It was more convenient for me so I can get to class and work without having to worry about being late. Because I was closer, I was able to pick up more opening and closing shifts. It was tough getting hours at the Urec at this time because there was an expansion project full underway. So, only half of the facility was usable, which means only half of us were needed for work. Most of the Urec fam were gone, and the rest of us was pretty much taking our hardest classes in prospective colleges.

We were still trying our best to celebrate like we usually do, but things started to go downhill.

When September came, I was able to declare for graduation for this Fall. It was a great ass feeling to know that I made it out here. But that feeling was short lived because I was informed shortly after that I wouldn't be able to graduate since I did not meet all of the requirements. I was trying to ignore it at first and just not think about it, but eventually it crept into my mind. After countless meetings with the administration, financial aid, and bursars' office, I still wasn't given the green light that I could graduate in the fall. It was hard fighting alone with no family behind me, no support from anyone on campus, and no one with enough power or pull to talk to them about a potential solution. I literally begged the bursar's to just let me be this semester and let me graduate. Whatever payments was left, I would get a job with my math degree and pay it.

Just please let me be to graduate.

I been here this long, there's no point in stopping me in my last semester. Fall 2015 became the second worst semester of my life. As the semester went on, I was stressing so much, which led to me being behind in my classes. I had five classes left and these were the hardest undergraduate math classes in the program. Since day one, I felt as though the university was against me. My family doesn't call or support me. It seemed like no one cared for my well-being or anything. All of this was taking a heavy toll on me. As the semester progressed, the effects of that heaviness started to show. My anger and sadness were in constant battle for superiority. People I was close with were becoming more distant by the day.

People true colors were starting to show as time went on. It seemed like everyone I was close to was becoming an enemy. I never thought I'd say this, but I started to hate going to the Urec. Negativity on top of negativity occurred, and the tension was growing everyday as you walked into the facility.

It definitely wasn't home anymore.

BE GREAT TODAY! NO DAYS OFF!

I was falling apart on the inside, and I had no one to turn to.

As a result, I started to distance myself from people, and that only made things worse. Since I wasn't in a good head space mentally nor was I emotionally stable, I was failing my classes like no tomorrow. The only good thing that happened in September was my niece Aubrey being born. That provided a little light at the end of the tunnel, but it wasn't enough to get back on track. Despite how I was feeling, I made up in my mind that I was going to keep fighting hard every day no matter what. I was going to make it a better day no matter what.

But adversity had different plans.

It's like adversity overheard my thoughts and decided that it wasn't going to let up no matter what either. When October came, I kid you not, I had an F in every class I had. I was losing my mind and every night I would have a nervous breakdown because I didn't know what to do or who to turn to. Even though I did this alone, the only good thing that was going on at the time was going to the football games to watch my boy Leonard Fournette bring pure chaos to the other teams. But it still wasn't enough to get me out of that funk. Man, I was ready to quit and walk away from everything swiftly. My life was in turmoil, I legit had everything to lose and didn't care.

I remember texting Nicole and Alex separately. I was pretty much begging them to come home and just get the gang back together. I hated everything that was going on in my life. I even started hating the Urec and everybody that work there more and more as the days went by. I was starting to lose the love I was once had for the place I would give my all to. The words being said and the actions being shown weren't aligning together. They told two different stories. The bad part about it is no one was willing to admit they were wrong or at least see it from another perspective. How quickly they forget that I was the picking up all the closing and weekend shifts that no one wanted. How quickly they forget that I was the one that motivated them when they needed it the most. I'm relevant or valued because I'm convenient, not because I'm loved.

How quickly they forget.

DARNELLE CUYLER

I run the Urec, don't get me wrong, but at this point I was ready to quit. And sadly, it felt like they wanted me too.

The next day I just sat in darkness and had a pep talk with myself.

"Get it together D. I know everything and everybody against you right now, but fuck that. You must keep fighting. You can't give up. Not now."

I sat there for a long reassessing the situation I was in and accepted for what it really was. Everyone wasn't against me, and I needed to accept that. I couldn't hold that against everyone. It was just one problem after the other that added more negative thoughts to everything that was going on. The university whether it's bursar, financial aid, or even the administration, weren't against me. They're just following protocol. It's not their job to have sympathy or care about my personal problems. My personal problems weren't going to stop any of their operations. In their eyes, they might be thinking I'm playing the victim and trying to get by on them, even though that definitely isn't the case. All I'm trying to do is graduate in peace, but the road to crossing that stage with my diploma in my hand just got harder to navigate through. But I can't change that. However, I can change me and I'm going to do what I always do.

Work harder.

That's the only thing I can do. That's the only thing I've ever known. The situation may change but the mentality doesn't.

No days off!

The following week, I remember walking through the quad and seeing my boy Nethaneel. We started talking about the things we were going through and working day by day to push through. He wasn't even running track at this time, and he was going through it just as much as I was.

"Aye, come to the rec with me," I said. "I'll get you right mentally. The track team trains you to be physically strong, but do they train you mentally? I've been going through a lot lately but I'm still good at training the mind."

We started going to the Urec and working out together every day. And we were putting in work.

BE GREAT TODAY! NO DAYS OFF!

"This position you're in is just temporary. I'mma train your mind to be more focused and aggressive. You have to fight adversity harder than what you've been already doing. You going to get back on the track team and then you going to go to the Olympic games. I promise you, you're going to make it."

He thought I was wild.

He crossed his arms and had a stern look. "Yo, your thought process is crazy. How can you really see me going to the Olympics in the midst of all of this? My guy, no offense, you are really insane."

"You got the work ethic to make it happen. Every time you step on the track next year, you're going to be a problem. No days off, my boy. No days off!"

All those times Working out with Blake was really a life saver. It enabled me to be stronger. It allowed me to be a better version of myself despite how hard things got around me. It gave the courage and strength to push pass my own endeavors, my issues, to be there for someone else. To be a helping hand, to motivate someone else. It kept me from stressing about my own problems. There were some losses in my hometown, but I was trying to do everything in my power to not get distracted and focus on graduating. Getting those phone calls, it was never a pleasant conversation. It was always some kind of family drama, or a shooting.

It was getting closer to November now and the only thing I was doing was at this time was grinding and going to work. I was still keeping my interactions with everyone at the Urec to a minimum. The tension was still heavy, but that wasn't my focus. My focus was trying to figure something out so I can graduate.

Just change your mindset and do better, I thought.

I know I'm much better that what I think I am. If people don't want to be around me or deal with me, then so be it. That's not my problem, that's theirs. I'm not going to give up on myself nor the grind. I worked too fucking hard to get here. What used to be bother me, I'm letting that shit go today. Graduation is the only thing on my mind and I'm going to graduate! They can shun me, misrepresent me, talk bad about me, or even hate me. They'll never be able to replace, but I can replace them.

DARNELLE CUYLER

November came, I finally stopped having nervous break-downs. I stopped trying to feel like everyone was against me and whenever I worked, I just stayed to myself. I started back working fully on the weekends because it was quieter, and I didn't have to deal with anyone. I also started doing better in my classes.

I was slowly getting myself out of a hole, but adversity wasn't too far behind.

"Hey," Haley bumped into me. "What are you doing for the game?"

"I don't know to be honest. I might stay in, but if I go, I'm probably going to go by myself."

"Nah," she had the biggest smile on her face. "We're going together. I feel like I haven't seen you or heard from you in a while. Everything just been off lately. I miss when me, you, Alex, and Abby would go to games together. Hell, I miss all of us hanging out so much."

I chuckled a bit.

"Yeah, we were a squad. It was always live at the games with us."

"Always! I'll text you and we can meet up for the game."

The next day was game day, and Haley & I met up. I was telling her what was going on with me and the situation concerning me graduating this year. After venting for a little bit, we kept it positive and just focused on the game. Especially since this the last football season we'll get to experience as students. We saw Julie, Micah, and Zach come up to us in front of the *Student Union* section. We all talked for about five minutes, and then we went to the game.

Early the next day, I sent a text to Nicole, Alex, and Carlis, talking about how we were going to grind all November, be great, and finished strong. The text I got from Nicole after was not what I was expecting.

"Did you hear about Zach?"

"No, but I saw him last night with Julie and Micah before I went to the game."

She called me.

BE GREAT TODAY! NO DAYS OFF!

Zach died in an accident last night, and hearing that destroyed me emotionally. After we talked, I sent a text to a couple of people, and I was crying so hard. I didn't even know what to do at this point. Everything in my life was going to shit. I been fighting every single day relentlessly. Every time things start to go right; things suddenly go left.

We loss an amazing member of the Urec.

He was definitely fam to me. He understood the passion behind the grind and accepted me for who I am. I felt it the most because his death was the same week as my birthday. We had a funeral service for him, and the old Urec fam came out to give their thoughts, prayers, and condolences. We was so happy and sad at the same time because we remembered the man we knew and all of the funny moments. Then we would remember he was no longer here with us. I spoke at his service and shared some words that would help soothe the pain, and some uplifting words that would help them move forward. I tried my best to deliver my speech without breaking down, but I was struggling a-bit myself.

Afterwards, I told the original OGs what was happening to me behind closed doors, and they were devastated. Then the professional staff found out what was really happening and a few of them put forth the effort to help me. We celebrated my birthday as usual. All the pain and mourning were put on pause for 48 hours.

I was trying hard to end November on a good note.

I was still trying to do better in my classes and grind in the weight room with Nethaneel. Nethaneel and I was using the Urec to the maximum capacity so we can get better. We were putting in work until the end of November.

Breathing heavily, he said, "my guy, we haven't taken a day off in a month. I'm exhausted. We really put work in."

"Yeah, but how you feeling though? Do you not feel mentally and physically stronger?"

He laughed. "Your mindset belongs in asylum. You really train the mind to be better. And you're a math major? You're nuts. But I'm glad this happened because this adversity making us solid. People don't understand the trenches like us. We're putting in work to be better, and to overcome the obstacles that stand in our way.

DARNELLE CUYLER

Don't ever change bro. I mean that. Don't ever change for nothing man."

"Honestly, I couldn't change even if I tried. This is all I know. Fighting to be better and to uplift others in the mist of my own hardships is all I know how to do. As long as I live by my motto, then I'll make it."

Be Great Today! No Days Off!

The following week, Nethaneel and I no longer worked out at the Urec together anymore since we were trying to focus on our upcoming finals.

December has arrived, and it was time to put up or shut up. A do or die situation. I fought hard to pass my classes. I was trying to express to my professors what I was experiencing, but only one wasn't willing to at least hear me out. They made a deal with for extra course work and for the final exam. That way it can at least save me from failing the class. I still failed one of my classes and they did not have any sympathy for me. I was stressing out so much this semester, and had so much unexpected pain, that I was just ready to give up. And honestly, I didn't have the money to pay for another semester.

I was doing everything I could to make it and all I did is fail. This university been against me since day 1. Chris, Lois, and Julie were trying hard to tell me that it's ok to comeback another semester, but I was done. I gave all I had and didn't have nothing else to give. I had a couple people trying to talk me into coming back, but it was over with. When the semester ended, I went back to Orlando. I was so down and out mentally. I told my mom everything that happened and was hoping she would at least be comforting.

It wasn't comforting. It just made it worse all honestly. I can't talk to no one in this house about my struggles. I went and talked to Peanut and a few others about it. The more I talked about it the worse I was getting mentally. Everyone was getting pissed more and more. The only thing that was getting processed was that I wasn't graduating. It's the holidays and I was trying to be peaceful but, how can I? I was going through hell. Not to mention, all the family drama I was trying to avoid was front and center in my face.

BE GREAT TODAY! NO DAYS OFF!

Altamonte was the last place I was trying to be, but I had no choice. On Christmas, I did everything in my power to not think about it. I just told myself to let it be because stressing was not going to help. The next day, all the stress and hardships started showing up little by little. I was over everything at this point. As we get ready to approach to the new year, the negativity came back at full force.

"I got to get back on Sanford Ave. I have to go to *The Trenches*. I have to talk to God."

I went and started running. It was late one evening and I was angry. Extremely angry.

"God, why you did this to me? I did everything you asked time and time again. Every time I tried to better everything get worse. I did everything possible at that University. I was a stem major, I did research, I worked at the rec center, I strengthened and brought competition to the athletes. I brought diversity to the University. I did everything that could've been done. Why is this always happening to me? I have everything and everyone going against me! I'm even getting death threats thrown at me because of this situation I can't control. I fought every single day and most people sat there and watched me suffer. I can't talk to my family or people around here about it because no one understand the requirements and protocols. I can never talk to anyone at school about my hood and family problems because none of them never been through this level of adversity. I'm always struggling and I'm always alone. The good people I had in my life pretty much gone. I can't keep throwing my problems on Chris and Lois because they have their own problems."

I was crying and something just told me to go home.

I had just got home, and I was just thinking about Julie and the Urec and suddenly, she messaged me. She told me that everything was going to be okay, and that good people were fighting for me. I emailed the administration the next day and didn't get a response. Granted, everyone was on their holiday break as well.

One day I started thinking positive. I went to *The Trenches* and did the sessions.

"It is ok to go back one more semester. The end goal was always to graduate from LSU. We can't let nothing, or nobody stop that. Whatever solution that the people that are fighting for you bring to the table, take it. When you go back to Louisiana, work harder. Don't leave no stone left unturned. Grind harder but make it more precise. Don't only go back to the Urec, do more than you ever did before. Be more influential and more uplifting. A lot of them are graduating and need support. Step up and ease the tension off the professional staff. Go back and bring your best. All the hard work we put in can't go to waste. We will be the first to ever do it. You will graduate from Louisiana State University."

I felt better, lighter, and uplifted. I started messing my Urec fam, telling them that I was coming back, and we going to grind hard one last semester. The next day emails came in from professional staff and administration to come up with a reasonable solution. I took it and headed back to Louisiana. January 2016, right before classes started, I had to be real with myself. I had to let go of sports and focused on graduation.

I went back the next week.

I was with Chris, Lois, and Ally at a track meet. I went to go show support since Nethaneel was back on the track team. He was a whole problem like I said he would be. I had to instill my dreams into him because graduation was my number one priority. You can see the aggression in his performance. He was wrecking shut all season and did run in the Olympic Games like I said he would. He became one of the fastest sprinter's to ever wear an LSU uniform. I told him to keep the aggressive mentality.

"Don't be humble and don't let up for none of them. They don't know about adversity or the trenches. We built different."

After track meet was over, I went the Urec to put in work, and Chris, Ally, and Lois went home. I wanted to put up some shots for Zach. As I was shooting, there was man that walked on the court dribbling a basketball.

It was Dr. Allen.

He was a well-known and valued professor between LSU and Southern University. He knew what was happening in my life and he gave me some advice. I told him I don't know what to do at this point because they were already saying I wouldn't be able to go to grad school because of my GPA and GRE test scores.

BE GREAT TODAY! NO DAYS OFF!

"You're still going to go grad school. You have to make it for you. You have to continue to pave the way for others to come in after. You can't stop because of what other people say. Yeah, you have a low GPA right now and a few bad test scores, but who cares? You don't have to go the traditional route. When you go back to Florida, go to one of the schools and apply as a non-degree student. You show them that you can handle the classes and ask for a fighting chance. It's not going to always work but professors and some administration love to see students who try. I'm on many boards here and I always fight for the students to be given a chance. You've been fighting and making it work this long, you'll be alright. You will make it."

That was probably some of the most influential words I've ever heard in my life. That gave me so much hope, strength, and motivation.

~On a side note. R.I.P Dr. Allen, I made it work it. It was all thanks to you. I'm forever grateful for the words that you spoke into me. Thank you for believing in me~.

As classes began, I was putting in work. I told the fam I will give everything I have one last time and I was not going to let up. I was picking up the opening and closing shifts. I didn't want to work the openings, but I told myself I would step up and keep my word to Julie. I was on the closing shifts with Lois. Lois and I had a friendly competition that we had six minutes to get home and must text each other soon as we got there. We stayed in the opposite direction. We did that for the entire semester. I was also applying to graduate schools too and I knew I was going to more than likely get rejected, but I had to try anyway. I was going above and beyond by grinding in the library with my coworkers that also had goals to get into graduate school. I was grinding with my coworkers that were striving to get into medical school too. I prayed for them every day until they got their acceptance letter. I prayed for my people to get a new job in their field as well.

School wasn't for everyone.

Some people wanted and needed a break from it. It was a hard grind this semester, but I kept the tempo at full throttle every day. Most of us didn't really celebrate *Mardi Gras* and *Spring break* this year. We were really focused on graduating. We all made it through midterms alive and then we had our *Urec Employee Appreciation* ceremony. I was nominated for Employee of the Year for the third time which was excited. I felt like I should have won it, but I also felt as though I shouldn't have been nominated. 2015 was rough towards the end, but nevertheless, I was grateful for everything.

Now, it's May, and it was final's week. I made it out alive, and by the grace of God, I was officially able to graduate.

The day finally came. May 13th, 2016, I graduated from Louisiana State University with a B.S. in Applied Mathematics. It was by far one of the happiest days of my life. My brother, sister, and my nieces came to watch me walk across the stage. The next day they went back home. No one from my hometown said a word to me until my brother posted a picture of me on his Facebook. My notifications were going off for days. I didn't care for none of the praises because most of them never said a word prior to me graduating. They never said a word during the struggle, and I don't need an applause when the success come. People only support you when it's cool to support you.

I stayed in Louisiana for about another week or so. I partied and spent time with the fam, but I also took time to reflect on my life. One night, I sat in my apartment remembering what my uncle said to me. *Everyone one have one family member that make it. You'll be the one in our family to make it.* Now, I'm sitting here crying because I did make it. Not only that, but this just the beginning. I was the only African American male to graduate in my class with a math degree. I was the first person in my family to graduate from college. I was the first person from my hometown of Altamonte Springs, Florida to graduate from LSU.

I beat the odds.

I struggled and starved since day one. I was even homeless. I fought against everything possible. I pushed through all the deaths and devastating events happening to me and my family. I motivated people to chase their dreams and accomplish their goal I stopped people from giving up, committing suicide, and helped them with

BE GREAT TODAY! NO DAYS OFF!

making boss moves by chasing greatness. I met so many extraordinary people. Some of them not only became friends but they became my family. Especially Carlis and Chris because we really were taking losses, living, and surviving with each other. Literally staying at each other houses cause we ain't have nothing but each other. I wouldn't trade them for nothing in the world. This will be a memorable time of my life whether I want it to be or not. I will deliver more strength, support, and motivational speeches from what I've been through here. I'll be back to pay back them out-of-state fees. I will also start a scholarship fund for students like me.

I'm a man of my word.

Tomorrow, I say goodbye to LSU, and I head back to Florida.

To Louisiana State University, I'm grateful that you took on chance on a nobody like me. To help me prove that with all the hard work and effort put in, you can make it. Thanks for the things you've taught me. Thank you for letting me be a part of your culture and family. I can't wait to pave the way for the future students coming, and to share my experiences to inspire others. Thank you for turning me into the first ever LSU Alumnus from a small part in Altamonte Springs, Florida.

Thank you for giving me the opportunity to chase a better life.

Thank you for everything!

I can now scream this from the bottom of my heart and soul.

GEAUX TIGERS! LOVE PURPLE LIVE GOLD!

Forever LSU.

DARNELLE CUYLER

Remembering Katherine

As I sit here and think of all the memories you and I shared, it's hard to even put my thoughts into words. We had really good times and we also had our struggles but despite everything, despite all of the obstacles that stood in our way, we made it through.

I hope my work, my words, and my experience being shared does you justice.

I don't know whether to talk about the good times or the bad times, but knowing you, you'll want me to do both. I don't know if they're ready for this roller coaster, but that was my experience with you. Ups, down, turns, and curves, but exciting, memorable, and enjoyable. It's a lot of things that was never mentioned from my standpoint but also from yours. As I think about some of the times we shared, I think it was completely unnecessary for you to have me working the way you had me working. Every day, you had me doing yard work and you would sit there and just watch me. You would call me every day to come by and it was so much work that sometimes I grew annoyed. Annoyed to be in the way of Florida's unwavering sun that had no sympathy for my hydration or well-being. Continuously on my hands and knees transitioning from yard work to tidying up around the house.

It was never a time that I could just come by to say, *hey*.

It was work, work, and more work.

BE GREAT TODAY! NO DAYS OFF!

It was like you got a kick out of watching me constantly working. It didn't matter how much I did that day, you somehow still found something for to either clean or do.

I didn't know it then, but you created a work ethic in me that birth a drive that would never settle.

You did this to practically anybody that paid you a visit. Always putting someone to work no matter their conditions, intentions, or mission.

I remember watching an exchange between you and my uncle.

"Yeah, I know what I got a list of things to do for you."

You smiled. "I was only going to ask you to do one thing for me."

My uncle and I looked at each other like, *yeah right.*

"Yeah. but we all know that one thing will turn into a list of things to do before we know it."

We laughed so hard that I could feel it in the very depths of my soul, because it was true. There was no way for you to deny it. It was never do one thing and be done with it; it was always a list of things to do. Whenever we heard, "come here and do this real quick," we knew what type of time you were on.

Always on the move, never chilling, never relaxing, and that was crazy to me. But it was nice to see you enjoying yourself to good music and having a beer.

I personally hated to see you drink.

I knew that alcohol was bad for you, and even though I knew you would leave this world one day, I wanted you to live a long life. I sit here and think about the times when you'd try to lie while hurrying to put it down.

"What? this my only one. I promise"

That was definitely your third one, and not even minutes late, I saw them grab you another one out the cooler. You knew I was looking out for your health no matter. I used to hate how you could sit there enjoying a cold one, chilling, and watching others you put to work.

Nah, sit yo ass there with yo beer and leave people alone.

Of course, I never said that, but I definitely said it in my mind. I wonder if it was on everybody mind too, if we're being

DARNELLE CUYLER

honest. I couldn't even enjoy my hotdog in peace without you coming by.

Oh, come pick this up for me right quick. Do this for me. Do that for me please.

See, it's already time for me to go home because it's 100 people at this cookout and you steady asking me to do things. Thankfully, at least one of my uncles will step up and help me out so I can go back to minding my own business.

The worst is when we're at your house and you know we can't stay long, and you still try to put somebody to work. I knew you didn't care. But then you get mad when people don't come by the house because they know you're going to try to put them to work and potentially cuss them out. Anytime anybody mentioned you, there was always a resentment to go by your house.

"Nah, I'm not going to Mema house. She going to put me to work."

"I'm trying to give the quickest hi and bye because I already know what type of time she on."

I used to get so jealous and mad because I knew the truth. I was Mema's favorite.

"Man, shut yo ass up," I blurted out with a smile on my face. "We all know it don't matter who at her house, she's going to call me. Y'all know you just be filling in until she gets ahold of me. She'll call the whole family, and soon as one of y'all mention my name, it's over.

"Oh, tell him the come to the house right quick."

It was always a lie when you saying, 'right quick,' knowing damn well that it'll be a minimum of three hours if she caught you lacking. People think it's a game and don't even know, she'll have you doing work ALL DAY and won't think twice about it.

I remember the time you made me move a truck by myself.

"This truck needs to be move and I don't have the key."

Any logical person would think that the truck wouldn't be able to move, right?

"Nah, throw it in neutral and push it."

What the actual fuck?

"By myself? Can I at least call my uncle for some help?"

BE GREAT TODAY! NO DAYS OFF!

"Nah, they pissed me off yesterday," she took a gulp of her water. They better not come to my house."

"Mema, how am I supposed to move the truck?"

"Just rock it back and forth. It'll move it."

"Okay genius, then how am I supposed to stop it?"

"Boy, I don't know, figure it out. Just put something behind it."

"Man, I'm going home."

"No, you not. Get back over there and move that truck like I asked you to do."

She deadass thinks I can move this truck by myself.

Speaking of doing things by myself, that made me think of how you only call me for almost everything. It's funny because my cousins knew what time it was and how to get out of doing work for you. Their go-to was fighting. They knew if they start fighting, you'd tell them to leave. It was the perfect set up every time. See at first, I just thought they were being idiots, but they knew the whole time. I only noticed when they started laughing as they was leaving. I remember when we were doing yard work and cleaning the front porch, my back was turned but I can hear them arguing and cussing each other out.

Here they go with the bullshit.

I turn around and saw my cousins fighting.

"Both of y'all get out my yard and don't come back to my house today."

She ain't never have to say leave twice. They were already grabbing the game.

"So, y'all just going to leave me by myself knowing Mema don't like that?"

I laughed so hard that my eyes were closed. By the time I opened them again, they were gone.

This was the moment I knew, I fucked up. I had a bad habit of laughing in serious moments.

Ain't that a bitch.

They didn't do this all the time, but I peeped game when I knew they wasn't trying do slave work. Once I realized it, I would just tell both of them to leave before they started fighting so Mema wouldn't get mad.

DARNELLE CUYLER

"Yeah, y'all can go ahead and slide. You already know the routine."

For some reason, even when I got stuck doing the work by myself, we would laugh as they were leaving. It's wild because both their dads are my uncles, and they would do the same thing. I would be on Ronald Reagan, slaving away and they would ride by. You can hear the acceleration as they passed by. They would beep the horn and smile extra hard at me. I would smile hard because it really was funny to me how we all thought the same shit.

"Let me speed past Mema house, cause if we stop now, we doing work. Oh, look who out there? Oh, he is doing the work. Yes sir! He the realest one in the family."

"Y'all ain't shit," I would say to myself.

My uncles would laugh. "Chill out nephew, we'll be back."

We knew damn well they weren't coming back. A few times one of my uncle's would bring back Gatorade because he knew I was doing work she probably told him to do.

However, we all had to do yard work when it was time to put up Christmas lights. Christmas lights was your life. I just didn't understand how you was using the same Christmas lights in 2012 from 1998. Only thing we had to do was switch the bulbs and all the lights would still work. We could've easily brought new Christmas lights from the Dollar Store, but nah, let's spend the next 2-3 days fixing old ones. You made sure every year the outside was lit up. It always brought joy and peace to people riding down Ronald Reagan. During the holidays was the only time there was more peace and less yard work.

You mainly just wanted the Christmas lights up.

I remember there was a day I was aggravated about coming over and we got into it with one another. I was doing work for you day in and day out, and you just wouldn't give me a break. You didn't seem to care if I was sick, tired, hurt, busy, or nothing. The only thing that was on your mind was me coming over and getting work done. Even on Saturday mornings, we can never sleep in. You and my momma were always up extra early talking loud for no reason and telling everybody business.

Then my mom would lie unprovoked.

BE GREAT TODAY! NO DAYS OFF!

"Oh, I told momma you was sleep."

A bold face lie.

I can hear them talking loud as hell, and I heard my mom tell her she'll send me over there later.

Does peaceful sleep mean anything to y'all? I can never get no peace. None of us could.

"Every day," I had a little more authority in my voice. "You'd call me to do every little thing. I come over here to do one thing, I can't leave until I've done ten different things. I bring you food, I clean up around the house, and I do yard work. No matter what it was, everything have to be done every time I see you. I can't ever just come over here to chill. It's always work. You don't think about nothing else but working me like a white-mouthed mule."

We laughed for a slight second.

That's another one of her favorite sayings.

I'll work your ass like a white-mouthed mule.

"Anytime anybody come over here you do the same thing. Now, don't get me wrong, doing stuff for you is not a problem. It's doing it every time we come around that's a problem! You make a demand, and you take off before anyone could make an objection. I don't get why you laugh with all of us and then turn around and cuss people out knowing you need them."

She looked me right in my eyes and said, "I DON'T GIVE A DAMN! If they come to my house, I'm going to work they ass like a white mouthed mule. If they don't like it, then they don't need to come over here. I call you because you always do like I ask. You're going to always see what I and how I want it. I don't care how you feel about it and you can be mad all you want. Hell, you can even hate me, but I know when I call you, you're coming over to do what I ask or need you to do. I always call you because I know you're always going to get the job done!"

"Well, what are you going to do when I leave?"

She didn't look at me.

"I'll still call on you. Whatever I need done will wait until you get back. I sleep good at night knowing you're always going to come by and make sure I'm ok. You'll always get the job done."

I stood there briefly thinking about what she said.

DARNELLE CUYLER

"Yeah Mema, I'll always come get the job done. Just call tomorrow and I'll come sooner or later."

Then I left.

After having that talk with her, I never asked her what she wanted done. I just went over there every day and did work that I knew she would be satisfied with. Sometimes, while she was sleep, I would use the spare key to get in and clean up. Once I was done, I would just go home. I quit trying to get out of doing work or questioning why she won't call on the rest of our family as much as me. I just kept putting in work. I knew that I was getting ready for college and preparing for hard times.

I was noticing a few changes with my grandma, but I never examined things closely like I should because I was too focus on trying to get into school and leave Altamonte. I went to Bethune Cookman University for a semester, and everything really started taking a turn. I was brushing things aside with our family but as time progressed, it was one hardship after another.

It rained so hard that water started leaking from the roof. Then mold started building up in the roof of the house. I remember it like it was yesterday. It was August 2011. The roof got fixed immediately but they left your house in shambles until I came home from school for Christmas break. I cleaned inside and outside by myself per usual. Kind of strange how everyone had quick access to you but couldn't drive 30 seconds to go to Ronald Reagan to clean the house.

I let it slide and listen to the things you told me.

It was crazy how I had to come live with you shortly after and I don't regret it. It was to help you while I was going to Seminole State to stay in school. We stayed on Top sight for a few months, and I didn't like anything about the situation at all. I moved back home even though I should've stay with you. Especially when I told everyone I was going to LSU by any means necessary, and no one took me seriously. Everyone took me for a joke except you. We all say actions speak louder than words and I was putting forth maximum effort that showed I was going to do it.

I remember before I left for LSU, I was trying to stay positive because of Uncle Hodges being extremely sick from cancer. I was getting ready to move to a new state on my own and I was sad at the thought of leaving you here. But I had to go after my goals and dreams.

"I hate having to rely on people for help," I said in frustration. "It's always a problem or an excuse when it comes to me. One day I'll graduate from college and get me a good job to buy a big house. You'll be the only one that'll live there, and we wouldn't have to worry about none of them and the drama they got going on."

"I keep telling you, don't worry about me. I'll be at peace knowing you working hard and will be alright. You need to leave here and don't come back."

I hated that you said that. Why wouldn't I come back for you?

"That's so ignorant. Why would you tell me not to come back here for my family?"

"Because you don't belong here. As long as you work hard and stay the hell away from here, you'll be alright."

I knew going to LSU was going to change my life forever. You told me not to come back to Altamonte and I was trying to figure out why you kept talking like that.

"Just make sure you keep working hard and everything will work out. You'll make it. Make sure you smile and do right by people. Make sure you're always good to people, even the ones you don't know. You don't have to worry about me or nobody here no more. As long as you're working hard, I know you'll make it in life. And the thought of that puts me in peace.

I made sure to live by your words.

I'll always get the job done.

When I went to LSU, I knew you were so proud of me. I was trying my hardest out there. When I first moved to Louisiana, I was nervous, but I knew the game plan and goal in mind. I would call you almost every week to let you know that I was doing ok. It was rough at first, especially not having a job. It was hard for me when I would ask y'all for money. It was lowkey embarrassing to ask Peanut and Stevan to have Tweet put money in my account to get my rent paid. I was doing all I can to not worry you. I was trying to make friends and look at the brighter side of everything. I

DARNELLE CUYLER

was doing all I could to stay afloat until I got a job at the Urec in the Spring semester. Even though I was enduring a lot of sad & lonely nights behind closed doors, I made sure I smiled hard the next day. I was making sure I stayed focused on my goals and dreams.

In January I was so happy when I got the job at the LSU Urec. I knew I was able to work and not have to ask people for help. I can just work and pay for everything myself and not worry about being a burden to anybody. At least that's what I thought. It was hard because I didn't have the extra money coming in from Peanut anymore. I made the promise I wouldn't ask anymore, and I made sure I kept my promise. It was hard when I came home in February for Uncle Hodges funeral. I had just told you I was doing better because I finally got a job. I made sure I called you every Sunday when I was walking to my morning shift at the Urec to talk about my week and to tell you I was doing good. I was grateful for the friends I've made thus far at LSU and spending so much time at the Urec. Months went by and I was still struggling to get by. I remember when I called and was asking you to please send some money.

"If I had it, I would send it. I would give you my last dime, but I don't have anything right now."

I cried to myself to sleep that night. After that night, I just told myself, I'll never ask y'all for money again. I'll just take my L's every single day. Thank God I was blessed with friends that covered up my hardships and helped me through hard times. I had to swallow my pride and take the help and support that they were giving me.

It hurt me so bad internally when they used to help me. I felt like I was working so hard and it was in vein because I still had to rely on people that I barely even knew. I would be in tears after studying sessions with the crew and they would ask about my family supporting me on this journey.

It used to pain me so much.

Why these people keep helping me and I'm not even related to them?

I used to stress about it so much. One day I just said fuck it. I'll take whatever help that come my way. I will stop seeing them as

BE GREAT TODAY! NO DAYS OFF!

people who were not my blood family and I've only known them for less than a year. Hell, they won't even be these people anymore. They'll be my people. Some of them will be my family. A few of them want to see me doing better than my own family any way. I started going even harder for them. I was doing whatever it took to take the stress off them, and show them they can make it too. I was constantly supporting them and grinding with them too. I was putting in so much work behind them. Even if I was tired, sick, or hurt, I would still go to work and grind with my people. I would keep going just like you embedded into me. I didn't need to take a day off and to be honest, I didn't want to. I didn't make excuses or let them make excuses. If you became fam, we were grinding every day.

It started making sense, let down after let down after let down that you told me not to come back to Altamonte. So many phone calls and text messages kept pushing me away and leaving me in tears. During the semester in 2013, I finally got ahold of my life. I finally started getting everything together. I was able to make payments on my tuition, pay my bills, and pay for groceries without asking for help. I was finally able to get control of my grades to continue to do better at LSU. It wasn't until 2014 where I thought I truly had my life together and could do better. I was spending a lot of time trying to focus on the good times and let go of the bad. I didn't hold any grudges against anybody, but I knew I was going to work so I wouldn't have to rely on anybody. In 2014, I kept calling you every week telling you I'm doing so much better. I know sometimes I would skip a week whenever I had big exams. I kept calling you and telling you how much my job loves me, and how I'm getting the job done. I was doing everything you said I would and should do. I was doing good by people, and I was getting the job done every day. I didn't take a day off for weeks at a time because I was doing everything in my power to live up to your word. I came home Summer 2014, and I was telling you that I was going to make it. My grades were doing better, I was trying to be a student athlete to get scholarship money. I was doing research to get help with my tuition. I also still kept my job at the Urec and was making enough to pay rent and personal expenses. I was at my best and

DARNELLE CUYLER

you were so proud of me. I would talk about the good things that was happening to me and you would laugh so loud.

Things was really falling into place for me.

I remember taking you to the doctor when I was home and they said that everything was fine and that you were 100% health. You told the doctor that I was always trying to help you exercise and get some good sunlight. We knew I wanted you to live long. I went back to Louisiana for summer school because I was getting ready to make power moves. In the middle of the Summer I got a call saying you were sick and you were back in the hospital.

"When y'all go see her, call me." That's all I kept telling my family.

I kept trying to stay focused on my goals and dreams and not worry about you being in the hospital. When you finally called me, you assured me that everything was fine, and they was letting you go home in a couple of days.

OK, Cool. I didn't think much of it.

Why would I stress when they said that you were good to go? A week or so went by and we talked again you let me know they were letting you go home in a day or so.

"I thought you told me that a few weeks ago?"

They did let you go but you had to come back because your blood pressure was high. I tried every way possible not to stress or panic. I just told myself to pray on it and to stay focused. I called home and told them what I tell them every time.

"WHEN y'all go see Mema, CALL me."

I couldn't stress that enough. I had enough going on with barely being enrolled in school at this point, on top of trying to make ends meet. On top of trying be an athlete at LSU, add research to it, and finally let's add that I was taking really challenging math classes at that.

I remember like it was yesterday, I was sitting at the Urec on a Sunday shift at the equipment desk when my brother was trying to call me. I didn't answer his call until I was off work. I was so devastated when I got home and called him back. I never been so devastated in my life. I remember crying endlessly when you passed

BE GREAT TODAY! NO DAYS OFF!

away. I never experienced pain like that in my life. My chest was hurting so bad. My heart was hurting.

I remember you saying, "if your heart hurt, you will die."

Lord Knows I wanted to lay down and die from you leaving this earth. It was a power move for you to tell Lyric to go down the hall to get you some cookies instead of letting her watch you die. I struggled so hard trying to deal with your death. You took everything from me at that I was so close to doing what's never been done before and I lost it all because of you. I struggled mentally, emotionally, and spiritually for months on the inside. I couldn't talk to nobody about what I was going through because all anybody would say they didn't know how to respond or that I was trying to play victim. I didn't want to say that I could've been going through depression because of what I was always told growing up.

"Ain't nothing wrong with you and you don't need any help." I just kept it all to myself and tried to stay around people that made me laugh. It was so hard trying to deal with what was really going on, on the inside. All the drama that was going on in your house and I couldn't do anything about it. I was at the house looking for all of your things.

"Where's Mema's stuff? Where's her clothes, her jewelry, her antique stuff? Where are all of her family photos?

"Oh," my mom said. "They bagged it up and got rid of it."

When I asked who touched your stuff, no one would answer me. I was dealing with too much at LSU and I didn't need to get into more problems in Altamonte. I had to tell myself to let it go. She no longer exists in this world and I needed to come to terms with that so I can move forward.

The next few months after your passing were the hardest months of my life. I was constantly crying myself to sleep. I would wake up shaking to a point where it felt like I was having a seizure. My muscles would get so tense that if I moved too fast or moved the wrong way, I would be in a world of pain.

Pep talks with myself in the morning were always rough.

"Fix your face before you open the door. Smile harder today and above all, put in work."

Once I was able to stop crying and get myself to a better place, I would go even harder whenever I went to the Urec. I made new friends that were genuinely good-hearted people. They always brought good vibes to the table. I was trying to find every way possible to not think about you and not stress about everything that was going on in my life. I tried focusing on my classes, celebrating with my friends, and working out more. Time was a great friend because over time the pain eased up, but the pain kept coming randomly every now and then. It would come when I least suspect it. Different time periods and even at different events over the course of a couple years.

I tried to keep myself busy with school, work, and spending a lot of time around people. It helped me hide from the anguish that tormented me but eventually, like a game of hide and seek, it would always find me. I was always honest with everyone about my circumstances, but I never told them about how hard it was for me dealing with your passing. To be honest, I don't think expressing that particular detail would've made a difference. But, I do apologize to the people that I would dump my thoughts, emotions, and problems on when I should've faced them head on.

Even if I tried to fall in love it wouldn't have changed anything. I wanted to so badly, but deep down inside, I knew it wouldn't have healed anything that I was dealing with on the inside. I was trying to think of any logical thing to do to cope with the pain.

So, I went back to the one thing I knew how to do and that's work harder. The pain was still there though. During the Spring and Summer semester, when I was either working on something or hanging out with my friends, the pain was still there. Pain met adversity and decided to fuse together and make chaos. I was at the point where I wasn't going to graduate from LSU, I didn't make the track team, my grades were dropping, and I was losing myself all over again.

Pain wasn't my friend. It also wasn't my enemy. It was an entity that didn't discriminate between the just and the unjust. It didn't live its life by greed or money. It was something that everyone experienced. Energy that can neither be created nor destroyed, just passed from one person to another. So, I contained that pain and channeled it for my benefit. It was pain that forced me get my-

BE GREAT TODAY! NO DAYS OFF!

self together and take better care of my well-being. But one day I told myself to let it all go. I had to psychologically alter my mindset to accept everything for what it is.

Mema's cause of death was heart failure. And when I look back on things, she was going through a lot of pain. She's the one that said, "if your heart hurt you'll die." She'd just lost another son, the rest wouldn't get right, and I was no longer living in Florida. She also said that she's at peace knowing that I was away from Altamonte and making something of my life.

If we look at that stand-point, up until now, prior to her death, I was making it. I was doing things that was never done before by anyone in her family. I was working hard and I didn't have to ask for help or depend on anyone. It was a peaceful time for her to exit this world. If I weren't making it, she'd still be alive until she found out I was.

I am making it through. I WILL make it.

I'm at a point now where I have to make it at Louisiana State University. My grandma will continue to sleep in peace because I'm putting in the work every day. Be at peace with this death. I felt so much weight lifted off my shoulders once I told myself that. I still had a lot of other things to let go at that time and I was tackling it one by one.

If your friends don't want to make time for you or make you feel worthy, let them go. Be at peace with all of this. If your family don't want to help during hard times, let them go. Be at peace with all of this. The number one focus in this time frame was to graduate. All and All after everything that happened, I went into another semester fighting to graduate.

"I'm not from here!"

I kept telling them that since day one. I have to make it out here. Through many trials and tribulations, I had to take whatever was thrown at me and press through no matter what. I had to do whatever it took to be the first in the family to do it. They kept telling me that I wouldn't make it, but I knew I had to make it because my grandma believed in me, and I had to do it for my hometown.

There are those that didn't want us to be great in life in Altamonte. They'd rather we lie 6 feet deep in the graveyard. People

DARNELLE CUYLER

have always told me that I was aggressive, but how was I supposed to act when a lot of people wanted me to fail?

They don't know me or where I'm from. We built different over here. I graduated from LSU for my family and for my city. I really couldn't let up on it because history was being made. Generational curses were being broken.

Put me in the book of greats.

I've been putting in so much work to the point I was obsessed with the grind because of you. It's because of you that a lot of people don't want nothing to do with me and that's perfectly okay. I'd rather run until my heart give out than sit still and chill. I'd rather take the unknown path, the hard route, and struggle than to take the easy way out.

I've dealt with so many hardships since you've been gone. I was offered sell drugs to get by, but I turned it down because I didn't want to let you down. I stayed solid in the trenches. Starving and struggling were my closest friends. We were a perfect trio made to be. I was grinding for the hood, even the ones that hated me. I'm the only one that went against the grain and stepped out on faith. I didn't give into the circumstances. I made a game plan and I stuck to it. I could care less about what others say, I will out work all of them every day! You don't have to act humble on the other side of the grave, you can let them know you made me! I'll go to any section, any trenches, and put in work. I'm not afraid of failure. I know if you were still alive, I wouldn't have had to face so many problems alone. I had people send me death threats and did all they could to sabotage to my dreams. People shook my hand promising one thing and ended up doing another. The only reason I didn't retaliate because you always showed up in my mind in the nick of time.

"Let it go. You have work to do."

I can't go to work or graduate if I'm sitting in jail. I had to deal with being homeless time and time again, and one of the things that kept me going was the thought of you being here and knowing I wouldn't have to worry about a place to sleep. I could've stayed with you until I got my life together. I won't ever forget the

BE GREAT TODAY! NO DAYS OFF!

death threats and attempts thrown at me, but I know one thing, their efforts weren't going to stop me from working hard.

No one will outwork me.

I'm doing what you said. I'm living by what you instilled in me and I'm pressing forward.

I been put in so much work everywhere I go but sometimes I can't understand why I struggled so much. I never took time off to spend time with my loved ones in our time of need. I lost friends and loved ones. I don't mourn properly because the only thing I know how to do is work. I just go to work and cry at home if I have time. Your funeral was the last one that I've been too. A lot of deaths happen since then, and the closure was me going hard at work the next few days on their behalf. I prayed hard over them and kept it moving.

Certain things will let it be known why I grind so hard and why I act the way I do. I be putting in work to help the people around me get through their own trials and tribulations. I be praying for them to get through their hardships and to prosper. I stayed strong to keep my people motivated. Every day I put forth the effort to show them that we can make it out. I work harder for the people from the hood to let be known WE CAN AND WE WILL make it in life!

I represent the struggle.

I'm not afraid to let it be known that I really came from the trenches. I never hated on anybody from the hood or the support they had to make it out. All I did was work harder to keep them motivated and to show others there's more than one way to make it out. I let people feel my pain and show them I'm a survivor. That if I can make it through, so can you. I refuse to give up on my goals and dreams no matter the circumstances because you always said that I'll get the job done.

I hold my friends to a higher standard. I don't let them make excuses because I was never allowed to make excuses. I don't have sympathy or pity because it was never given. Some people like to complain about the struggle, I'd rather grind through it. I keep talking about my friends because God really blessed me to be around so many extraordinary people. I'm not afraid to fail or fall because of them. I know they'll be right there to pick me up and push me forward. They really accept me, my passion for the grind, and my obsession with Oreos. Instead of laughing at me, they'll come grind with me and eat Oreos with me too. I don't question if they have the same amount of faith in me as you do. I wouldn't expect them to be as proud of me as you.

I do everything to make them laugh out loud and hard until they cry. Even though you probably had one of the most annoying laughs I've ever heard in my life, I loved it so much because it brought me so much happiness and peace. Whenever you laughed super loud, I knew it was whole-heartedly and you would wipe the tears from your eyes. Every day I try make people smile hard and bring them that same type of Joy.

I never told anyone but every time I think of your laugh, I would literally cry. Even as I type this message, I'm in tears right now because I miss it so much and as much as I would to go to your house to hear it, I know it's not possible right now. I've been going so hard behind my loved ones and friends. One of my friends told her mom that I'm the realest person she has ever met. When I met her at graduation, she smiled, hugged me, and called me that.

I just laughed.

Since she called me that, I had no choice but to live up to it. I promise I'm not letting up. I'll message, call, or post to my people every day to let them know that I'm proud of them, I love them, and that I miss them. I try my best to let them know I value them more than anything.

Well, anything except the grind. But they know that.

I stayed strong during hard times to pave a way for them. I showed them they can achieve anything because I'm right there with them. I stayed down with them during hard times too. I cried with them during their hardships and the deaths they experienced in their own lives. I showed them how to work through it and press-ing forward when obstacles keep coming. One of my closest friend's was losing family members back-to-back since I've known him and not once, have I ever seen him down. I think it's because he saw what I was going through when I lost you and he was there to watch me pick myself back up and grind it out. I have other friends that lost loved ones and I'm one of the first people they look

BE GREAT TODAY! NO DAYS OFF!

too for positive affirmations, support, comfort, and of course, good vibes. I'll do whatever it takes for them to growth their pain and grind harder despite the circumstances.

Whenever my friends were going through any type of hard times, or there was new goals they wanted to achieve, I was one of the first people they contacted for motivation and a game plan. I try my best to help my people prosper in life. I feel like their goals and dreams are my goals and dreams. Their hard times are my hard times. I promise no matter how far or how hard they fall, I'll pick them up every time. No matter how dark, or how deep in the trenches they get and lose their way, I'll always go find them and bring them back to the light.

I promise to love them and not trade them for anything in the world. I'll show them how to grind every day. I wouldn't trade the grind and motivation for nothing in the world. In this game called life, I'm giving it all I got.

I promise.

Every day I'm putting forth the effort to achieve bigger goals and to do better in life.

I will donate and strive to help programs that my friends establish and are a part of. I broke the barriers for first generation graduates. I'm going to make sure African Americans can be proud of being a STEM major and have a love for science. I promise I'm not letting up. I don't have no faith in my siblings to put money away. I put money away for each of my nieces and nephews to go to college. I understand the value of saving, endowments, and investments. I'm doing all I can to pave the way for future generations. They hate an aggressive black man but hate an articulate black man even more.

I'm at my best when I'm doing numbers or involved with money. Some call me a Mathematician, but I don't go by titles. I just give it all I got and bring my best to the table. I try my best to stay focus on my goals in life.

I will put in the work and let it be known that your grandson is a beast when it comes to this grinding life.

It was already predestined for me to achieve greatness.

I just wanted to say thank you Mema. I want to thank you from the bottom of my heart and soul. I want to thank you for making me who I am today. I want to thank you for putting me through hell and preparing me for hard times. I thank you for instilling the grind into me. I thank you for putting all your Faith and love into me. I thank you for constantly telling me that it'll be ok and that I'll make it. I thank you for leading by example and constantly telling me to do right by people and that it'll always come back to me.

I tried to keep my life simple like you did. As long as I can eat Oreos and go to work, I won't complain. Thank you for helping me stay strong and to grind through the hard times. I thank you for not giving up on me. I thank you for showing me how to laugh out loud and whole-heartedly even when it's not that funny or funny at all. I thank you for bringing me tears of joy. I promise that one day I'll get a house so nice that you'll be laughing from the other side of the grave. I promise the outside will be lit up with Christmas lights. I will keep your tradition alive.

I'm not going to lie to you though, I'm not using the same lights for damn near 20 years. I will keep putting in work and chasing my goals and dreams. I will fight hard in this life I live. I will make my life a great one. I will go down in history for doing what most said was unachievable. I will continue to show people the power of consistency. I will continue to keep going hard for my friends. I will continue to be their number one fan and hype man. I will keep bringing motivation to others when I talk and inspire them to do better in life. I thank you so much for praying for me. I pray that I'm blessed to be around people that believe in me as much as you did. I know that seems like a fairytale, but one can dream. I will continue to live by your word, and I will continue to get the job done. I will try my best to let go of things that brought me so much pain and chase the things that bring me so much joy.

Hopefully one day, the love of my life will bring some of your tendencies to the table. If we can laugh together, and she believes in me like you did, then I'll make it work. I'll feel like I'm cursed if her laugh sounds like yours though. It'll suck trying to enjoy something funny while I'm mad, happy, and sad all at the same time. The good thing is, at least the memories of you will always be with me. I promise will continue to always want more out of life. I will continue to always yearn for more. I will show people that I can do more because you showed me and instilled that into me. I will always get back up and keep fighting after I fall. I will use the fire in me to keep fighting.

"It's ok," you said as you watched gasp for air. "Just get some water"

"I don't want water! I want to go home!"

"Just get some water and keep going."

I know now, I had to keep going because I didn't have a home. Whenever people say, *Go Hard Or Go Home* I promise I'm going to always choose to go hard because I can never go home! I'm grateful for you accepting me and loving me for who I am. I'm always going to let the passion show. Even when I'm laid out on the track. I always tell myself, "I don't need no water. I'm strong! I can keep going because my grandma said I can endure more. She showed me that I can endure more in life. I can keep going because my grandma believed in me. My grandma proud of me. I don't have to question her thoughts towards me."

It was like pouring gasoline on a small lit fire.

I was back up and I wasn't tired anymore.

I was born and raised in the heat. I was born and raised in hard times. I was born and raised to grind. I will give my last breath when it comes to the grind. I know you on the other side of the grave sitting with our family. I know they are asking you how you have so much peace. Then you, Uncle Hodge, Uncle Butch, everybody else in our family can say proudly, "because he is working."

I promise I won't give up on our family. I promise I will keep working hard and doing it the right way. I thank you for understanding that I'm not perfect nor do I want to be, but I am obsessed with putting in work.

I know you're not coming home, but I'm letting you know I'm still doing what you told me to do. I turned your words into a lifestyle. I feel like I am a decent human being because of this, because of you. Maybe one day I will be a true inspiration for people in need. I'm grateful for being born into our family. I'm grateful for the dark skin that I have. I'm grateful for the mentality and the drive you told me to have. Living the life you want me to live is hard sometimes, but it's worth it. I wouldn't be here if it weren't for you. I wouldn't be one of the realest from Altamonte Springs, Florida. I had to tell my people about you. Now they can understand one of the main reasons why I work so hard. They can see why I constantly put more effort than others. They can see why I'm such a die-hard grinder.

I proud to be your grandson.

I want to say thank you for it all and I will get the job done. *I promise.*

I love you. I miss you. I pray you continue to rest in peace. Every day I will make you proud. Until we meet again.

Being An Inspiration

Anyone can be an inspiration.

You can be an inspiration at any time and any place.

Inspiration comes from the root word inspire. The definition of inspire is to fill someone with the urge or ability to do or feel something, especially to do something creative.

You can inspire someone or become inspired by someone else. The definition of inspired is of extraordinary quality, as if arising from some external creative impulse. To me, the quickest way to be inspired is to watch the action of others. Watching others perform will lead to the thought process and concept of doing better. To be an inspiration it states that one has the process of being mentally stimulated to do or feel something, especially to do something creative. A lot of people feel as though the only way they can be an inspiration is by being rich, a celebrity, or professional athlete. Those aren't the only ways to inspire people, to be inspired, or to be an inspiration. I see so many people throw themselves or their goals away because of this thought process. They feel like if they aren't rich or have a big-time job, they can't inspire others to make it or do better.

The smallest things in life can make the difference.

The constant commitment and dedication you bring every day will inspire someone. Most people don't know that the people they inspire the most aren't in their family or anyone they know personally. I've been inspired by so many people that I've met at LSU alone and not one of them are from where I'm from. I see the downfall of people because they do so much comparison to others and blocking the glow and the light they bring to so many other people on a day to day basis. I hate the fact that some people don't

DARNELLE CUYLER

realize how much they truly inspire others just for showing up every day. Just because no one tells you every day, you're still an inspiration.

Some of you are truly genuine, good-hearted people and that makes you one of the purest forms of inspiration there is. That's something you can't teach, that's something that's embedded in the soul. You can't train that.

I feel like I try my hardest day in and day out while being around people that do it so easily. To sit there and continue to make people smile, uplift others, and to make them laugh wholeheartedly daily is simply amazing. And to think that you do it all while covering up your own hardships and struggles is truly an inspiration. I can only dream of performing these acts as if it's second nature. I've seen people just walk through the door and the entire atmosphere change. To walk into a work setting and everyone becomes in such a better mood just because you showed up today. Even when you're not at your best, your presence alone lift the burden off so many people. I laugh at the fact that I worked with people that really brought this energy to the table and every time I see them, I just laugh and thank God for them.

Thinking back on it, I was internally beefing with my friends. I envied the vibe they produced because it was so natural instead of being forced. I was praying and begging God every night to help me smile every day and bring that type of energy. Thanking him continuously for putting them in my life because they made me a better man every day just by genuinely being themselves. It made me want to be better. I was constantly trying to reevaluate my hardships and situations to learn how to keep my composure. I wasn't humble enough. I was trying to figure how can I pick people up if I kept falling. Being around these types of people help me develop the mindset that I'm not afraid to fail.

If you're unwilling to fail, you will never succeed.

You inspire others when you keep getting back up every time you fall. I was fighting every day to keep picking up the people to the point they would never fall. I would be there to catch them every time they stumbled. Even if they fell in the dark, I would always go back into the dark to pick them up and to bring them back

BE GREAT TODAY! NO DAYS OFF!

to the light. Being around inspiring people help endure the dark times and helped me face my fears head on. To navigate in dark times was tough, but it became easier to get back up because I knew my purpose. I knew I needed to be there for someone and help them through their trials and tribulations. Helping them helped me find strength in the struggle and laugh in the face of hard times.

Failing wasn't something I feared because failing is a part of life. It's a part of the journey and it's necessary for growth. Plus, I knew it was a couple of people that was proud of me regardless. I think that's so dope to help someone develop a better mindset. To reassure them that they are amazing and loved no matter the end result of something. I was going hard every day to deliver that energy to other people. Afterwhile, I wasn't afraid to fail anymore because I knew there were people that was going to pick me up and cheer me on to the finish line. The only thing I can do is thank God for that and keep going hard behind them.

I ask myself the same questions every day.

How do I get better at it?

How can I do better at uplifting people?

But the only answer that came to me was to be consistent. To keep bringing positive energy to the table every day. Bring it even when you're not getting acknowledged for it. Keep bringing it to the table even when you're feeling down and out.

Keep going.

You have to keep going because you never know that a day may come that you may potentially save someone's life. I've seen so many inspirational acts and people don't even know it. I can go into depth talking about the actions of inspiration and you wouldn't believe me.

TO THE PEOPLE:

To The Students: Waking up every day and showing up for school make you an inspiration whether you believe it or not. We all be there where we don't feel the need to go to deal with what's going on. I know it's tough trying to find your way, make friends, and accel in the classroom. It's even tougher to the students

DARNELLE CUYLER

that want to be involved in extra-curricular activities. Going to practice and not skipping a rep or set, make you an inspiration. I know and see some athletes skip reps and sets and still accel which is elite in itself, but for those to not take a rep for granted because someone else watching them. You're an inspiration for going to college even though it's not a D1 university. You're an inspiration for still going to college to accel in academics even though you wanted to continue to play sports. I feel your pain but it's still amazing to go off to continue your education to better yourself. To all the long nights of studying for an exam or to pass class, to show the dedication is inspiring. It's also powerful for those to shake back off the procrastination to prove they can get the job done at last minute. Some of you never realized how you made a difference in the classroom till the day you didn't show up and everyone asking about you. Just because you never talk in doesn't mean your presence going unnoticed. Keep showing up. I think the most inspiring is coming along and only knowing someone for a few months and create a friendship so strong y'all become family. Keep showing up and changing lives.

Teachers and Coaches: You're an inspiration for being a teacher. The fact that you take your time with them because they lack discipline and support at home. The fact that you sit up there and bring joy to them kids every time they see you.

You're an inspiration to coach kids to be better and to excel in sports. To let them know not only to be a great athlete but to be a great human being. That's such a powerful impact because it helped so many people in the long run learn to do better and to lend a helping hand. You helped individuals understand that yes you can be great individually but there are times where you can be better with a team. You're an inspiration helping students find something their good at in extra-curricular activities. You're an inspiration taking kids to and from practice every day. You're inspiration for wanting to teach and coach other kids even if they parents don't have the funds. That's something that effect so many young people. This keep them out of trouble or being in situation they never wanted to see or be apart of. A lot of kids need this type of

BE GREAT TODAY! NO DAYS OFF!

support in their life. The fact that you're putting forth the effort to do that is simply amazing. I support that to the end of time. You're an inspiration for going home and making time for your family after a long day of work. You're an inspiration being able to teach every day. You're an inspiration to go above beyond to let a student know they matter and they're safe. A lot of students never feel safe or valued but instilling that into them every day is nothing but love. REAL Love.

You're an inspiration to continue to put your best foot forward to educate students to stride in life. You're an inspiration for doing research and inspiring people to have a mind of their own. You're an inspiration for not giving up on students that lack the financial stability. You're an inspiration for stepping up for the students that lack the moral support and attention they need at home. You're an inspiration for uplifting students when they're in need instead of degrading them in front of other students. You're an inspiration when you provide other students a meal, not knowing it's their only meal for the day. You teacher and Coaches are a very critical asset to this society and I apologize that the system doesn't show or support you the way they should. Please Keep going and fighting for the students and the future of this world.

Professional Jobs: You're an inspiration picking up trash every day. You're an inspiration flipping burgers at a fast food restaurant. You're an inspiration working in retail and customer service. You're an inspiration when you working overtime for little or no pay. I know society strive to degrade you for everything you stand for but you're a huge necessity to our modern day society. You're an inspiration to work in any part of the medical field to save lives and not do it for your own benefits. You're an inspiration to work during natural disasters. To put your life on the line to benefit society doing the time of need is no easy task. I can't imagine the life of storm trackers. I'm from Orlando, FL. I know all too well that once that hurricane go past a Category 3, you're 100% playing with life and death. You're an inspiration taking care of people in a life and death situation regardless of they have insurance or not. You're an inspiration showing gratitude. You're an inspiration by saying good morning every single day. A lot of people

DARNELLE CUYLER

don't understand what a simple "Good Morning" can do to alter someone's day. You're an inspiration when you take people away from the pain they've endured behind closed doors. You're an inspiration the way you uplift people in their time of need. You're an inspiration when put forth the time and effort into others because they don't have anyone else to depend on. You're an inspiration for going to fight fires and bringing families out alive. You're an inspiration when you're fighting to protect and save lives instead of killing black people and letting us know that we don't matter.

You're an inspiration when you're fighting to help people for the greater good and letting others know they matter regardless of gender, race, religion, and so forth. You're an inspiration for going to foreign lands to start a new life so your kids won't have to struggle. You're an inspiration for working in harsh conditions because the job needed to be done. You're an inspiration for dealing with racism every day and continue to bring your best foot forward. You're an inspiration for being a guidance counselor. You're an inspiration for being a mentor. You're an inspiration for being You're an inspiration for doing numbers for people so they can feel financially safe. You're an inspiration for fighting for a country that keep showing us there's no love for your people. You're an inspiration at the fact that people can come to you and feel trust and safe. You're an inspiration for stopping an active shooter even though you weren't put on the news or glorified. You're an inspiration for finding lost kids from human trafficking. You're an inspiration for sheltering others during a natural disaster. There's so many jobs and careers that are undervalued when they're the backbone to sustain life. I promise you bring a bigger impact that others give you credit for. I wish I could acknowledge you all but please understand you are valued. If you stop showing up, it'll cause more harm than you realize. I'm not the one to overlook you, I promise I hear you. I promise I value you. Keeping Inspiring.

The Forgotten: I know it's a lot of people that feel like they don't belong, nor should they continue to exist but that's not true. There's been plenty of times where I was in a place where I felt as

BE GREAT TODAY! NO DAYS OFF!

though I don't belong, so don't worry I know how you feel. You're inspiration for not giving up on yourself and trying to find value to your own life. You're an inspiration for overcoming your drug habit. You're an inspiration for telling others your hardships so they can learn how to deal with their own. You're an inspiration for standing in the crowd rooting for someone kid when their family won't show up to support them. You're an inspiration for beating any form of Cancer. You're an inspiration for dealing with diabetes. You're an inspiration for still having joy while dealing with any sort of syndrome or disease. You're an inspiration for finding love again after the worse of the worse took place. You're an inspiration for finding happiness in the small things in life. You're an inspiration for bringing people joy. You're an inspiration for just being you...

To The Families: The fact that you stepped up to the plate for taking care of someone else's child, don't ever downplay yourself because that's truly extraordinary. You're an inspiration for being a father to your kids. A lot of people grew up without a father regardless of the situation of how it happened. To be a father figure is so important to life. You're an inspiration for breaking the cycle and taking care of your kids even though you were fatherless. You're an inspiration for stepping up and taking care of your nieces and nephews no matter the situation was with their parents. You're an inspiration for stepping up for your nieces and nephews or grandkids when their deadbeat mother or father could take care of their responsibility! You're an inspiration for providing for kids that's not biologically yours. You're an inspiration for making sure all their needs are met on the day to day basis. You're an inspiration for staying strong and taking care of your kids when their father walked out of their life. You're an inspiration for always providing for your kids and their friends so they wouldn't feel left out. You're an inspiration for helping someone else child feel loved. You're an inspiration for constantly stepping up to the plate. You're an inspiration for providing your kids and someone else kids a place to sleep at night. You're an inspiration for rooting for their kids because you all they have. A lot of people don't understand the darkness and pain that some people had to or have to endure because

DARNELLE CUYLER

they don't have a parental figure in they life. To show up to an event to support your child's friends is one of the more sincere heart warming thing a person can do. It's a different ball game when you have someone supporting you regardless. Please keep stepping up and continue to support the young.

To The Streets: A lot of people don't know how to approach a topic because they don't understand. I understand and I'll let you know too. You're an inspiration for covering up the premediated thoughts that was leading to murder due to misfortunate events. You're inspiration for dealing with rape when none came to your rescue. You're an inspiration for staying strong when they false accused you of rape. For either side of the story, I'm sorry you have to endure that type of fear and pain. For you to keep going forward and not letting it stop you from finding life again is simply amazing. You're an inspiration for staying real when she was cheating on you. To continue providing for your family after she tried to take them away from you, you real for that. You're an inspiration for being in your kids life after she threw you on child support and took everything. You're an inspiration for getting out of that relationship when he was beating on you. You're an inspiration for taking care of the baby after he was cheating on you with your with closest. That's a power move for showing that you don't need someone that's constantly putting you down in order to have a happy life. You're an inspiration for putting down selling drugs and going to school. Some don't understand the courage it took to change but I've seen it done before and I promise I'm proud. You're an inspiration for putting the drugs down and going to get a 9-5 to provide for your kids. You're an inspiration for working 7 days a week just so someone have food to eat. It's hard to do better in life when you're sitting in jail. You're an inspiration for staying solid when they were laughing at you for walking every day. You're an inspiration for riding a bus every day and not making excuses for getting to and from work. I'm glad you understand the grind stop for temporary obstacles. You're an inspiration for keeping your priorities in order and not using your money to flex. You're an inspiration for making it out that shootout alive. You're an inspiration for staying

BE GREAT TODAY! NO DAYS OFF!

home for the kids after they gunned you down. You're inspiration for not retailing and returned all favors. It's hard for a lot of people to see that they are very much needed in this world and that life would be more difficult if they were dead or in jail. You're an inspiration for making it out of any unspoken hardship. I promise I haven't forgotten or gave up on you. Keep fighting to stay alive and maintain.

To the Fam: You're a blessing from God. You're an inspiration for constantly showing people they can be better. You're an inspiration for staying solid after went months without a job and never gave up. You're an inspiration for not giving up when opportunities didn't go your way. You're an inspiration when you volunteered your time to those in need. You're an inspiration for going to homeless shelters and helping feed families in need. I'm promise I'm proud of you. I promise I love you. I love the fact that you keep showing up and bringing value to people. You're an inspiration for working in career field that doesn't provide the best pay but you value helping others rather more than the money and you truly are an inspiration. You're an inspiration for being a social worker. You're an inspiration for being a therapist. You're an inspiration for being someone others can vent too. To the one's in the medical field, whether you're a doctor, nurse, a surgeon, or even a front desk clerk, please don't let up. I'm grateful for the fact you can take on such at task and provide hope in the darkest of times. You Powerful. You're an inspiration for being a dentist and helping people smile more. Helping people smile to bring sunshine on a clouded and hurt soul. Every day I personally strive to smile to make someone else laugh or have a brighter day. You're an inspiration for working in your family business and to those that's creating your own business. To handle that is no easy task but the work you bring to the table really make a difference. You're an inspiration for working in engineering. You're an inspiration for being a mathematician. You're an inspiration for moving back to your hometown and work until the right opportunity come. You're an inspiration for working in Higher Education. You're an inspiration for going back to get a diploma or a degree. You're an inspiration for becoming a professional athlete. You're an inspiration for taking tens of thousands or even millions out of your own money and start scholarships for students. You're an inspiration for putting homeless people into homes. You're an inspiration for moving back home until you're ready to be on your own. You're an inspiration for picking your head up when they left you in the rain. You're an inspiration for overcoming hard times that no one know about. You're inspiration even when no one believed in you. You're an inspiration for staying alive when you watched you're mom and dad break down and began dying in front of you. You're an inspiration for not committing suicide and falling in love with the grind. I promise I still pray on you. You're an inspiration for stepping up and taking care of your siblings when your parent passed away. I promise I pray that you continue to prosper and lead. You're an inspiration the way you pray over people every day. I think that's one of the purest forms of love. Regardless of what you do in life I promise on my life, I'm proud. The work ethic and passion you bring to the table is unmatched. The way you know the difference in self and mental care. The way you willing to put forth the effort and not settle for less, really inspire me. I'm obsessed that you can easily influence people to be better without trying. I'm glad that we've crossed paths because I wouldn't be where I am today. Thank you for being inspiration and bringing joy and light to me on clouded days.

To The Few: You're an inspiration for putting everything on the line so someone else can survive. You're an inspiration for going against the payroll to keep someone else enrolled. You're an inspiration for going against the policy and making exception for someone else to make it. You're an inspiration for covering up someone else's hard time. For going back and paying on someone else's tuition. For fighting to keep a worthless soul alive just to leave it up to Faith that He Will BE GREAT in life. To go out your way to stop so many tears from streaming because a dream was all he had. To telling you proud of him and you love him when nobody else gave a damn. I promise y'all one of the most extraordinary inspirational people to ever do it. Don't ever change.

BE GREAT TODAY! NO DAYS OFF!

To The One: You're an inspiration going against the odds and making it out. You're an inspiration for being a first-generation graduate. I know it's hard breaking generational curses. You're an inspiration for constantly bringing motivation to the ones that needed it the most. You're an inspiration for never giving up. You're an inspiration for following your own dreams.

To The Real: You're an inspiration for accepting me for who I am. You're an inspiration for befriending me. You're an inspiration for believing in Be Great Today! No Days Off!

Finding Strength During Hard Times

Finding strength during hard times is something that's easier said than done. I talk about my life a lot, but I think this is the motivation that some people were looking for. This probably the strongest message I've ever delivered. I think about this a lot because it's such a critical factor in life. Sometimes in life that's the only thing we can do to keep going. It doesn't matter who you are or where you from, everybody goes through something. A lot of people aren't going to care about your hardships, trials, or tribulations. And honestly, some people won't be able to understand the problems that you're going through. So, talking to some people will seem like a waste of time.

Then next thing you know you find yourself in a deep dark place feeling lost and alone. Me, personally, I had to find out on my own that not every hardship is meant to hurt you. Some hardships are meant to help you get to where you need to be in life. So many times, I saw myself being alone and isolated from everyone because of my personal problems but it was to help me. I understand not everyone is built to handle extreme hardships or dealing with them time after time. I know it's hard wanting to have someone to talk to, but no one can relate to you. I know it is hard seeing people get more help and support than you. It was very tough for me because

BE GREAT TODAY! NO DAYS OFF!

I would automatically get labeled the problem even if I was the victim in the situation.

So, I understand when people feel that way. I understand when you're feeling stuck at a dead end wand it seems like there's nowhere to turn. I've been there, time and time again.

This is why I say it's important to find strength during hard times. You can also view this as having faith, trusting in God's word, or keeping positive energy through the situation. It's all in your choosing or beliefs. I know that not everyone believes in God or is a Christian, so word it how you see fit.

It's hard to say that everything happens for a reason, but depending on the event, maybe it did happen for a reason. I found myself struggling from time and time, but my hardships brought strength to other people. I've seen people get their life taken away from them and couldn't do anything about it. I always tell myself that no matter what, If I can do something about it, I will. I've seen some people get their life, goals, and dreams taken away then turn around and achieve even more greatness. I felt like all my life I just smiled and worked hard, I never thought that it was pretty much my way of life.

I didn't notice it at first and I didn't really practice it until I graduated from high school. I know that it's considered being a genuinely a good person, but I've been through some many trials and tribulations to the point that I had to practice smiling through the pain and still pushing myself to work hard. I had to continue to fight for my sanity and push through the bullshit at all cost. I never in my life thought that I would come to a point where I had to practice smiling to hold back tears. I was constantly drowning in my own tears and wallowing in my misery, but I knew I couldn't give up or give in.

I refuse to sit there and watch my life get thrown away.

I refuse to quit!

It didn't matter if I was all alone and I felt like crap at times, I had to find strength during hard times to keep going. This became part of my discipline, dedication, and passion, and I was fortunate enough to come across people that made this practice happen with ease. All my friends ever did was motivate me to work harder.

DARNELLE CUYLER

What's the reason that keeps me going? I had to ask myself that when things got harder and the nights got longer. I sat in the dark in a puddle of my own tears so many nights trying to figure out why is this happening to me. I had to constantly change my perspective to look for the brighter side and to work harder. It was a spiritual and a psychological warfare with a lot of migraines and sleepless nights.

Sometimes, anger makes you stronger. Sometimes the pain help you develop more strength. Diamonds are just rocks that were pressurized by fire and pressure. I excelled in the weight room because I was dealing with my own weight in my personal life. I wasn't going to let the weight weigh me down.

I was going to rise up.

I was going to win.

I had to remind myself that I am worthy, that I am strong. I had to be strong for my friends and remind them of their own strength. It took me awhile for me to realize this but not all every trial was meant to be a tribulation. Sometimes, it was triumph. The trials was support to show you how strong you are. It was necessary for you to grow and find hope, serenity, and strength in hard times. I started to understand that not everyone is going to have sympathy for you and that's okay. Keep moving forward anyway. Sometimes the only thing you can do is stay true to yourself and know that you are going to out of this better than ever.

I came to this point in life, time and time and time again. Whenever I would talk to my friends or motivate them, it became more clear. I saw myself stepping up from a personal and motivational standpoint. I felt like I couldn't be the friend I needed to be for them if I wasn't giving them my all and encouraging them. I feel like what type of friend am I, if I'm not supporting them, encouraging, and holding them accountable to a higher standard? I'll always want you to do better.

We will fight through it together regardless of the situation.

I had many instances when I had to dig down deep and redefine the grind. I only had two options, give up or grind more. Hell, I really only had one option because giving up wasn't on the

BE GREAT TODAY! NO DAYS OFF!

table. I would never let my people give up nor will I ever give up on myself.

We're chasing greatness every day.

No Days Off.

I'm coming for everything I want and everything I lost with aggression because that's the only way to approach it. Sometimes you must fight fire with fire, or you're going to get burned. And you can ask my closest friends, when it was time to put in work, I was never idle about it. Soft spoken has never been me and I will forever be loud and proud when it comes to the grind. I'm not giving you a pass or accepting any excuses. No, we will put in the work and get the job done. If we fail, we will try again until we achieve what's needed to be done.

I know how it feels to reach out to people through social media, call, or text, and people do not respond. Sometimes sending something uplifting to others is just as beneficial to you as it is to them. Even if they do not respond. I know it's hard to uplift others and spread positive energy when you're going through your own storms. To fight negativity with positivity and feel like you're on the losing end.

I understand.

Do it anyway.

Finding the strength to push through it and still be there should not only be motivation but inspiration to change others' lives. I tend to go into overdrive whenever I feel my friends or myself giving up due to misfortunes. I feel like it's my job to keep them going. My closest friends will tell you that I don't tolerate slacking or even the thought of giving up.

What are we talking about? Why you got your head down? Oh, you must be thanking God.

What are you crying for? You must be crying tears of joy because we putting in work and it's paying off.

You can't get down on yourself with every single hardship, otherwise it will hinder you from achieving the greatness you are meant to have. Sometimes the only thing you can do is fight for it. For a few of us, it's the only option we have.

Always remember this, someone is always watching you. How you handle the situation plays a direct part of their view and

DARNELLE CUYLER

growth for their life. Your strength enables their strength. Not everything is about you and honestly, showing up and being present is sometimes enough for others to keep going. Pushing through that dead-end job, keeping your head up through unemployment, and fighting through homelessness. A lot of people complain about the situation that they're in, but never do anything to get themselves out of it. It is much easier to complain about your circumstances than to put in the work to change your circumstances. When I didn't like the situations I was in, I did everything possible to change it by putting in the work.

You have to give yourself a fighting chance!

I've starved many nights and even been homeless a couple times thus far, but I never gave up. I will fight my way through and find a way out of the situation. Despite the circumstances I was in, whether in or out of my control, I knew I had to do whatever was necessary. I had to the light and the strength to keep going. I am a black man living in America, so I already have two strikes against me. Misrepresentation, stereotypes, and false statistics have been against me since day one. Sometimes, I was perceived as a suspect, criminal, and even a threat. Every day I strive to help people find their own purpose and strength because adversity will consume if you're not prepared.

I never thought about committing suicide, but I know people that have. They feel like everything will be better if they were no longer here, but that's not true at all. So many times, I wanted to give up, but I always thought about others that were going through similar trials as me. I couldn't give up; I couldn't let them down. It made me think of the younger generations in my community. I wanted them to know that it didn't matter what their circumstances were, it didn't matter how bad things seemed at the moment, it didn't have to stay like that. They do not have to be a product of their environment and I wanted to see that I was a living example of that.

What will happen when they want to go to college but can't afford it?

How would they feel if they knew that there are those who do not want to support you or see you succeed?

BE GREAT TODAY! NO DAYS OFF!

If they never seen someone beat those odds regardless of the deck being stacked against them, they wouldn't be as confident in themselves and possibly give up. And I don't want them to give up.

So, you see now? I had to keep working harder. I don't have any hatred or jealousy in my heart. I love to see people make it, especially black people. It allows us to pave the way for others to follow in our footsteps and succeed.

You have to understand you're a blessing to someone when you keep fighting. I used to think that no one can be proud of you if they didn't pray for you, but that's a lie. There are people that's proud of you whether you know them or not. There are people that heard of you and feel proud that you gave their loved one a reason to keep going. There are people that's praying for you to make it through every misfortunate that comes your way. Plenty of my friends told me they told their family, colleagues, and even friends back in their hometowns about the positive impact that I've had on their lives. And even though we've never met, you prayed for me and extended grace towards me, and I'm grateful for it.

I used to question that a lot at first, but It made me feel honored to be a voice of tranquility. The genuineness of just wanting someone to be do and be better. I've seen people helping others in a little way and yet, it was big thing for the other person. It was the fact that they genuinely wanted to see others prosper and succeed without being selfish.

They were just naturally good-spirited people.

Finding strength during hard times is having faith that it will work out no matter things appear. You find yourself overworking out of fear instead of trusting the process. If it worked itself out before, it'll work itself out again. I can admit, I struggled with this concept as well. Whether it was academics, athletics, or even work, I found myself putting a lot of wear and tear on my mind and body because I feared being rejected. I feared going back to Altamonte Springs the same as I left it.

I feared failure.

But I let all that go and trusted the process. I couldn't see it at the time, but I was putting in too much work, in which there is no such thing. *At least that's what I thought.*

DARNELLE CUYLER

But I needed to know when to rest my body and give my mind time to refresh for a new day.

Finding strength during hard times meant pushing through knowing that some people don't support you. People always pray for shade, but ignore that before shade can be given, it must rain. The rain represents trials, it represents the process. God will give you a seed, which is a blessing of opportunity, but it is up to you to do what it takes to make it grow.

Faith without work is dead.

Carlis used to always quote Galatians 6:9.

"Let us not become weary in doing good, for at the proper time we will reap a harvest if we do not give up."

He said it so much that it was damn near ingrained into my skull. And because of that, it just pushed me to further no matter the hardship that came my way.

You reap what you sow.

I always pictured myself growing a harvest, metaphorically speaking. I feel as though I have to put in the work every day to achieve the goals that I've created in my heart. The goals that I've set for myself was never achieved the way I wanted but they always did happen.

I remember the words spoke from Proverbs 16:9.

"A man's heart plans his way, but the Lord directs his steps."

Things don't always go according to plan, but I know God will direct my path so I can achieve the goals I set out for myself. Just because you didn't accomplish the goal within the time frame you wanted it, doesn't mean that it's not coming your way.

Keep putting in work.

Stay the course.

Trust the process.

New Beginnings: FSU 2016

I had a lot of my mind when I got back to Altamonte. I went over to Peanut house. Everyone was surprised to see me when I stepped foot in the yard.

"Look who it is" Peanut uttered.

I looked at Peanut and we started laughing.

"I told you I was going to get my degree," we hugged. "It was hard, but I got it."

I hung out with them for a little while before heading back home. When I was getting ready to leave, Ed stopped and asked if I wanted to work with him to make some money in the meantime. I still needed to make payments on my bill with LSU and since I'm not working right now, I definitely needed to put some extra money in my pocket.

"Yes," I said without hesitation.

I was still sticking to my routine and running on *Sanford Ave* every day. I still had the *No Days Off* mentality and knew this wasn't the time for me to get complacent. I was still talking to my closest friends from the Urec every day. I was still staying on top of them every day so they can stay focused and motivated for anything coming their way. Our relationship stayed strong, and the flames only grew over time. There were days we didn't have anything to say to one another, but we would still let each other we were still

DARNELLE CUYLER

alive. As the summer progressed, I was still trying to figure out what was next adventure for me. I didn't get accepted into any of the grad school programs that I applied for. The jobs that I applied for, a few of which I thought I had for sure, sent their denial emails.

I didn't want to come back home, but with all of the denied applications and no call backs for jobs I applied for, it didn't really seem like I had a choice. I didn't have an opportunity to connect and network with people with family businesses or go to career fairs at LSU because I was always working. Because of my financial position at that time, I couldn't take a day off. A day off meant not having enough money to pay my rent or feed myself at least. I didn't want to ask my family for help or assistance with job search simply because of the bad experiences I had when I was away for school.

Why did I come back here?

But it wasn't time to have a pity party, I had to tell myself to create opportunities instead of looking or hoping that they would come to me.

When July started everything started to go south and I immediately knew it was time for me to leave Altamonte. Over the next couple of days, I was configuring a plan to relocate, but none of those avenues were working. I didn't have anywhere to go, but I knew I needed to get away from here.

I was jogging up and down Sanford Ave and I remembered what Dr. Allen told me.

"You need to make a game plan and don't just wing it. You can still chase your dreams, you can still accomplish your goals. Take the road less traveled. But I think you should apply to Florida State University. I think it'll be a great fit."

When I got home after my run, I applied to FSU. I still kept in contact with the graduate math coordinator at FSU and she was extremely helpful throughout the whole process. The following week, I got accepted into Florida State. I got accepted as a non-degree student like Dr. Allen suggested. I didn't tell anyone at first because it was a lot of things I needed to get figured out before I announce everything.

BE GREAT TODAY! NO DAYS OFF!

This isn't the sexiest thing in the world, but I did what I had to do. I took the Mega Bus from Orlando to Tallahassee to get things settled. Now I know what you're thinking, you have a degree. Why the hell are you taking a bus? I have to the mindset of getting where I need to be by any means necessary to create the opportunities that I want. Whether I have to walk or catch the bus, I will get to where I need to go.

Everything went smooth when I got there and once, I was done, I returned to Orlando, the same way I came.

July was a rough month because as each day went by, things weren't the greatest at home. But I accepted it for what it was, and I knew it was time for me to go. I was never the kind of person to stay in a place I didn't feel welcomed.

I reached out to Jorge and told him I was moving to Tallahassee. This came out a shocker for him because he knew that meant I got into FSU. When I told Jorge that I was going to Florida State, he was so hype for me. Mostly because he got a job there after we graduated from LSU. While I didn't tell him why I wanted to get away from Altamonte, he was thrilled for me to leave for the next adventure.

He was excited. "Yo! Why didn't you say anything about getting accepted?"

"It was a last-minute thing, and I didn't really intend on applying. But I needed to get away from Altamonte."

He talked with a coordinator from FSU, and he let me live with them for a few weeks. We talked it over with Ben who was a coordinator at FSU to allow me to live with them for a few weeks. I was extremely grateful. I told them I would pay rent or whatever was needed so they knew I appreciated the kind gesture.

I moved to Tallahassee with the same mindset, but with new goals.

"Aye," Jorge called out to me. "You want a job at the campus rec center?"

I was debating in my mind if I wanted to stay or not because the experience I had at LSU. But I needed money to stay afloat and to cover the bills I had.

"Sure." I told him.

DARNELLE CUYLER

I couldn't start work until August because I had to register for classes first.

Jorge and I were close at LSU but our friendship more and more after. I met Jorge at LSU Urec in 2014. We had the same mindset when it came to people who thought they had a position of power whenever they walked into the facility. We strive to influence people to do better. We had a lot of in-depth conversations and really got to know one another.

One day he asked, "why does everyone think so highly of you? The way you carry yourself and how you handle things stood out for some people. Everyone respects you, and I didn't see why at the time because I didn't know you. Now, I get it."

"Everything takes time."

Everyone comes around eventually.

Slowly but surely.

I earned my respect the hard way. Julie, at the time, always needed certain shifts covered and no one would pick them up. So, I would pick up the slack. When someone constantly didn't show up I would be the one filling in those gaps.

On random days, Jorge would be walking by the facility and see me throwing weight around with the powerlifting team with ease. Hell, some days he even saw me pushing weight without a spotter or pads on the bar. Running up and down on the indoor track envisioning myself running against the greats. Every day I was committed, dedicated, and disciplined. I turned aggression into passion, and trials into motivation. Jorge saw me being positive and uplifting others beyond where they were, and he understood what I truly meant to the Urec.

Being calm and humble is commendable but it did not get me to this point in my life. I got here because I had the audacity. I had to be aggressive to keep fighting adversity whenever she came lurking on a regular basis. I fought so many battles alone that I feel like I am a whole army by myself. I will not make it trying to be something that I'm not. I will make it being me. I'm not changing who I am for nobody. I'm not trying to be liked. I can care less if someone doesn't like me, but they will respect the grind.

BE GREAT TODAY! NO DAYS OFF!

Jorge watched me go through situation after situation, conflict after conflict, pain after pain, and still watched me rise above it
all. His level of respect was noticeable. I can tell by him seeing me
push through things and come out victorious, it motivated him to
push through things whenever things got harder. I can't take all the
credit. He had that mentality before he met me. I just think that my
effort to keep fighting added fuel to his fire.

The next day we went to FSU campus rec center. There
were two gyms on campus, the *Bobby E. Leach Center,* and *the Fitness
and Movement Clinic* which is also known as FMC. Jorge introduced
me to a few people on the staff. I arrived at the *Leach Center* and
seen some old faces. The Bolings, Lauren and Alex. We were reunited and it was a feeling I could never forget. People at Leach
didn't know I went to high school with them. The next person I
met was Jorge's boss, Darryl. As we talked to Darryl, I told him a
little about myself. He seemed to be admiring my accomplishments
and everything I was bringing to the table. He was getting hyped.

"We need that type of passion and energy around here,"
Darryl was excited.

I knew he would let me grind how I really wanted to. I
don't think he understood the gravity of this kind of freedom, but
he won't regret it.

Jorge showed me around the facility and met a few more of
the staff members.

I remember the next day I was playing basketball and
needed ice because I strained my hamstring. I forgot about the
workout I did a couple days prior, and my legs were still sore. I met
the supervisor that day. Her name was Chloe. Before the semester
started, I was able to pick up shifts at FMC. FMC was a smaller but
sufficient gym, and it was the spot to be. Well to me at least. A lot
of the staff didn't like it because the pace was slow, but I loved it.
Slow meant nothing is happening, and nothing happening meant
easy money.

I only worked two days and I already being talked about.

"Hey man," Jorge called out to me. "Everybody already
talking about you. They're saying how friendly you are and how
many shifts you already picked up."

A big smile slithered across my face.

DARNELLE CUYLER

"Yeah man. Just trying to keep the LSU grind going."

"This isn't LSU anymore, my boy. You can grind more. We're going to be elites over and you're going to be a supervisor. You can't be dropping the F-bomb left and right. Plus, we have people that really be grinding. You'll meet people like Matt, Katelyn, and couple others that grind just as hard as you." The first thing that came to mind was *man, fuck that*. I'm not trying to be a supervisor. Secondly, my competitive nature kicked in when he said they grind just as hard as I do. I wanted them to know that no matter how hard they worked that I was going to work harder.

"I can't wait to meet these people! I feel like we'll be great friends because it sounds to me like they respect the grind. I honestly don't care for being a supervisor. But I will put in the work regardless. My mission isn't to get everyone to like me, but to uplift and motivation others until I prevail. I will lead when it's time and where I see fit. I will grind and put in the work every day nevertheless."

"We are grinding!" Jorge said.

I continued to pick up shifts and I could feel a certain energy lingering around. A lot people thought that since Jorge and I are friends I was going to do whatever I wanted to do whenever and however I wanted to do that. I didn't have that mindset though, and I knew it wasn't going to be easy for people to see that. I was there to put in the work. One thing I needed to do was to make sure I connected with all of the people that worked at the campus rec center that shared my complexion. I need to connect with them so they knew we were in this together, and that I was here to help them in any way I can, motivate them, and uplift them to exceed beyond expectations. I already had a degree despite striving to get another one, and I felt it was my duty to make sure they get theirs. I need them to know that they had someone to be there with them and for them during their hardships. I'm not here to just hang out with you. I'm here to motivate you and help you break generational curses and be the first-generation college graduates in your family.

I've been that person for my family.

Whatever problems you have, I'll do whatever it takes to see you through it. I promise we will make it. I know talking with them about the hood and the conditions back in their hometowns made other coworkers feel uncomfortable. I didn't care. They'd never understand the hardships and trauma we had to endure growing up. They'll never know the pressure some of us are going through as first- generation college students. Especially as a Black college student. They don't know what it feels like to have your family and community wanting to see you succeed or fail. I know how it feel to be the only African American in your class and feel like you don't belong, or people clowning you for taking STEM courses because it's not the traditional route people take in our community.

I always thought it was crazy for people to frown upon you for taking math classes but praise you when you have an engineering degree. It's a little ass-backwards if you asked me.

It was all love after I was able to talk with everyone. Every time any of us saw each other, it was all smiles. I was able to give them that sense of comfort that they aren't alone, were understood, and have visual proof that they can succeed.

As time got closer for classes to start, I had to make sure I had everything in order. From my experience at LSU, I knew how left things could go if I didn't act quickly. I had two objectives, register for classes and find a place to live quick, fast, and in a hurry. I moved into *Villa Cristina* on Belle Vue street. I had a roommate named Justin and he was cool people. He was an LSU fan as well, so we were definitely going to get along. Especially when LSU played. We developed a close relationship and about once a week, we would come home and say, "bro, story time." We knew it was going to something crazy, wild, or disrespectfully. They were all funny, nevertheless.

It's the first week of school and I was officially a student at Florida State University. I didn't really tell anyone at first because I was slightly embarrassed since I was a non-degree seeking student trying to get into the master's program. I was trying to make sure I had it all together before I tell people. I was going to take my classes more seriously than I did at LSU and the first thing I needed to find was a place to study in peace. The Dirac Library became my sanctuary, and it was for the STEM majors. At least that's where most of the STEM majors studied at. To me, it was the new Middleton. I was in there every single day of my college career. I studied in Strozier, which is another FSU library, a few times but it wasn't the same as Dirac. I was in Dirac studying for hours even on the weekends.

Nothing's changed. It's still *No Days Off*.

I would study in the computer lab room all the way in the front left if no one haven't already taken my seat. Man, I was faithful to Dirac. The librarians and the door watcher knew that I was coming through. I had Boosie and Kevin Gates in rotation in the headphones. Sometimes, I would go there two to three times a day if needed. It would mainly be before and after class and work. It didn't matter what time of day or the kind of weather we were having, I was going to Dirac Library one way or another. I was in Dirac from the first day of classes until I finished all of my courses and earned my degree. Dirac was considered my second home. I've spent more time there than in my own apartment.

Right before school started, we had a scheduled meeting at the campus rec center. I sat in the front with this guy name Marvel. I worked with him for a couple weeks before school started. A few people were a little confused by who I was because they never seen before.

"Who is that?"

"We don't know him."

"When did we hire new people?"

Those that did work with me had my back though.

"DC? Oh, you'll love him. He came in from LSU. He's Jorge friend."

As the meeting was coming to a close, they touched based on the shifts and it was the same shifts that nobody wanted or spoke up for. The weekend shifts, the closing shifts, and the Friday evening shifts. I picked them all up so we can hurry up and leave. Everyone was hyped about it.

My first shift when the semester started was a Thursday morning opener. Every Thursday morning, I would walk to the Leach doors and this girl would walk by going the other way. She even had on the same uniform as me, so it was safe to assume she worked for campus rec as well.

So, the first week I didn't really think nothing of it.

BE GREAT TODAY! NO DAYS OFF!

The following week, I saw her again and really paid attention that we're wearing the same thing. The third week I broke the ice.

"So, we both work for campus rec, I see. I'll get a shift with you one day. It was getting weird that we would walk by and not say anything, and we have on the same clothes."

She laughed. "Yeah, it was getting weird. But now, we can say hey."

Her name was Valeria. I didn't fnd that out until we worked a shift together at FMC. My Thursday opening was a squad shift. I met Kiana, who taught me how to do my tasks at Leach, and Taylor, who I found out we were both from Altamonte-Longwood area. We bonded instantly. Whenever I would work, I would always play Kevin Gates song *I Don't Get Tired*. I would always think of Ally because she would always play his music too. I would come to my shifts hyped, and Kiana & Taylor would laugh. I would tell them we have to be hyped this early or we'd die of boredom on this shift.

We had one rule on shift though.

NO YAWNING!

It got rough as the semester progress, because classes were beating us down and it was getting cold. We were getting tired.

The next shift I had was at the FMC. I was trying to turn every shift into a squad shift. Squad shifts were always a good time working alongside good people. I kept meeting new people throughout the week around the campus rec center. I had a shift working with one of my boy's Clayton, who was giving me vital information on others I would work with. I wanted to know who they were before we got a chance to work together. It was important for me to understand them so I can figure out a way to make our shifts better, or at least, turn them into squad shifts. I met Ashley and Claudia, who were both were supervisors as well. I remember meeting Claudia and Malinda because they were STEM majors and we had some of the same classes.

They witnessed my losses firsthand when it came to some assignments.

I remember having a conversation with one of my coworkers and they were trying to warn me about Claudia.

DARNELLE CUYLER

"She majors in geology. She'll talk to you about rocks the whole shift if you don't stop her."

"I think that's cool for someone to be passionate about their studies. I don't know if I ever worked with someone who talks about rocks, but I'm actually hyped to work with her to hear about it. I want to learn about everybody major because I know there's not a soul that wants to hear about math problems from me."

I met the boss of FMC the same day and her name is April. She was so nice. I was a bad influence on April's progression with working out. Every time I saw her it was bad. She would be in her office or just now finishing a workout and I would come causing trouble.

"Hey April," I would startled her with my excitement. "Would you like some Oreos?"

She was confused at first and then looked at Jorge to see if he shared her same sentiment.

"What," She asked. "Who just asks someone if they want Oreos randomly?"

Jorge and Alex laughed. "Yeah, that's just how he is."

"I offer people Oreos because they make people happy. I haven't met anyone yet that doesn't like Oreos."

She stood there for a second and thought about it.

"You're right. They do make me happy." I was a problem ever since.

That first weekend I worked at the FMC with Claudia and Clayton. I remember that shift like it was yesterday because there was a real bad accident, and it took the paramedics over 45 minutes to arrive. Despite that, all FMC shifts were squad shifts. Especially on the weekend. The next week I was walking to Jorge, and we met some more of the Leach workers. He introduced me to the staff and then he introduced me to Matt.

"This is Matt," Jorge said. "When you talk about the grind, that's Matt. He works at least 30 hours a week."

"In that case, I will also be joining the 30 hours a week club. Probably more. I don't take days off. I love the grind."

Matt chuckled. "30 hours mandatory." I said.

"Light work." We shook hands.

BE GREAT TODAY! NO DAYS OFF!

It was nothing else to say after that. Real recognize real and we looked familiar to one another. We both knew what time it was after that and we were friends ever since. Thing about Matt is he was considered *The Cool Kid*. A little too cool for some people. I liked that. I like meeting different people here and figuring out what made them stand out.

Then I saw Alex standing behind the desk and I went back there to touch base with him.

"Did you meet everyone that work here yet?"

"No, not yet. But I've been meeting them as I go."

"Did you meet Andrew yet? He's from Altamonte too."

Andrew came off the basketball court to the desk and we talked. He had this huge grin when he was telling me a story about him playing ball at Sanlando and East Monte Park. We became great friends. Better yet, we became family.

After a couple weeks into the semester, I picked up a closing shift at the FMC. This was my first closing shift during the week. I met one of the supervisors, JJ. It was JJ, Ethan, and I for the whole shift. Tuesday and Thursday were closing shifts for us. We introduced ourselves and talked about where we were from. We were day 1's ever since.

JJ interrupted randomly. "Oh, you have to meet Maurizio. He cool peoples!"

When any of us was on shift together we always went to Wendy's after and got a 4 for $4. It was always a power move.

Around October, I remember when I was on a shift with Clayton, and he asked me did I play smash. The game was called Super Smash Bros., and it was created for Nintendo games.

"You can go get whoever and I will give you problems." I was extremely confident.

"Bet. You tell whoever and we'll all play."

I told Andrew, both Nicks, Ethan, Anthony since they lived across the street, and Alex. Once or twice a week we would all go over to Clayton's place and play smash. This helped strengthen our friendship and enjoy each other's company outside of work.

I was hanging out with Andrew a lot. Not only did we play Smash with Clayton on regular, but we also always played basketball together. This was at least two to three times a week where we

DARNELLE CUYLER

would play each other in a one on one at the Leach center. Andrew loved basketball and I'm extremely competitive, so I was always down to play.

Andrew would text me, "you trying to play one on one."

"Yeah, I'm down. We both know I'm winning."

"That's a lie. I beat you every time."

"BET! Soon as class over I'm running to Leach to bust yo ass."

As soon as class was over, I would literally be running from The Love building to the Leach center. It would never be one or two games. We would go to at least ten every time. It was always first to 11 by 1's and 2's. 2's would be from the 3pt line, and 1 point would be from everywhere else in between. He admired my competitive drive because I would go hard every single game.

Even when he won, I would immediately say "run it back." He would laugh and check the ball up. Then we would start all over again. I helped fuel his drive for the love of the game. We all know *Ball Is Life*. To Andrew, Ball really was life. I peeped his game pretty early, but it was hard to stop. I wasn't really a basketball player, but I love the cardio and competition. He would always run to the right side and go for a lay-up, and I would push him at the left side of his hip and push him out of bounds.

"AANNNDDD 1"

And 1 is when you get fouled on the play and still score. He wouldn't score all the time, but he would scream that all the time. His second shot was the left corner of the free-throw line. He would make that 90% of the time. I could not stop it. I remember one day, after ten games of straight losing I would tell him, "One more."

He would say, "Ok."

I would still be going hard and he wouldn't let up either. The game would be tied, and he would not let me come inside for an easy win. I would go to about the half court.

"You're not going to make it."

I said, "all I ever needed in life was an opportunity and I will make it every time."

BE GREAT TODAY! NO DAYS OFF!

I shot the shot and made it. We laughed and sat on the court. I was telling him about my life and told him how every day I come to Leach I would have to put up shots for my friend Zach Woods that passed away while we were at LSU. He challenged me to get better at it, so I stuck with it. Even when I travel back to LSU's recreational center, I still had to put up a few shots because that's what he challenged me to do. The ending of our games would be us being motivational or trash talking each other. From a motivational standpoint it was always reassuring one another that we got each other's backs and that we're praying for each other to get through our exams. From the trash talking standpoint it was aggressive. I would scream and go off if I made the game winner three.

"You know you're still trash, right," he'd laugh. "You just loss ten games straight!"

"Yeah, but you just lost!"

"You need to stop fouling and work on your shot. But what are you doing tomorrow, kid?"

"bussing yo ass in basketball again if need be."

We'd laugh and then we would figure out our schedule to see if we had time to play the next day or not.

We would always shake each other's hand followed by a hug. and leave the gym.

"Love you bro."

"Love you too man."

We definitely did some hard bonding on the basketball court. It was a place where we can escape our problems and be around someone who value and care for us. A lot of times we would always check in on each other make sure we had everything together or he would call me to cover his shift. Sometimes, I would be pissed because I need to study but he knew I was never going to tell him no. It was tough because the way our schedules were set up, I don't think I ever worked a shift with Andrew. We always had class during each other's shifts. He always brought the best out of the people he hung around. He was really a standup guy.

Working at campus rec center really brought great people into my life. Whenever we were on a shift together, it was always a great time. Everyone showed unconditional support and love for me, for the person that I am, and respected my passion. I'm eternally grateful for Alex, Clayton, Claudia C., Claudia R., Ricky, JJ, Ethan T., Maurizio, Kiana, Taylor, Katie aka "Cousin", Malinda, Andrew, Matt, Valeria, Nick D., Kelly, Nick L., Pete, Jordan S., Zach G., Caroline, Idris, Kyani, Pat and Ryan Hall, Jordan, Sisqo, and Forever, for keeping the FMC live. I'm extremely grateful for the professional staff that always showed support, especially, Chris M., Chris, Ben, Ian and Jen, Kari, Darryl, April, Dave, Lizzie, Jorge, and the janitorial staff. I was trying to keep the people I spent the most time with uplifted as possible.

I was also a bad influence well. I'm not going to act like I was a saint. I was constantly bringing unhealthy food to the front desk, especially at the FMC. I was continuously forcing them to pick up shifts so we can have Squad shifts for my own entertainment. I was dropping the f-bomb way too often, being overly excited when I should have been cool, calm, and collected.
One of the worse things that could've happened was me finding a deck of cards behind the FMC desk. I remember it like it was yesterday. One evening shift it was so boring at the FMC and I was looking for something to do. I was looking around and stumbled across them.

"Aye yo," I yelled across the gym. "You know how to play Tonk?"

My coworker said she knew but I didn't trust that. So, I taught her anyway. I was too bored, and I aggravated her until she gave in.

"We can play the last five minutes before we leave when we closed."

That wasn't good enough for me. I gave her ever reason to play.

"I'll even take the blame and say I forced you to play. We know Jorge don't get tired of yelling at me." But she didn't budge.

So, the last five minutes before we locked the building down, we would play cards. Walking out the door we would play cards. I was addicted to them and it only got worse over time because it went from the last five minutes, to the last ten, to the last thirty minutes of the shift. FMC was slow, and no one ever actually paid attention to us. The good thing about the FMC was no one ever spoke about the FMC outside the FMC. They knew the code: No snitching. I was playing cards with mainly just one person anyway. The next semester we played in front of JJ and kept it going. It was wild because during *Spring* break, I worked every shift from open to close and played with whoever was on shift. We were even playing with one of the patrons. She was an old lady that loved to talk. She watched the game one time and figured it out. She even brought us another deck of cards. I was playing cards for year straight before getting caught.

Another reason why I enjoyed the FMC so much was the radio. The radio station had the best music, especially on the weekends. No pro-staff or professors came to the FMC, so the music was always rap and hip-hop with no filter. Bangers was always being played left and right. I had love for the Leach too. People thought I spent more time at FMC, but if you looked at my time sheets, it was always roughly an even split. I met a lot of great people on my Leach shifts too. The radio in the laundry room at Leach ALWAYS had the jams on. I would go wash and fold the towels just to sit back there and listen to music. Leach was definitely a fast-paced facility. What I enjoyed the most was when I worked the weekend shifts was watching the LSU and FSU's games while getting paid.

In both facilities I tried to let my presence be known so everyone can be at ease. One of the janitors always called me "Easy Money" because I told him you can't beat getting paid to watch football on a slow shift. It was easy money.

Every day I strived to make sure every department and staff member know, regardless of their role at the campus rec, that they are valued and appreciated. Even when I'm not working or working out, I try to bring that energy to the table. I try to bring the same presence to the table when I'm working out as well. It's a different energy when you're in the weight room. I showed a few people in the fitness department that it doesn't matter about what you've read in a book, genetics, or even the diet someone utilizes, you can still grow from having mental strength. It's another critical factor that no one focused on but it's something I live off of. I made sure I stayed out of the fitness staff way because some felt

DARNELLE CUYLER

they knew it all, but I wasn't going to be the one to argue with
them. Some people lacked mental strength and didn't realize it. I
had to prove to some of them the difference in their perspective in
transition to their performance. I was telling people how real I am,
and they didn't believe me until I had to show them. One day,
someone challenged me.

"We never seen you lift heavy"

I smirked. "That's because I don't need too. I only lift
heavy when it's on my mind too. If you want me to show you I
will."

The thing that makes me different from everyone else is
that I earn my respect the hard way. 90% of the time I'm in the
weight room, I'm working my mental game. My physical strength
and conditioning will catch up. I earned my respect in the weight
room. I know how to turn on elite performance and turn aggression
into passion. I will show you how it's done. The only one I felt that
truly respected me and knew what time it was when I was in the
weight room was a man named Chris Matos. I was always working
out early in the morning. I would do light weight and some days I
would go heavy. Chris and I would never say a word, just passed
by each other. Then he started to speak when he seen me doing
numbers. It was rare for me to lift heavy in the weight room because I felt as though I didn't have anything to prove nor was I
around people that motivated me.

One week it was that time.

One day I walked into Leach, and I knew it was a day for me to go
heavy on squats. I ran on the indoor track to get some blood flow
and then I went to the squat rack. I turned it up that day. I started to
get hyped so I can bring out everything and everyone that motivate
me. It's just me by myself with no spotters. I'm only putting 25's
and 45's on the bar, nothing in between. I started off with a plate
on each side and went from there. The aggression started coming
out, every time I added more weight on the bar, it better look
smoother and better than the last set. Once I got to 225lbs I had to
envision my people around me. These the ones that played no
games in the weight room and had no sympathy. I earned my re-

BE GREAT TODAY! NO DAYS OFF!

spect in front of the greats. Then pop up is A-Rod, Andre, Chip, Coleman, Big Taylor, Conor, Carlis, and Kaleb.

None of them smiling.

Well, Kaleb smiling. I can't picture him being serious because he always smiling when I'm lifting. I met these people in different time periods of my life and they always let me be me in the weight room. I have *Set It Off* by Boosie playing, so now I'm really bringing all or nothing to the table. Each rep, smooth transition. Too easy. Add another 25 on each side. Too Easy. Three 45's on each side. It's still too easy. I stopped but I can see a few people trying hard not to stare me down, but they showed love and commented afterwards. Chris was one of those people because from now on he smiled whenever I walked into the weight room.

The next time he saw me I was leaving the weight room and he was going in. I was doing a heavy bench press that day. I approached the same as I did when I was squatting. Once I got 225lbs, I was feeling good. I told myself I got to go harder. It's go hard or go home, and I can't go home! It's time to put 275lbs on the bar. I only lifted 275lbs one other time in my life and that was when I was at Bethune-Cookman. I put it on the bar. I had to have the Chip mindset

"Either get the weight off or die. You'll die a bum because you should've got the weight off."

I hated his motto so much, but he understood mental toughness. It's a dumb ass theology in my opinion, but it'll saved a life or two. I went under, took it off and went down. On the way up, shit got real! I barely got passed my sticking point. The sticking point is when a person stops in mid lift and cannot continue. I was pushing and I felt muscles straining and getting tight.

"You will literally die right now if you don't get this weight off!!"

I got the weight up and I felt everything in my right shoulder shred and tear. I got up and grabbed my shoulder in so much pain. I was leaving out of the annex and the person I saw was Chris.

"I tore my shoulder from benching 275lbs."

"ATTABOY!," he yelled. "It's worth it every time!"

DARNELLE CUYLER

If this man don't go get me some ice. He was too hyped about me putting up big boy weight that I don't think he could tell that I'm in pain right now. I knew I earned his respect though.

There were unwritten laws in the weight room. A lot of people break these unwritten laws every day. I'll explain these unwritten laws.

Rule number 1: Never skip leg day. The disrespect is just devasting to see.

Rule number 2: Never talk to someone while they are lifting or in then zone. I can't stress this enough because people think it's cool to try to spark a thirty-minute conversation in the middle of your set. Please stop.

Rule number 3: When you see someone doing numbers, you pay homage.

Real recognize real. Working out in the Leach and FMC helped me strengthen myself and helped a few of my coworkers do numbers in the weight room too. Thank y'all for grinding with me.

Mike E. Long Track and Field stadium is where I spent most of my free time on campus when I wasn't at the library. This place was my new *Trenches*. This was my temple, my place of peace, and it was truly extraordinary. I remember the day I found out it was open to the public. I was shocked because at LSU, it was closed off to the public and only the track team were allowed inside. But FSU, it is open for all the students.

I dedicated so much time there it was unreal. At the entrance you will see a sign with all the elite athletes and records that was held on that track.

I will run a track meet here, I thought.

This place got me through some difficult times and I prayed for some great times here as well. It helped me grow and develop as a person. It helped me find new strength time and time again. At the stadium, I practiced discipline and dedication every single day. If I didn't run on the outdoor track, I would substitute the leach indoor track if needed be. Every morning before or after work, I was on the track putting in work. If I couldn't get there in the morning, I was there early afternoon. Weekends included. I was at my best when I was on Mike E. Long stadium. I trained every as-

BE GREAT TODAY! NO DAYS OFF!

pect of my very being out there. I trained and conditioned myself for intramural football with campus rec.

This is where I generated a lot of my best work when it came to motivational posts or speeches. I remember running to get better every single day. Mike E. Long was where I felt closest to God during my time at Florida State. I would mostly run alone, until Nick Diaz started pulling up with me.

He was a real one for that.

I had a couple other friends that showed up every now and then, but Nick came the most. Every time a track coach or an athletic coach would see me, they would give a light nod and a smile. They see the form and the performance. They knew I wasn't a rookie at the starting line. The throwing coach showed the most love though. He was out there most the time I was out there. I actually attempted to run for Florida State, but according to NCAA rules, my time slot had ran out.

I've spent a lot of time in Dirac, the Love building, Leach and FMC. I wasn't hard to find on Florida State campus. Every day I was grinding to get better. I was chasing a dream. This semester was the start of a new beginning. I played intramural sports with my new friends. I was still able to showcase my speed whenever needed. I was still able to showcase these hands, on Smash Bros. on a weekly basis. Most of all, I was able to continue my goals to motivate the people around me. I went to the football games at FSU. They weren't as exciting as LSU games, but I did enjoy myself. I went to just about every home game my entire tenure there. I had to find myself when it came to balance. I felt as though as long as I was progressing, I wasn't really stressing about anything serious. I still got hit with a lot of stress and adversity, nonetheless.

I remember when November came, I went to the LSU vs UF game for my birthday. After we went to the football game, we went to Fred's and then celebrated at Julie's house. It's always holiday season for my birthday. This year, Julie made me an Oreo-Red Velvet Cake. They all knew how to keep me happy, even though it don't take much. We were celebrating hard since I don't live in Louisiana no more. I turned back around and stayed at Lois house for Thanksgiving. For three years in a row, I went to Lois house for

DARNELLE CUYLER
Thanksgiving. I love my Korean family and we always had Korean BBQ.

Don't sleep on Korean BBQ. If you haven't tried it, you should.

I ended my first semester at Florida State on a rough note academically. I failed both the classes I signed up for. I was upset and embarrassed. I had to take undergrad courses because I couldn't afford graduate classes. Since I wasn't a degree-seeking student, I didn't qualify to get financial aid. I thought I was going to get kicked out of school, but I was put on academic probation instead. I talked to some of the administration and staff in the math department and explained to them why I had done so terrible in my classes this semester. I worked almost 500 hours that semester to pay for my classes, pay rent and living, as well as saving up to pay for my classes the next semester. They weren't mad about the outcome because some of them loved going to the Leach Center and saw that I was trying and doing everything on my own. I had taken two courses that I received an D and an F.

I don't mind sharing my failures. I continue to grind and overcome all obstacles. I knew I had to do better when the next semester started. I set big goals for myself this year and I didn't accomplish them all. I had set new goals for myself for 2017. I will do better academically and get into Florida State graduate program, I will run at a track meet here, and I will do better at motivating and uplifting everyone around me.

I tried to set goals that will keep me focused and keep me disciplined. Going into the holiday break I had a lot on my mind. I thought it was best for me to go home and spend time with my family, especially my niece's.

Looking back at this year as a whole, it was constant battle of trying to better. I graduated from my dream school and attended one of the best schools in the state. I've been through so much adversity, and it brought me strength to push forward. I am now able to have a better perspective of certain situations. I can use my adversity and hardships to motivate and help others even more. I am a prime example of what it's like to go through obstacles and continue to look forward to a better tomorrow.

BE GREAT TODAY! NO DAYS OFF!

I always tell myself that it can't get worse than 2014 and whatever it is, I can get through it. I can talk and show people that no two struggles are the same. I tell myself all the time that I'm proud of what I've accomplished and what I will accomplish everything I set out for in the future. I understand that my work ethic will get me where I need and want to be.

I have to trust the process.

I have to put my upmost faith in God and let him take control of the situation.

I have to use this year to prosper at this university.

This is the next step in my life, and I will make the most of it.

DARNELLE CUYLER

FSU 2017

I went into this year with strong but doable goals. I was enrolled in two math courses and told myself that school needed to be my focus this semester. I had to take a graduate level math class and an undergrad level math class to be considered full time. I was putting more effort into time management this year because I noticed this was something I needed to improve on. I continued to play ball with Andrew and do my daily track workouts. I was promoted to member service representative with the campus rec center, and it paid a little more.

Every penny counts and although I wanted to slow down with work, the grind in me wouldn't let up. I just had to prioritize when I worked.

I tried to focus more on keeping my stress down and had the faith that everything would work out. I was still talking to a lot of my LSU friends every day or every other day. We all still had the *No Days Off* mentality even when we weren't around each other. The grind remained the same. It was hard because some of us were hard grinding alone. We weren't hanging out nor spending time together after a long week of the grind like we used too. Messaging each other or calling each other was helping us get by, but it's still not the same of our actual presence. I liked and enjoyed my

BE GREAT TODAY! NO DAYS OFF!

new coworkers and friends here at Florida State, but we haven't reached that level yet.

As the semester progressed, I can honestly say with confidence that I was doing well. Although the classes weren't easier, I wasn't stressed, and I was performing better. We had our campus rec center banquet in April, and everyone definitely enjoyed themselves. I watched them hand one of the student the *Employee of the Year Award*.

"I didn't get Employee of the Year back-to-back like Alex, but it would be legit if I won it at two different Universities. I will make that as another goal to keep myself from slacking."

I tried my best to keep myself focused on the goals at hand and not getting off track. I constantly tried to find new ways to live up to my motto and to make myself do better. I'm not perfect and I always felt that there was something that can be worked on. I can't settle nor become complacent. If you're not disciplined, you can't excel to where you want to be in life. Personally, I feel like if I don't stay disciplined, I won't make it. I have to keep going, I have to keep showing up every day and giving it my all. If I don't, then all of this work would've been for nothing. I know this has not been a crystal staircase and everything thrown at me was meant to make me quit.

But I'm still here, I'm still standing, and I'm still strong.

Getting this master's degree is not an easy feat but I knew what I wanted out of life and how I was going to get there. So, I had to keep putting in the work.

I had to become self-disciplined and understand the true meaning of it. I constantly heard my teachers, coaches, parents, and others constantly say that being disciplined will get you where you want to be in life. That going the extra mile was worth it and sometimes, always necessary.

Do the right thing and stay on task.

I had to learn how to be disciplined and then master it. I had to be self-disciplined because no one cared if I was going to make it or not. I needed to change my mindset if I was going to accomplish the goals, I set out for myself. It's something I had to work on every day because if I wasn't, the weight of adversity would've broken me.

DARNELLE CUYLER

I had a lot of practice being self-disciplined no matter how I felt physically or emotionally. I would do extra core work before bed or extra running to get in better condition for sports. It was doing work for my grandma day-in and day-out whether I wanted to or not. It was making sacrifices when it came to saving money. I try my hardest help people understand this concept because it is what separate the goods from the greats. I even get on myself about being disciplined and not slacking.

Being self-disciplined is what help strengthen the dedication and the desire you have towards something. Take Monday for example. Most people don't like Mondays, but I actually love them because it's the beginning of the week. If you start of the week on a good note, you'll end on a good note. It makes getting through the week much easier. Being self-disciplined allows you to create habits and having healthy-sustainable habits will help you progress towards your goals.

For example, being self-disciplined was doing extra core workouts so the next day when Coach Sampson would walk off and leave us in a plank position until he came back, I was able to keep going because I put in the extra work. His core workouts were crazy, but it got easier for me once I started going the extra mile and doing it on my own. Another example is studying on the weekends. I knew that if I didn't put forth all those extra hours in the library, I wouldn't pass my classes. Even though I've failed a lot of my classes at LSU, I was still better off due to the extra studying.

I think that it's such a critical skill in life and a lot of people do not have it. It's the slight difference that separates people achieving their goals and failing at it. I don't think it's because they lack the support and resources. They simply lack the notion that they have to put in more work than they're accustomed too. If I weren't self-disciplined, I would not be where I am today nor will I have achieved the goals that I set for myself. I knew I wanted to go to school, so I had to save and pay a lot of it out of pocket instead of spending it on other things. I knew I had to pay my own tuition instead of spending it on cars and clothes and other things that I probably wanted at that time. I had to have self-control when it

BE GREAT TODAY! NO DAYS OFF!

came to dealing with adversity. It helped me develop the strength to keep going forward and go harder.

I had to master being self-disciplined in order to chase my dreams and accomplish my goals. It's what helps me keep my side of the deal I made with God all those years ago on *Sanford Avenue*. People seen what I've been through and wonder how do I keep going. Simply put, self-discipline. It's allowed me to push pass all of my pain, my desires, and even failures. This is one of those things that was instilled into me for me to continue to chase greatness. I used to tell my friends all the time that you can't have big goals if you aren't willing to put in big work. You can't expect to go to the *Olympic Games* if you're not training your body even on days you're not feeling it. You can't have goals to be a lawyer or a doctor and not study on the weekends.

You think going out and partying is going to get you into those programs? It's not. You think just because you know someone in that program that you will have a breeze getting through? It doesn't always work like that. Some people may have it easier than you. Some will probably be smarter, but do not let them outwork you.

Work harder.

Study harder.

Always remember, the longer you slack, someone is out there outworking you. Do not be outworked.

I've seen people get blessed with once in a lifetime opportunity and they blew it because they didn't put the work in. Meanwhile, there's someone begging God for that same opportunity and would give our last for it.

Self-Disciplined is more than a word. It is a concept that you place at the foundation of everything you do. When building anything, you need consistency and repetition but how can you build that without having self-discipline? I know a lot of athletic coaches eat, sleep, and breathe self-discipline into their athletes because it really is what will get you to the next level. People can only push you so far, but if you don't have it in you to want it from yourself, then you'll only go so far in life. I see it as a self-commitment too. I try to tell myself that I will be committed to myself and give my last to everything I do. If I don't see myself doing better than I

DARNELLE CUYLER

need to figure out I need to be better. I also put being disciplined in the spot where people can justify a way of life. I see it as you mastering your craft and doing what you need to do to get the job done. It's the focus of seeing an end goal and doing whatever it takes to meet that end goal. I see it as the grit being brought out to keep you moving forward and getting after it. I yearn to be around these types of people because I want to know what make you grind hard. What make you become so focused, that being self-disciplined become a state of mind and a way of life. I try to be very diverse when it comes to making friends and meeting people in general. Doing this helps me get a better understanding of life.

I'm not a 'know it all' person, but I do my best to help motivate those who need it.

The semester was coming to a close quickly and I, for the first time in a while, had everything in order. I got a passing grade in both my graduate and undergraduate courses. I was so damn proud of myself. After my finals, there was a track meet going on at campus. I competed in the track meet. I ran the 200 meters. It was 30 degrees that day and I was so cold. I felt like I was running in slow motion. My time was bad, but it wasn't as bad as I thought.

I was excited as hell. I accomplished two goals in one day. I passed a graduate class and ran at a track meet at Florida State.

The following week I went to talk to one of the professors in the Math department about getting in the program. I told him that I was going to try to take another summer course to excel in so it would help me into the graduate program. After our talk, I felt good about it despite the fact that it wasn't guaranteed.

Keep fighting and it'll work out. It always do.

I was thinking about everything I've been through at LSU while I was walking back to my apartment. I made it through all of it. I overcame every trial and tribulations every single time. I just had to stay disciplined and keep the faith.

There was one small hiccup. I didn't have the money upfront to pay for my class and you don't get financial aid for taking one class. I knew everything was on the line. I knew that I had to get the money one way or another. I was stuck in a sticky situation because if I paid the tuition in full, I wouldn't have enough to pay

BE GREAT TODAY! NO DAYS OFF!

my rent. I knew I wasn't going back to the same hardships from LSU, but what was I to do? It was beating me down all weekend long. I was stressing. I had to go to Mike E. Long stadium to talk to God. I went to the track and worked out to come up with a game plan. But I didn't like the plan.

Swallow your pride and ask for help.

I got to find a couple people to get some of the money from and then pay them back fully as soon as you get it. I was getting mad because I didn't want to ask anyone for help. My pride was keeping me from asking because what if they get mad one day and decide to throw it back in my face. The problem that I had was relying on people. I was so used to being let down and I was tired of it. I was finally in a place where I didn't have to say anything about my personal problems or the financial issues I was having. I can keep everything to myself and grind it out. I didn't want to empty my bank account for this one class, because what if it don't work out?

NAH, IT WILL WORK OUT! We only got one opportunity and I have to make the most of it. Who is three people we can trust, and they not say anything about it? Jorge, Matt, and Kyani. Jorge knew the struggle and he knew the grind. Matt, because he going through hard times personally and he knows how it feels to be in this position. I already talked to him at the FMC that he needs his mental game worked on. I told him I will show him how to grind every day this Summer to excel in the classroom, work, and the weight room. We've been putting in work all semester. Kyani is the only level-headed person that understand the grind on a much deeper level than anyone else I know. She the only one I can think of when I think of grad school, grinding, and chasing a dream the hard way. She the only one I can think of that look at the aggression that I show and know it is passion. She know that I'm bringing everything I have to the table without me having to explain myself.

Now that I have the three people, how do I ask them for money? I think it's best that I talk to them individually. I was getting mad a little because my pride was killing me. I can't have any doubts about this. I have to make this work. I have to get what I can from them and make it work.

DARNELLE CUYLER

I have to pray and give thanks in advance that this will happen. I was thinking about Dr. Allen from LSU, and I was praying about it. Man, this better work. You said it would work and you had faith in me that I can get it done. So, I'm going to take a chance and make it happen. I will give everything I have in me and grind like it was *Summer* 2014. I will not let up for nothing or nobody.

I talked to them, and they didn't mind giving me the remaining funds to cover the course.

I assured them that I will not let this be in vain, and I will get into the graduate program. I got promoted to Supervisor for Campus Rec. My first supervisor shift was a Leach closing shift and I had all the FMC veterans working. They never worked Leach but since I was the supervisor, they said they would. All supervisors worked the shift. It was JJ, Claudia R., Ashley, Malinda, and me. I was so glad they worked my first shift to help me out. I told them I would still pickup CSR shifts to work with them regardless if I'm a supervisor or not. Now that I am a supervisor, I can help my staff and do more for the campus rec center. I was on a Tuesday shift from 11:00 AM to 2:00 PM with Matt and Valeria. We always had a question of the day to keep all the patrons on their toes and something to look forward to besides working out. We would always ask random questions like: What's your favorite Holiday? If you can be an animal, what would you be? What's your favorite movie? It was always something different every week. I kept my word about helping Matt grind. We grind the hard way every day of the summer.

As a supervisor, I tried to bring more support to the table. The new incoming students would look up to me since I was older, but I still let them know we're all equal.

"Just because I'm a supervisor does not mean I'm better than you, nor do I think I am. I'm here to help support and motivate you in any way that I can. When we work on shifts together, we will treat each other with the same level of respect. I'm not one of these other supervisors. I'm not here for the title. I'm not going to belittle or disrespect you. I'm not here to write you up or get you

BE GREAT TODAY! NO DAYS OFF!

in trouble. We don't get any rewards or prize for writing someone up."

On my FMC shifts, we have a few rules I follow. We will not be gossiping and spreading rumors. This is not Leach, and I'm not having that occur here. We will not share our coworkers personal business. On my shifts, if someone is having problems, we will come up with a game plan to help them get through it. Whether it's school, work, or anything, I will do what I can to support and motivate you. I don't want anyone giving up on school or life because they didn't have anyone to talk too. If you feel like you need to talk to me on a one on one, we can do that too. My ultimate rule, please don't get beside yourself and say some racist shit. It's not cool and it will not fly here. Long as we're on shift together, we're chilling. I'm not going to over work you but I'm not going to let you be a bum either. If you need to use your phone or anything, let me know. Other than that, we can eat, play cards, or whatever.

I didn't want to be seen as a micromanaging supervisor because that is just not me as a person. I tried to be as stressed-free as possible. The summer grind was relentless.

As the summer was coming to an end, I was doing everything possible to keep this dream alive. Matt made it out the summer alive, he pretty much aced all of his classes and was putting up major weight in the weight room.

"As long as you put in the work every day, it'll always pay off in the long run."

Matt had introduced me to his barber, Mike. He cut in a barbershop called *Shear Design*, right along with Levi, B, and Ike. They were cool people. If you ever need a haircut, I'd recommend going to them every time. Jorge was cutting my hair for the longest but only a couple people knew that. It was always a good time whenever I went to the shop. We always talked about sports. Game day was always hyped whenever I came in to get a cut. Everyone in the black community knows that your barber is practically part of the family. They always show love. I remember telling them I got a math degree from LSU and going to FSU to get my masters.

"You graduated from LSU," Mike asked. "The Tigers, with a math degree? And now you're at Florida State to get your masters? You're in a different league kid."

DARNELLE CUYLER

The other barbers lightly laughed, and head nodded. Every time I walked through the door; I would be laughing because they knew I was coming with some bullshit. I was repping LSU like a true diehard fan. We always talked about what our team would do against other teams. Mike, who was my barber, was a University of Florida fan. So, it was always a debate when it came to those games. Another thing that made Matt and I really enjoyed the shop was that we can always talk to them about life and some of the issues we were dealing with. Now, I'm not saying, to talk to them like they're a therapist, but they definitely were understanding of the problems we encountered. I know when they see us walking through the door, they knew a good laugh was coming. They supported the grind and the goals. They told me it will all work out, and that I came too far to let up now.

Summer ended and I passed my second graduate level math class by the grace of God. The math department gave me a chance and I got into the FSU graduate program to get my master's in Applied and Computational Mathematics. The grind was so real for Matt and I, and it finally paid off. I was glad that Jorge, Kyani, and Matt was able to help me out. We were all hyped about it.

Jorge told the supervisors we were having a "Supervisor Retreat." It was a few days on the beach where we were to get to know each other better and have a team bonding session. Jorge always emphasized that we were a team. At the retreat we got to learn about each other, our backgrounds, and future goals that we had planned. We had some great moments out there. Especially with Volleyball. It got real! It was 4 versus 4. It was Ryan Hall, Scott, Dylan, and me versus JJ, Thiago, John, and Zack G.

Competition was onsite.

If we weren't doing a team activity, we were playing volleyball. I LOVE the competition. I had Ryan, who never talk, trash talking left and right. I couldn't stop laughing. No Diss was ever repeated.

"Is this what be on your mind, when walking through Leach and FMC? I thank God I'm on your team, because God knows the disses you have under your sleeve about me."

BE GREAT TODAY! NO DAYS OFF!

"Nah, you pick up everybody slack at work, so I never thought anything bad about you."

"Jesus take the wheel! This the only time my work ethic has been recognized."

We all started laughing.

One memorable moment was when we all walked on the beach and had to talk to someone to get to know them better. One walk in particular was when I walked with JJ.

"Man, I never told anyone this, but I really like Anime. I heard someone trashing a person for watching so I never say anything about it."

"Hell yeah," I screeched. "I watch Anime too. I got to a point in my life that I can careless what people think of me. I'm a math major and people already say I'm lame for that. Adding anime into it isn't going to make a difference. Whenever I'm not crying over math problems or grinding, I watch some anime. I tweet about it and all. I like it for the fact it's a protagonist that's fighting to be someone or a hero. But I mostly like it for the animation of fighting."

JJ instantly felt relieved and settled. We began talking about different shows that we watched. We became closer after that.

Another person I felt I became close to and made a major impact on was Malinda. We were African Americans in the STEM program, and we always felt alone because you're the only black person in your class as well as lack the financial and moral support to succeed. I let her know that no matter what, we will make it and graduate from Florida State University.

We left the retreat on a good note and was ready to take on the Fall Semester as supervisors.

Matt and I became roommates and lived in an apartment on the edge of campus. I felt like I was at LSU all over again for the fact that I was literally on the edge of campus and the walk only took three minutes. Matt introduced me to our other two roommates, Kole and Chase, the Forehand brothers. One was already in medical school and that other one was working on getting into the program as well. In the end, they both ended up going to FSU for Med school. We always had *Spade* or *Tonk* competitions at

DARNELLE CUYLER

the apartment and played Catan from time to time. Chase's girl-friend Chessa was always down to play cards with us too.

Chase blurted out, "every time I would come ask you some-thing, you would already be gone."

Chessa chuckled. "I like how your bed is already made and everything. The only time we know your home is if we hear you brushing your hair."

"Yeah, I usually will be working out before class or having to open the gym for work." I responded. "Y'all can hear me brush-ing my hair? I have to keep my waves flowing."

"Yeah, you the Wave God," Kole chimed in.

We always enjoyed each other's company when we were at the house. Kole would also do early track workouts with me some mornings.

When fall started, I was still bringing positive vibes to the table when it came to managing our shifts, but I also felt the more responsibility within myself to become more motivational now that I am a graduate student as well. I realized I can bring more to the table when I talk about overcoming adversity.

One day I remember I was at the FMC talking with one of my coworkers and letting them that they can make it if they put in the work. I understand how it feel when you're constantly coming across adversity. I've failed ten classes in undergrad. I've failed classes here at Florida State. I've had semesters where my GPA was under a 2.0 and I was on the brink of getting released from the university. I know what hard times feel like. I was released from LSU seven times due to the lack of financial instability. I was on academic probation at least 5 times at LSU. I've been at FSU for a year, and I have already been on academic probation twice for hav-ing a low GPA. I've failed hundreds of exams. I've failed the GRE five times and each exam was $200. I still owe LSU money right now. I have a balance of roughly $9500. I have the Perkins Loan that's owed to them that's $2000, and the interest being added so, that'll end up being a couple hundred dollars extra. They sent my balance to collections, and it got up-charged $2500 for Collections fee. I can't get my degree until I pay off everything. I have the de-partment of Collections calling and threating me that I need to

BE GREAT TODAY! NO DAYS OFF!

send their money or I'll be sued, but I don't have a dime to spare. I understand when it came to struggling and failing because that's all I do. Yet, I refuse to give up. Even after all of that I still got into graduate school.

Failure is not an option for me.

I will continue to put in work every day. I know that I will struggle in graduate school but that's okay. I know from the bottom of my heart I can be a failure in everybody else eyes but as long as I don't give up on myself, I'll never be a failure. I will pay back every dime I owe to LSU, but first things first, I have pay back Jorge, Kyani, and Matt, every check I get. I know how to settle for less and make sacrifices to get the job done.

During the first semester of graduate school, I was in the 'weed-out' classes. These were the classes they make you take to weed out those who would not succeed in the program. The hardest class I've ever taken in my life was the first and second semester. What was worse was they were computer programming classes. I hated computer-programming so much. I can do the math, but coding was not for me. In my classes I stayed quiet and only spoke unless I had too. I didn't want to say I felt uncomfortable, but I felt like I was on eggshells. I was back at being the only black person in all my classes and on top of that, I didn't get into the program the traditional way. I got in because a couple people were giving me a chance to showcase myself. One failed class and I will be released from the university, expeditiously." I felt this way because this was constantly the case that I had to deal with behind closed doors.

I knew the professors weren't focused on my history but on my work ethic and the performance I bring to the table each day. This semester was going to be intense every day and I knew I wasn't taking a day off from anything. It was grind mode around the clock. My most intense math class, I would spend days on one problem. Some nights Matt would beg me to come out the room and hang because I've been studying since I got home. Only way I'm studying at home is if it's too late or my spot was taken in Dirac. On the weekends nothing changed. I would be in rotation from working FMC to Dirac to Leach. Either way the rotation went I was studying and working. If it was a home game, I would wake up early and study. I would go to the game and then go back

DARNELLE CUYLER

to studying. I didn't tailgate at Florida State because it wasn't the same as LSU and plus, I wasn't really close with anyone. All my friends at FMC had their own friends that they hung with before they met me, and I wasn't trying to be a random at someone's tailgate. One the nights where LSU had a home game after I got off work, I would go to Fuzzy's by myself and watch the game. Fuzzy's was a little restaurant that I was introduced too while I was at LSU. So, I would go there in honor of my LSU Urec Fam and rep LSU while watching the game.

I tried to enjoy myself on the day-to-day basis while dealing with constant hardships. I don't want the weight of adversity to consume me, and I end up giving up. I would still do things that made me happy even if I was alone. Slowly as the semester progressed, I would feel like I belonged more, but I still stayed to myself most of the time. Even though I was closer to home, I didn't have a reason to return to Altamonte. I didn't go home to run on *Sanford Ave*. So, I went to the temple instead.

Mike E. Long Track and Field stadium.

Sunday morning was when my sessions took place. I would thank and praise God in advance for allowing me to go to Florida State. I already knew I wasn't going to catch a break, but I kept going anyway.

"Thank you for bringing me this far. Thank you for allowing me to be a student at FSU and officially getting into grad school. Please renew my mind. Please assure me that I do belong here, and that I will graduate from here. Every type of adversity that come my way, please help me find a way to rise above it. Let me understand that the grind comes before all. Let me know that's what will pull me through. I will not dwell on the actions of the people around me. Please, if death comes my way, let me grind through it. I will continue to grind for those that are never coming home. Let me continue to follow my path and do what's best for me. The grind never let me down before, don't let up me now. God let me always lean to you for help and support. Let me love myself, especially when I feel like there's no love for me. Let me praise you through it all. Let me continue to push and fight even when I feel like I can't endure no more. I'll put in work regardless of what anyone says or feels. I'm grateful for it all. I promise. Thank you for everything. In Jesus name we pray, Amen."

It was a constant battle with adversity day in and day out, so I knew I had to keep myself motivated at all costs.

Not much changed in September. I also came back for a 2nd year of intramural football with Campus Rec. I enjoyed that a lot. One thing I got a kick out of playing flag football was being Kari's hype-man. Kari was our coordinator with Jorge who came to play football for the fun of it. I took it to a whole other level. I would be hyping Kari up to everyone. I would be bragging about her stats and drawing so much attention to her. Everyone would come out to see her play just because I kept bragging about her.

Kari would be standing there trying to be calm and play it cool.

"Darnelle always hyping me up. I just came to have fun."

"Nah, Kari a triple threat athlete. Last week she had over 100 yards and 3 touchdowns."

I'm pretty sure she was a bit embarrassed. No matter what sport Kari played I would hype her up and gloat her stats like she all-world. She was athletic though. I'm just glad she let me be her hype-man because that was my specialty and I finally found someone who'll let me just be me and be great.

I was still going at it with Andrew on the court, and I was still going hard at everything I do. It was a long month, but the grind was worth it. It always is. I was always going at it with Andrew about picking up his shifts and constantly getting in trouble for going over hours. September started off rough because we had got hit with category five hurricane name Irma. A lot of people across the state went without power and almost no shelter for days. I stepped up to the plate as a supervisor. I was working open to close making sure that I was able to provide security and comfort to the entire FSU Campus Rec staff, FSU students, and FSU community as a whole. I grew up in hurricanes all my life in Central Florida, so I know how it feel to be without power. I was grateful that I was able to help, and I will continue to help whenever need be. I was grateful beyond measures for this job.

One good thing about September was I went back home to Altamonte and celebrated my niece birthday. I really try to put

DARNELLE CUYLER

forth effort to be in their life but school and work always stopped that.

When October came, things became more intense. My math classes were really tearing me down. I was failing like no tomorrow. I was trying hard as I can but it's grad school math. Time and effort can't save me from the L's I'm taking. One the worse weeks of my life was here. I had an exam in my most intense math class. I already knew I was going to fail but I will still give my best effort. I been in the library, work, and pulling all-nighters and that F was still screaming "I'M COMING!"

I remember walking home from closing the Leach center after our supervisor meeting and I saw a lot of police lights way down *West Call Street*. I wondering what happened, but I said, Nah, I have to go home and study. I got home and thought of Andrew.

"Man, what happened to Andrew? He missed the damn supervisor meeting. I bet he was sleep again. Watch tomorrow he going to call me talking shit and blaming me."

I kept checking my phone while I was studying but he never texted me. The next day I was walking to campus and noticed Andrew still haven't texted me complaining. As awkward as it sound I just knew the text was coming because it happen after every meeting. Literally. I was sitting in class and needed to go to the bathroom. I went to the bathroom and soon as I was about to open the classroom door, I got a text. The text was from Matt.

"Andrew was in a car wreck last night."

I literally froze and sat down on the floor in the hallway. I was thinking to myself that he'll pull through, but we found out later that day he had passed away. I felt so broken. Then it started spreading like wildfire throughout the campus rec center and Facebook. I told my professor that my coworker had passed away and he pushed the exam back for me. I told myself get through the exam, but no matter how much I studied, I still felt like I was going to fail. I might as well take the exam and get it over with. Jorge was calling and showing support, but I told him I'm good. I was still picking up shifts. I made sure I picked up Andrew shifts and people that were affected about what was going on. I kept my composure around my coworkers. I didn't show any emotions, I didn't mourn around them, nor did I speak with them about it. His death still hurt though. I just wasn't trying cry with them, in front of them, or around them. I just kept it to myself. I just went home and cried by myself.

Whenever I saw Matt, I just told him I'm straight. The next few weeks of my life felt like a living hell.

October was a very rough month for me. I had to fight through a lot mentally and academically just to make it to November.

When November came, I was trying to make the best of every situation. I tried to stay motivated, dedicated, and elevated. Andrew's funeral was held in our hometown. I didn't go since I already had plans set in stone. I went to Louisiana to celebrate the union between Conor and Amy. It was a lovely wedding. While I was there, I went to LSU to spend time with Lois and the rest of the fam that was still in Baton Rouge.

On that Greyhound I was just there all night trying to figure out what to do. I literally lost one of the closest people to me at FSU. Everyone was sad, but I felt destroyed. Every time my life starts going well, something devastating happens.

Why does this keep happening to me?

I went to tailgate and caught up with some of the Urec fam, but they knew it was rough for me. I went to the LSU Urec and shot on the court that was in honor of Zach Wood. I played Andrew in basketball in my head.

"AANNNDDD 1!"

I started crying and I just envisioned Zack and Andrew standing at the free throw line while I put up shots. I made sure I wasn't missing. I was telling myself that I will still keep putting up shots for the both of them every single time I step in LSU and FSU recreational center. I'll keep my work ethic. I'll keep my word to you guys.

I went back to Florida and I was still doing my best to keep my composure. I did a lot of praying on the bus ride back home. I didn't know how to mourn after someone passes. I handle it the best way I know how.

I just went to work.

DARNELLE CUYLER

All I knew was that I needed to go hard for the people who weren't coming home. I ran on the track until I couldn't run anymore. I was trying to figure how I was going to get through the semester. I had to remind myself that I needed to stay discipline and consistent. I was trying to shake back from what happened this past month.

As usual, I didn't go home for my birthday because I had to work. I haven't celebrated my birthday in Altamonte in years. Instead of going home for the holidays, I went back to Louisiana and had Thanksgiving with Lois and the fam.

When December came, it felt like everything going back downhill. I kept working all I could over the break. I made it out of my first semester alive. I knew I was going to be placed on academic probation but at least I'm not getting released. I'm so grateful to God for making it this far. I was still making it despite all the adversity I was going through. I just had to keep the faith and keep going. There were times I wanted to walk away but I didn't. I'm still here. I went to Altamonte for a few days for the holidays and to spend time with my nieces. I spent most of my time with them. We watched a lot of Moana, Home and other movies and ate a lot of Oreos. Spending time with them helped me shake off the funk that was on me.

It was time to bounce back.

FSU 2018

2018 started off the right way. I was with my LSU UREC family, Haley and Taylor B. We went to watched LSU play in a bowl game in Orlando. This was a great way to start a New Year on a Monday. After we graduated from LSU, Haley and I started a tradition that we would see each other at least once a year and go to LSU's bowl game no matter where it was. Sadly we enough we had to watch LSU lose to Notre Dame by 5.

This year I had big goals for myself, and I made it my business to accomplish them. The goals this year were to compete at more track meets, pay off my balance at LSU, and most importantly graduate from Florida State University. As soon as the game was over, I rode the Greyhound back to Tallahassee. When the campus rec center opened up, I've worked from open to close. You know my motto by now, *No Days Off*. I made it my mission to be consistent with myself, my staff, the New Year resolutioners, the gym rats, and anyone I could help achieve their goals. I wanted to make sure everyone was comfortable and felt like they belong in the facility.

This was a tough semester, but I was going to surpass all of it. I was taking the hardest math classes at FSU, another computer programming class, a seminar math class, and a neuro bio math class. This is going to be challenging since I was doing everything I can to better my time management. I wanted to put in more time and effort for my classes. Claudia and I made sure we still made time to go to the weight room and get a good lift in on Tuesday and Thursday mornings. My track workouts were mandatory regardless of what I had going on. I was still putting up shots on the

DARNELLE CUYLER

court for Andrew Sun and Zach Woods in remembrance of them. I'm keeping my promise to my boys.

Ball is life. Forever.

I was keeping myself accountable by making sure I was motivating and uplifting those around me. I was helping Claudia and a few others work on their applications to get into grad school, med school, or whatever else program they were striving for. I was more than happy to help people excel at their goals and dreams because it helped me feel like I was living in my purpose. Whether it's at work, the library, or through text messages, I was always making sure I was available to help. I want to see them succeed so I was doing everything possible to make sure it came into fruition.

I've been praying for them and everything.

I remember when I was thinking about Clayton and I randomly hit him up.

"Hey bro," I sent him a message. "I was praying for you hard last night and that your acceptance letter come today."

When he saw the message, he immediately went to go check his email. He got accepted into the program he applied for. I told Claudia the same thing will happen for her. She just needed to keep the faith and putting in the work in the meantime. From January through March, we are going to grind relentless.

I was getting after it every day.

I was becoming good friends with some of my classmates in my math classes. I think what brought us closer together was knowing we were all failing the class.

"I promise to God," I said. I couldn't stop laughing. "When I saw you take your glasses off and started rubbing your eyes, I knew all was lost for me. I thought you were crying. I swear if I saw a tear dropped, my face would've been flooded!"

She laughed. "I did almost cry though! Hell, if I knew you would cry with me I would've cried too."

"I'd leave tear drops in places where answers were supposed to be." We all laughed.

We always tried to make light of this situation because it felt like a nightmare that we endured day in and day out. I remember one night we were all studying for a final together and we played music to lighten the mood. I rarely studied with people because I can't compartmentalize the side conversations and figure out solutions at the same time. But about this upcoming final, Colton, Julia, Dan, Hui, David and I really bonded together over the stress from that class. I told them I eat Oreos every time I leave that class or whenever I can't figure out the answers to the homework problems. Even though the material was intense as hell, I learned a lot in those classes. Especially the computer programming class and I hate coding. So, that says a lot. I did enjoy the Neuro-bio math class with Angie and Virginia. That class was interesting and easy for the most part. We looked at how different Neurons affected the human brain from a quantitative standpoint. My Seminar class was a breeze I did a presentation on why the Omega for the stopwatch and photos were so critical in Track and Field.

My commitment and consistency this semester were un-measurable. The hardest part of any semester is staying dedicated in the middle of the semester, and I was doing my best to keep it going. I was doing better with my time management, and I wasn't overworking myself until I burned out.

One Day I was working a shift at Leach center, and I heard someone call out to me. I was walking to the gym courts, and I hear someone say,

"Is that Darnelle," the unfamiliar voice asked. "Is that great Darnelle I've been hearing so much about?"

Don't believe the hype.

Then I heard, "dad, stop."

"Hello, I'm Dr. Parrino," he introduced himself. "I'm Rosa's Dad."

"Nice to meet you Dr. Parrino." I smiled.

"Rosa's told me so much about you and how great you are."

I looked at Rosa who looked slightly embarrassed. I couldn't help but smile harder and give a *oh, really* look in her direction. Rosa was smiling but she gave me a look and I already knew what it meant.

Don't feed into my dad's bullshit. But, when do I ever listen?

"Really? That's crazy."

DARNELLE CUYLER

"Yes, really. She always talks about how you're such hard worker. How smart you are. She even told me you graduated from LSU. I also graduated from LSU."

We started talking about LSU afterwards and our time there. The more we conversed, the more we connected. He asked me what my goals were, and I told him that I wanted to be a motivational speaker. I told him I really like uplifting people and that it felt like it was my life's purpose to help those push beyond their limits and succeed at whatever they put their minds too. I did admit that I struggled with speeches and having certain topics to touch base on.

"Listen," he said as he pointed to my heart. "Speak from here. Always speak from here. It'll never steer you wrong."

This was great advice, and I appreciated the insight. He helped me realize to keep everything natural and fluent. It's not about how I deliver the message, but rather speaking on what's in my heart. Because what's in my heart will guide me to how I deliver the message. It's better to just speak from the heart instead of writing it down or writing out a speech. The message will get delivered to the right people. I took that to heart and try to live by those words.

The semester started to slow down and now, it's the campus rec center appreciate banquet, where we celebrated another year of service. It was at a nice venue, and it was really nice to see everyone dressed up. We all got our plates and ate until they made the announcements.

I put in so much work this year. There's no way I don't leave here with the Employee of the Year award. I was hyping myself up and Malinda came and killed all of that without the slightest hesitation.

"I don't know why you're hyping yourself up like this. You're not getting the award."

Well, damn. That hurt. We laughed together.

"But in all honestly, I really don't think they're going to give it to you."

"Who outwork me," I asked. "I did everything possible and then some. That award leaving with me tonight."

BE GREAT TODAY! NO DAYS OFF!

"You know it's not coming to DC."

"Alright, watch."

The ceremony began and then they started calling people up for the awards. And then they announced the recipient of the Employee of the Year award. It went to another coworker. She looked at me like 'I told you so'. I applauded along with everyone, but I was a little salty. From the looks of some of my other coworkers as well, they didn't necessarily agree with the final verdict. Some people made their way over to me and they were not happy. Despite how others may have felt, I was happy for my coworker.

"What the Hell? I was so ready to scream your name."

"You should've won that award."

"You're always helping every department."

The more they talked about it, the more I was getting upset because it really should've been me. Once the banquet was over I got up and left in silence.

I went home and started doing my math work. I opened a pack of Oreos as well. Matt came home and came to my room instantly.

"You straight?"

"Yeah, I'm straight. It didn't really bother me until people kept saying I should've won."

"Because you should've! Everyone knows it. I'm glad they won, they're a beast but be let's be honest, they didn't outwork you."

"Definitely didn't. I was in a league of my own and no one was keeping up with me."

"No one came close to you. I couldn't even come close to you."

"It's cool. Can't change it now. Tomorrow, we're just going to grind and let it be."

"Let me know if you need anything."

He shut my door and continued with his night. I kept studying and doing my math homework until almost one in the morning. I told myself it was time to go to bed because I have a hard track workout after work tomorrow and I need all the rest I can get.

I went to work and then went to the track stadium.

DARNELLE CUYLER

Damn, I really didn't win Employee of the Year. The longer I thought about it, the more it made me upset. Every negative thought you could imagine flooded my mind before I could blink. This was one of the biggest goals I had for myself, and I got snubbed. I put in so much work and gave the campus rec center everything I had day in and day out. I work more opens and closes than anyone here for two-years straight. A lot of times, I closed during the night shift and had to turn right back around to open for the morning shift. We called that a *clopening*. I worked every Friday, worked almost every weekend. worked open to close on the weekends. I worked every single Friday close that the gym was open. Some of my coworkers and other supervisors always found a problem with me on every shift I've worked since I've been here. I never complained. But one day I did confront Alex about it.

"Hey bro," I stopped him. "Why am I always getting written up and yelled at? I'm the one that picks up everyone's slack and help every day when I don't have to."

He shrugged his shoulders. "Because you came in different than everyone else and your work ethic is insane. You will be the biggest target here until you graduate. But don't let it get to you. Keep doing what you're doing and keep working harder."

Every day I have to deal with the stress of these math classes on top of paying for everything by myself. The pressure of getting release from the university every semester was always on my mind. The one place I thought I had peace was a lie.

There was never any peace.

It seemed like I was always targeted by entitled kids that never been through any adversity in their life. No one really understood what I was going through on a day to day basis. Those were the ones that were constantly trying to cause problems. I was the one picking up everybody shift when they didn't feel like working, and despite the excuses they gave for missing their shifts, I picked them up anyway.

"Aye, I'm trying to go to this party by the Nupes or some other frat and sorority."

"Aye DC, I'm a bit hungover. I'm not going to be able to make it."

BE GREAT TODAY! NO DAYS OFF!

"Darnelle, bro, I just don't feel like going. You got me?"

Meanwhile, it felt like I had to fend for my life during the closing shifts sometimes because I was by myself. I didn't have any help or support. Being down staff on shift was the worse. Plenty of nights I had to walk home and pray that the police, or even a random stranger, doesn't bother me or shoot me. Plenty of nights I put aside my pride and begged JJ or Kiana to give me ride home so I wouldn't be harassed or worse, end up dead before morning. There were some nights the police would literally creep down my street slow as possible with the lights off. Everyone swears that they were here to serve and protect, but my experience with them was far away from serve and protect. On the nights I would walk home, I feared being pulled aside simply for being black, and losing my life for simply being black. What I feared most was them getting away with it. It didn't matter that I had on FSU Campus Rec uniform or that I even had a campus ID.

I'm not going to lie to you, there were some nights I cried on the way home because that day could possibly be my last and I thought no one would give a damn. Even though I didn't have a criminal record or anything, but the way people treat me, I know this will be the easiest way to be done with me. I always tell myself the only way anyone would know something would happen and even care is if I didn't send a snapchat out at 9:00 pm and again when I got home from work after closing. I didn't want anything to do with the law enforcement because a few situations that happened while I was growing up.

The place I enjoyed the most brought me the most problems. I picked up shifts for people that never stepped up to the plate to help me or anyone else on the staff. It was worse when I became supervisor. We always had supervisor meetings, that I always thought were pointless, to talk about things that could've been sent in an email. They would always put emphasis on "we're a team!"

We ain't shit.

How are we a team when there's over twenty people on this staff but only a select group of people voice their opinions in the meeting? How are we a team when certain supervisors are bias towards other supervisors and make sure there's no advancement? I'm not the voice of the people nor do I want to be, but it's clear as

DARNELLE CUYLER

day as to why some people don't speak in these meetings because they feel as though their words won't be taken into consideration. How are we a team the I'm only one a few people pick up everybody slack? I pick up everyone shift when they have an exam but not once has anyone ever helped me with my classes here. I failed exams left and right because I didn't have enough time to study, and I was constantly on the brink of being release from the university because of it. There were so many times I asked, even begged, for someone to cover my shifts and no one stepped up for me. There was always an excuse. Whenever I did take time off, which was rare, I was looked at like I was the bad guy.

"You're not being a time player."

The audacity, bro. Instead of going off on them, I just made time to study and stayed out of the way.

Don't get me wrong, not every meeting was pointless or negative. I just felt that most of the time it was an inconvenience for me because I worked so much. How are we a team when there's three people working 30 plus hours a week, and the other 20 can't even work a two-hour shift on Friday's? I asked for help so many times and they couldn't even split none of my shifts so I can handle my personal business. I haven't celebrated my birthday with my twin in 8 years and the only time I could have, I couldn't because we had a pointless work meeting, and no one would cover my shift after. But when it comes to anyone else, they jump up quickly to help them.

I worked here for the past two years and had coworkers try to get me fired simply because they didn't like me. I work hard to pay all my bills, tuition, rent, and everything else that needs to be paid based off this income, and yet, I'm constantly in a position of losing my job because someone didn't know me, or didn't take the time to get to know me. No one knew how important this job was to me. No one knew why I was giving this job my last.

FSU Campus Rec was my life. It was how I survive.

If anyone had a problem with me, I never understood why they never pulled me aside to talk to me about it. If someone ever messed up during the shift before mine, I would just text them that I fixed it and let it be.

BE GREAT TODAY! NO DAYS OFF!

It was not the same energy for me.

I was basically getting cussed out on sight as soon as I walk into the facility. Whenever I did report someone for messing up on the shift before mine, it felt like I was be called childish and petty for not talking to them first. I never hear a word about my mistakes from my coworkers until I'm in the office. I questioned it almost every time.

"Well, did you know why I did what I did? Or are you just taking their side like always?"

Sometimes, I don't even waste my breath trying to defend myself because there's no point. Almost every week, one of the CSRs would always warn me before I walked into some mess.

"You're in trouble again, bro. You can never catch a break."

I laughed. "Yeah, I know. It's always something. Just have to accept it and keep it pushing."

I gave my last, and because of the person that I am, I'd do it again. Not many people could say that. I worked during hurricanes and other natural events for nothing in return. I can never go to anyone here when I'm in need. Seems like I'm only valuable here when I'm picking up everybody else shifts.

When I needed time off, it wasn't approved since no one would cover for me. When friends and family were passing away from gun violence back in my hometown, I could never go home to mourn with them. All because I had to work! My family and people in my community were starting to hate me because I would never come home. If only they knew I couldn't.

"Oh, I can't come home fam. I have to work."

Even though I blame my family on that part because I literally couldn't afford to take a day.

I couldn't celebrate anything with my family because I had to work! I can never get help with all the problems I was going through because I had to work. When Andrew Sun died, I didn't asked to take off because I knew my shifts wouldn't get covered. I just worked through it all until I left town.

This job reminded of one thing and one thing only. I only mattered when it was convenient for others.

I gave it my all day in and day out, but I always get pushed to the side like a redheaded stepchild and put down like I'm noth-

DARNELLE CUYLER

ing. Any time there was something wrong or I needed help, I wouldn't get the help I needed.

"There's nothing wrong here."

"I don't know what to tell you."

"Just deal with it."

Straight bullshit.

Never lending a helping hand. Never giving any resolutions.

"Oh, I'm here for you." but no help ever there.

Bullshit.

I can never explain or express how I feel because everyone always going to tell me I'm being aggressive, or they're going to tell how to act or react to a situation. I never understood people telling me that something isn't racist when I, a black man, tell them I feel like this is racist, especially with supporting evidence. I always had to keep my emotions to myself because I already knew someone was going to turn it against me, and somehow, make me the problem.

I never went to human resources because I didn't want them to tell me how to feel about a situation or tell me what necessary steps, I should take to prevent it. Even if they would handle the situation properly, I didn't trust them enough to do that. It was just easier to stay away from everyone than to risk potential wrongful termination in case one of them found out that there was a problem. I enjoy this job to much to let that happen. In honesty, I needed this job to stay afloat. I couldn't let them mess up my livelihood.

People always show their true colors and turn their backs against me. Even the people that haven't done that, I feel like I needed to keep my distance from them because I didn't want to give them the opportunity to do the same. I feel like I don't have no one to lean on. Only thing I can lean here at FSU is the gate at Mike E. Long when I'm dying from running 200's.

The longer I sat on this bench, the worse my thoughts became. It was negative thought after negative thought with no signs of letting up.

I just can't believe that I'm not good enough, I thought.

BE GREAT TODAY! NO DAYS OFF!

It felt like no one could ever point out the good I do here. I was constantly stopping people from quitting when they were fed up and motivating them to pick up more shifts. I sacrificed birthdays, holidays, and even my safety by working during natural disasters so the gym can be open to others. I was there for several students when life wasn't going so well for them and they wanted to commit suicide. It was me working over 500 hours a semester including the Summer to make sure the facilities were operational so people could come by and do what they needed to do for themselves. It was me being uplifting and motivational to the patrons by letting them know I was proud of them for coming to the gym. It was me helping beginners get out of their comfort zones when it came to living an active life.

I did everything possible and yet I wasn't good enough to be Employee of the Year.

I felt the tears about roll down my face, but my pride wouldn't let them fall.

Pick your head up!

I can hear the voice in my head, and I knew it was time to stop having a pity party and move forward.

Do you really care about winning Employee of the Year? No.

You don't need an award to validate you or the things you've done at this job. Tomorrow you will tell them you're proud of them and glad they won. No matter what people think, say, or feel, you're still the hardest worker here. You have a huge target on your back and it doesn't even matter anymore because they can't stop you. We're going to grind every single day until we leave.

Yes, it sucks the police make you feel uncomfortable but after today we will no longer walk anywhere in fear. Until the police pull you to side, keep grinding. We're no longer living in fear from this day forth.

Yes, it sucks that the people make you feel undervalued, but we will continue to grind despite that. We're here to grind and get our master's degree. We're not here to be liked, we're here to grind. And one way or another, they will respect it. If they try to put you in a situation that'll cost you your job, just leave and get a new one. The plan may change but the goal always stays the same.

DARNELLE CUYLER

We're grinding for everything! Always have and always will! We're not supposed to be here so we will continue to keep our head held high and keep driving. We will step up and work harder for campus rec during any disaster or scenario that take place. We won't complain or cry about not having help but work harder and stay level-headed. Whenever someone passes away, just keep your head down and grind it out for the people that can never come home. We will grind for them and go to work for them. We will keep this mentality for jobs to come.

Just eliminate the thought process of being let down. You already know that you don't have any extra help, so you must keep grinding so you can pay the bills yourself. We already know it's hard to save like you want to because you must pay for everything by yourself but at least you don't have to call anyone for help. You're upset about not going to funerals, but you don't even like funerals. I do understand the thought of wanting to take some time for yourself though. You let a lot of these small problems build up and you need to let it go. You going down the same path as LSU and we not having that again!

We need to focus on what's in front of us right now, which is to graduate from Florida State University.

You can't sit here and say that you're not valued here, but that is not true. You put in too much work for that to be true. There are people that will fight tooth and nail for you, and you know that. Sometimes that's hard to see when there's so much negativity and adversity being thrown at you every time you turn around. An award can never quantify the value you bring or even justify the amount of work you put into people and these facilities. The only reason why this bothered you more than it should have was because you turn it into a goal that you didn't achieve.

You picked up shifts from CSR to Supervisor since day one and will continue until you walk across that stage in December. The number of hours you put in this job is insane, but keep going. I'm sure, you worked more hours in the shortest time frame in the history of Campus Rec. If not, by the time we graduate we will.

BE GREAT TODAY! NO DAYS OFF!

Don't throw away all of your hard work and dedication just because we fell short of the goal. You're better than that so be better than that. Keep your head up and stick to the game plan.

We will continue to work hard and pay off the balance at LSU. We will get our second degree from FSU this year!

WE WILL KEEP THE DREAM ALIVE!

We will continue to grind and uplift people. We will continue to smile and be genuine towards others even when they're not genuine towards us. We will still create a scholarship fund for students struggling to make ends meet and need assistance. We will pave the way for those behind us and open the doors for those seeking to better their lives.

If one of us make it, ALL of us make it!

We will do our best to inspire those in our hometown to be better, do better, and do more for the community. We will open doors for future generations to come. We will not let go of the end goal just because the plan didn't work. We will grind and get this degree. The *Lambo* still coming! We're still grinding every day!

No Days Off!

Keep the game plan to the heart and keep the soul on fire. Now get up, we running 10 200 meter sprints. We will run each one at 85-95%. We will be fasting for 24 hours on top of that because you becoming mentally weak. We're not like them, we grind through hard times, not be consumed by it.

Pick your head up.

Lace your shoes up!

PICK YOUR HEAD UP!

It doesn't matter how many times I run 200 meters it never gets easier. However, I always get better. Afterwards, I went back home and studied hard. I made sure I stuck to the game plan. I fasted and it was tough. But I made it through. I was going to show them I was everything they didn't believe I was.

I'm not valuable? Stand on that.

I don't belong here? Stand on that.

You want to overlook my hard work? Stand on that!

I was putting in work like no tomorrow leading up to finals week.

DARNELLE CUYLER

Although I didn't pass one of my courses, I couldn't let that get to me. I had to stick to the game plan. Luckily, I got spared and the university put me on academic probation again. This Summer, I took four graduate level classes while working full time. I was working so hard with the math department so they would advocate for me to stay in the program, which ultimately meant me staying in school. I took two statistics courses, advance calculus, and probability. I was going pass these classes no matter what. I wasn't just going to survive and try to stay alive.

While it was tough, I was saving every dime I touched. In the middle of the summer, my family and I took a big loss in the family, and it took a huge toll on us. Everyone was asking me if I was coming home for the funeral. I couldn't be there considering I was in New Orleans for a wedding already. I was trying to escape the pain by being in an exciting setting, so I didn't have to think about it. I was happy to be reunited to be with the powerlifting family and to see Zach and Kayli get married.

I really enjoyed the food, especially the open bar. I had forty-eight hours to enjoy myself before I take the greyhound back to *Tallahassee* and get back to the grind.

When I got back to Florida, I turned it up a notch. I was working harder and studying longer. I ended up doing well academically over the Summer, which meant a lot. The math department was pleased with me. I was still on academic probation, but I was still in the program, nevertheless. I came up with a game plan to graduate and pitched it to the math department. They approved it and I was allowed to stay in school for the Fall semester. I was sitting at a 2.8 GPA and needed to have 3.0 to graduate.

I wasn't going to let 0.2 keep me from graduating. It's time to grind harder than ever before. I'm not letting up on my goals and dreams.

Everything was on the line during my last semester. I wasn't going to get another chance after this semester. I made sure I paid everything in advance regarding my tuition and rent so there weren't any issues. I took three classes this semester. I moved into a new apartment on High Road with another supervisor name John and a random roommate name Juan. We were all working so

BE GREAT TODAY! NO DAYS OFF!

much that we rarely saw one another. This semester I was making sure I was going all out. I still told myself that I would make time for myself care by going to a couple football games. This was important so I didn't get burnt out in the middle of the semester. I didn't run at any track meets this semester, but it was a small price to play for me to achieve all of my goals. It was a bit of a struggle during September and October, but I knew November was going to be a good month for me.

I can feel it.

I've been spending more time with my young bulls. I been trying to engrain it into the minds of Stephen, Kayla, Sofia R., Ethan, Josh, Kaelee, and a few others to step up to be leaders. I kept telling them every shift, I won't be here too much longer, you have to keep the motto alive. You have to be great and keep the incoming class motivated. I was probably harder on them then they'd like. I feel like at times I cared a little too much about Campus Rec. I was trying to leave them on a strong note.

Going into the next month, it started pretty rough due to hurricane season. We were hit by a category 5 hurricane. I was doing my best as a coworker and employee to make sure there was reassurance and peace in the midst of all the madness.

October I was a little down because I couldn't celebrate my two oldest nieces' birthdays and I also was trying to stay uplifted from Andrew's passing. I knew with November approaching, I had to bring my best. We're coming up on the final stretch.

November came and I was doing well in all my classes. I was able to have a little breathing room. I went to visit my LSU Urec fam. I know I always do, but this time it was more eventful. The reason this time was so special to me because I finally paid off my balance for LSU in full. I was able to get my degree on my birthday. I graduated from LSU two years ago, and now I finally have my degree on November 19th, 2018. I was also a month from graduating with my second degree and I had already paid my balance in full so there were no delays.

I was so excited about the way things were progressing.

After that weekend I went back to Florida.

I knew I just had to finish strong.

DARNELLE CUYLER

I went into overdrive once December arrived. I was working my ass off at the campus rec center and in my classes. I was studying harder and more efficiently than ever before. I was running my best runs over at Mike E. Long track stadium.

I started to feel bittersweet. I realized that my time here was winding down. As the days go by my coworkers and I were becoming sad about it. A few of them felt the need to express themselves and let me know what I really meant to them. I was trying to cover up the sad times on shifts by doing the usual.

Eating Oreos and laughing.

Then it was finals week. I had to dig deep so I can finish strong. The self-motivation was pretty much at an all-time high at this point. I gave my all and I saw it through. By the grace of God, I passed all my classes and was cleared to graduate from Florida State University. It was a bit nerve wrecking waiting until the last minute to see if I passed, but boy when I did, praises to God was continuously flowing from my mouth.

On December 15th, 2018, I graduated from Florida State University with a Master of Science degree in Applied and Computational Mathematics. I was officially a mathematician. I was also the only African American in my class. I was the first person in my family and community to graduate from FSU with a master's degree. I was so happy that I knocked down two of my biggest goals in life.

I was ready to do more.

My brother, sister, and my nieces came to see me graduate. It was raining during the ceremony, and I was soaked but I didn't care when I walked across that stage. After that, I stayed in *Tallahassee* for one more week and worked at the rec because they were short staffed. I moved back home afterwards. Soon as I got back to Altamonte, Ed gave me a call.

"Hey, you want to make a little bit of money over the holidays," he asked.

"Of course." I knew I needed some extra money coming in while I put in job applications. I needed a new job for 2019 and for the first time in years, it won't at a campus rec center.

BE GREAT TODAY! NO DAYS OFF!

To Florida State University, I'm grateful that you took a chance on me to let prove I was worthy enough to be in the program, but more importantly, I was worthy to myself. Thank you for allowing me to showcase my hard work and let my effort count for something. Thank you for the things you've taught me along my journey. Thank you for letting me be a part of your culture and family. I can't wait to pave the way for the future and share my experiences to others. Thank you for giving me the opportunity to chase a better life.

Go Noles!

I also want to thank Jorge for offering me a position at FSU campus rec center. I wouldn't have been able to complete my journey of graduating from Florida State. I wouldn't have been able to have met some extraordinary people that became life-long friends. I want you to know how much I appreciate you and grateful for you. I'm grateful that you took your time to understand the grind. I definitely felt that I had to keep stepping up to the plate because you reached out to your bosses and got me the job. I didn't want to be the one to let you down. I'm grateful that you let me showcase this work ethic and passion to those who admired and needed it the most. I'm grateful that you befriended me and stepped up for me when able too during hard times. If I had to do it all again, I would with no questions asked. I wouldn't let no one outwork me. I'll still show you how to grind through the hardships. I'll show you that you won't outwork me. I'll forever show you that it's ok to be aggressive, you don't always have to be humble and have humility for everything. I'll keep going hard so you can be at ease. Whenever you speak about growth and development you can use me as an example. Whenever you speak about greatness, you can use me, but don't forget to speak about yourself as well. Whenever you're in need of motivation and uplifting, you know where to find me.

Always remember that I'm proud of you for everything you do.

Always remember the motto,
It's No Days Off!

DARNELLE CUYLER

2019: Post Grad to Present

Moving back home wasn't exactly the plan but I knew it was necessary in order to regroup. I didn't have a job lined up after graduation since I was always working and didn't have time to go to career fairs or do job interviews. I know some people will say I should've made time but they don't know how my work schedule was set up. And despite the fact that I wanted to go, no one would've covered for me. And besides, less hours at work meant less money to cover bills necessary. It was either grind or be homeless. I prefer to grind. I wasn't going back to being homeless if I could prevent it. Everyone has a solution to a problem when they're not in that situation, but slow to provide support.

I was happy to at least see my nieces on Christmas and watch them open gifts. I was grateful that Ed was able to let me work with him to bring in some extra cash, but I knew I was on a time limit. I knew as soon as I got back home that I was only going to be there for a very short time frame. I started applying to jobs every night when I got off of work with Ed. I was constantly sending my resume to Chris, Julie, and Jorge to get feedback on revisions I should make. I wasn't good at doing resumes, but I was one hell of an interviewee.

All I needed was an opportunity.

I told myself that I was going to pump out as many as many applications as I can each day. That way, when the new year came, I can get a quick interview, and accept an offer so I can get out of

Altamonte. I was doing somewhere between 10-20 applications at the minimum a night. I did a little over 50 applications one day when I had some free time. I was determined to leave because of the environment I was in. People didn't believe my circumstances and I understand their perspective. However, I lived this every day, and it was obviously time for me to go.

Consistency was key for me.

I started back running up and down Sanford Avenue again to get my mind right and prepare for the New Year. I was still talking to some of the LSU Urec Fam every day, talking about our day and our plans. Our friendship was strong and very much alive. I also kept up with a few of my FSU campus rec fam as well.

I kept praying to God to send me a sign on the next steps. I needed to go into 2019 strong and focused. This was important because I was embarking on a different journey in unknown territory. Lord knows being back in the hood is the last place I want to be. I tried to make the best of it and spent most my time with my nieces when I wasn't working. We watched a lot of movies and ate Oreos. Whether I'm ready or not, 2019 was going to be a hard year.

But, let's do this.

2019 started I was still working with Ed at this job to help bring in extra cash. From the 2nd onward that timer started moving fast. I'm still being consistent with the job applications. I was starting to stress because I wasn't getting a call back for any job interviews. I was a black man with two degrees, a bachelors, and a masters. I can do whatever it is required of me. The same feedback I kept receiving wasn't regarding my education but my experience. I didn't have enough professional experience for the jobs I was applying to.

The following week I told Ed that it would be my last week because it's taking too much time away from me applying for jobs. After that week, I did exactly what I said I was going to do. I applied to more jobs.

Every time I walked in the house it was a problem. All I did was apply to jobs day in and day out. The only time I wasn't doing job applications was when I was outside running on *Sanford Avenue*

DARNELLE CUYLER

to pray and keep the faith. It's always a problem when you not giving people money.

I was being disrespected every day and keep putting me down like I was nothing.

I couldn't catch a break.

But I wasn't going to argue with anybody.

You got it.

This isn't my house. This isn't my first rodeo. I already knew I only had a few days left until I'm told I need to leave, and to be honest, I wasn't even mad nor worried. As soon as my degree come in the mail, I'm gone.

My degree literally came the next day and I was out without hesitation.

I made sure I took everything I owned so there was no reason for me to ever come back. It's crazy how after all these years of going to school I can't come home and catch a break. It's always about giving someone money. I was dumb to think that I could rely on family during this time, but I can't. They were willing to give to the streets and allow others to take from your household but was quick to turn me down on support that I may need.

It's the truth so I can't even be mad about it.

I watched so many people that I grew up with and ate off the same plate go through the struggles. Long as they were giving their check to their parents every time they got paid, there weren't any issues. But as soon as the money slow down, problems arose.

I promise they don't have to worry about me living with them again once I get back on my feet. I moved in with my sister temporarily. I already knew it was only a matter of time before things go left. I needed to speed up my timeline, but in the meantime, I was being useful. I offered to take my niece and sister to school and work every day. This allowed me to utilize the car to go to the library so I could apply for jobs or whenever I had interviews. A few days later my brother came and lived with us.

Yeah, I need to get a job asap, I thought.

I submitted about 200 job applications that week. I was praying something would break.

Nothing did.

BE GREAT TODAY! NO DAYS OFF!

One day I was hungry and went to *Dollar General*. I went in and got a couple things. Something told me to ask if they were hiring. It wouldn't be the greatest job, but it would be something to hold me over in the meantime. I spoke with the store manager, a Hispanic woman name Rosa, and for the most part, I could tell she didn't like me.

"No, we're not hiring," she said. "And we only hire part time for part positions when we are."

"That's fine with me. I'll do whatever is necessary."

I couldn't tell what she was thinking about me, but I knew it wasn't all positive thoughts. I couldn't shake the feeling of her thinking I wouldn't last two weeks if I was hired. Honestly, that very thought set a fire in my bones.

She doesn't know my work ethic.

She doesn't know my grind.

But she'll see in due time if she hires me.

"You can apply online to this store number, and I will call you once I see it come through."

I wasted no time. I went home and applied. The next day she called me while I was at the library to do an interview, and before the week was over, I was hired. Now, that I have a job, I can stay out of my sibling's way and vice versa. We were all working so we barely saw one another. My brother was contributing more than me. He was giving my sister more money for utilities and buying groceries. I, on the other hand, was giving just enough since I was saving everything to leave.

Before the week was over two other managers quit. The other three part-timers were there to work cash registers.

"It's just you and me now," Rosa said. "I'm putting you too full time."

None of the major jobs I applied for called me or emailed me back for interviews or a job offer. I figured I can stick it out here longer until then. It's the middle of February and I'm working full time at a Dollar General. The crazy thing was that most people from my neighborhood didn't know I was back in town, and quite frankly, I preferred it that way. I was being lowkey and staying out of the way. I walked to and from work every day since it was only a 20–30-minute walk.

DARNELLE CUYLER

Despite being full time now, my routine didn't change. I still worked out after work every day. I would ride my bike and lift the weights that were in the apartment complex gym. I knew this was temporary, so I had to stay discipline and focus so I didn't get complacent. The job started to get a bit demanding because for the next two months, Rosa and I were working every day from open to close. We may have had one day off during that time period until she was able to hire more people..

"You're my ride or die," She would say at the end of the shift sometimes.

I appreciated the compliment, even though I felt like we did more dying than riding. But I made the best of it. It wasn't the most lavish job to have, hell, you earned every dollar you made every day. It certainly wasn't for the faint of heart either. I would get cursed out every single day by crackheads over a pack of cigarettes and beer. Every day I would still be nice and friendly to people.

I laughed at everything mostly.

One day Rosa asked, "why are you always smiling? Nothing is funny! What's funny?"

"I am 26 years old and I sleep on the floor of my sister's apartment. I have two math degrees in my closet right now that cost over $100,000 to acquire and yet, I'm here getting cussed out by a crackhead for a pack of cigarettes. You don't think that's funny? That's not funny to you?"

She shook her head. No! You're crazy!"

Rosa and I kept working from open to close. We were working long 12 hour shifts while getting cussed out by customers from time to time.

"Man, I'm hungry."

"You're always hungry! Every time I turn around you want to eat something. I gained almost ten pounds because of you! Every time I turn around, we are eating!"

"So, you don't be hungry," I asked jokingly, "Man, I'm not going to keep working for you if I can't eat. We be in here all day long from open to close. You're crazy for not eating breakfast in the morning. But since I work open to close with you, we're getting breakfast every morning. That's mandatory. I have to eat before I leave here, I have to eat because I have to work out right after to get these gains. Since we're here all day, I get hungry out of boredom. I can't help that."

She walked off cursing in Spanish.

"So, are we getting wings or what?"

"Yes, Darnelle. Go get the damn wings."

I was still doing job applications every night before bed. I was trying to get out of my predicament as soon as possible. We had a big sale coming up in the middle of March so were working nearly 14-hour days to prep the store. The days was long and boring per usual. We listened to a Spanish radio station, and I felt like they recycled the same 12 songs over and over each hour. It only had 12 songs. My Spanish speaking skills were on point. Hispanic people would come in the store smiling thinking I was fluent in Spanish, but truthfully, it was all the radio.

I really didn't like working at the Dollar General. Every time someone from my neighborhood came come into the store and saw me, there was just this awkwardness that filled the room. Without saying any words to one another, we knew I wasn't supposed to be there. A few people were supportive and understood that this was only temporary.

Got to stay down until you come up.

There were these two guys that came to the store at different times and spoke to me. I didn't remember their names because I really haven't seen them in over 10 years. One had a bald head and a mouth full of golds.

"Dang young buck, I haven't seen you in a long time. The whole hood be talking about you. You still running track and going to school?"

"Nah, I just graduated. Now, I'm working here struggling."

"Keep doing what you're doing. God got you sitting here while he is getting your blessings ready. The whole hood knows what you did. I'm proud of you boy. Keep doing what you are doing! It won't be long. Be ready because it's coming! I'm proud."

Then he left the store.

I felt a lot better after hearing that because most people don't know how hard this journey has been.

DARNELLE CUYLER

The next encounter was a week later with a different guy.
He started laughing and was talking loud as hell. I'm trying to get
him to lower his tone because I knew Rosa was about to walk up in
any minute.

"Boy, boy, boy," he laughed hysterically. "They've been talking about you all over the hood. You still running track?"

I gave him the same response I gave the last guy.

"Young bull, keep going. This is only temporary. You gon
make it. Keep running."

His words of encouragement made me feel strong and
proud. I knew it was time for me to leave and do better. I still didn't
have any jobs calling me back for interviews nor job offers. My
mental strength was starting to fade a little. I signed up for a track
meet back at LSU. I rode the Greyhound to Louisiana and made a
pit stopped to Tallahassee along the way. I spent a few hours with
Jorge and then he had me speak to the graduating class. I delivered
a strong motivational message and let them know that life gets real
after you walk across that stage. I told them Campus Rec money
was the easiest money they'll ever make so enjoy it while they can.

I went to Louisiana and stayed at Conor house. I walked
five miles to the track meet. All the track meets I ran at LSU, I never ran at an outdoor meet. I only ran indoor. I ran the open 200-
meter dash.

I got dusted.

My take off and form was good. I died from the lack of
conditioning. I was still proud of the results. While I was there, I
spent time with Chris, Chip, Lois, and a couple others before going
back to Florida.

When I got back in town, I went back to working at Dollar
General. I knew time working here was winding down. I can feel
the shift changing in the atmosphere. At the end of April, I told
Rosa that I was leaving soon. She begged me to stay but it wasn't
hearing it. It was time for me to go. Then one-night things went
south between my siblings and I. I couldn't do it anymore. I sent a
message to Chip asking if I could crash with him for a bit. He told
me that he was moving back to New York at the first week of May
and then I can go move in once he gets settled. He told me to just

BE GREAT TODAY! NO DAYS OFF!

pay what I could for the rent and do what I can to land a job. I told my siblings I had a job lined up, but I didn't. I just knew I needed to leave Altamonte.

Before I left town, I helped my Rosa move into her new place because she was always nice to me. I felt like I was there to help Rosa get through hard times. She was going through some things she never spoke on, but I was trying to do everything I could to keep her happy and in good spirits while we worked together. I was grateful that she gave me a job.

While I was traveling back to Louisiana, I made a promise to myself that I will never move back to Altamonte again.

This was officially my last time living in my hometown. I have not moved back since.

I moved into Chip apartment with his roommates Greg and Blake. I got a job working with Blake and his uncle for a couple weeks to bring in some extra money. It was a simple job. I was just helping them move stuff.

I was thinking that since I was an LSU Alumni that it would have been easy to land a job in the area. I couldn't have been more wrong. It was just as hard here than it was back in Altamonte. I was talking to my mentor Dr. Sullivan and Micah and getting guidance on how I could get a job with the school, but there wasn't anything they could do. As the summer progressed, I was still cranking out job applications every day.

One good thing about moving back to Baton Rouge was that my LSU Urec membership was still active. I was able to go to the gym and keep working out regularly. I was still putting up shots for Zach and Andrew on the court. Mitch and I would go to the gym and then come hang with Greg and Blake. We would play Super Smash Bros every day, and that kept things at bay for a while. But I wanted to land a job in my field.

I was losing all hope on my situation changing. I was stressing behind closed doors and I wasn't in a place where I felt the need to discuss it with anyone. I just needed to suck it up and keep pushing forward. How can I motivate people when I don't have a job? How can I motivate people when I don't have a place to live? Why is this happening to me? I couldn't figure out why was I struggling so much. I was stressing but I knew I had to stay disciplined no matter how hard things are right now.

One day I applied to a job, and they called me three days later. They asked me what days would be best to do an interview and I told them I could do the following Monday or Tuesday. Once we had everything solidified, I rode the greyhound bus all the way back to Tallahassee to do a job interview. It was for a position working for a bank. I stayed at Matt house while I was in town, and he gave me a ride to the interview. After the interview, I rode the greyhound bus back to Louisiana a day later. When Chip moved out, I moved in with Micah because he had a spared room and bathroom that no one was using.

Micah was finishing up his doctoral program. Such a boss!

Micah and I got close because I was telling him everything that was going on with me and everything I was dealing with. The way I carried myself, he couldn't tell anything was wrong in my life now nor during the time I was at LSU. Because I was always uplifting everyone else, he couldn't imagine me, of all people, going through it like that. I was just focus on making those around me better. It helped me solidify my life's purpose, and it kept me from thinking about my own personal problems.

Once Micah graduated, he left Louisiana. Which ultimately means I have to find somewhere to live in the meantime. I moved in with Lois and Basem for a little bit. The banking job called me back and told me I got the job, but I wouldn't be able to start for another three weeks.

I was excited and happy as hell!

Until I started, the daily routine was watch tv on the couch with the dogs Kilo and Lilo. We would wait until Lois and Basem got home and then go from there. Basem and I would go to the gym before he went to work, which was usually after Lois most days. When Lois come home, we would argue.

"Did you eat?"

"No."

She squinted her eyes. "You sat in here all day and didn't eat? This is your house too. You can eat," she bellowed.

BE GREAT TODAY! NO DAYS OFF!

"I wasn't hungry." The growling coming from my stomach clearly said otherwise.

She would tell Basem to pick us up some food on his way home. We would talk about nonsense, LSU football, or play Madden afterwards. When Joey would come home, he would play with us too. Joey is Lois younger brother.

They were my Korean family.

I spent every Thanksgiving with them, and we would have Korean BBQ.

One day I was feeling down and thinking how I could not be working in my field when I graduated eight months ago. I don't have a job, don't have any money, and I sleep on my friend's couch. I didn't work so hard to get my degrees to be living like this. I quickly started to think positive because I didn't want to spiral in my own thoughts. I was so grateful to be back in Louisiana with my family. I was grateful that Chip, Micah, and Lois had given me a place to live during this transition period.

Finally, the day came for me to travel back to Tallahassee to start my knew banking job. I moved back into my old apartment on *High Road*. I had a random roommate named Arnoldo. Him and his girlfriend Ana was very nice. We didn't see each other that much because of our work schedule. The first day I started work was around the middle of August. I was working part time, so I was still able to run on the track. Because of my work ethic and my ability to grasp things faster than expected, I became full time 3 days later. It took me almost 3 hours to get to and from work every day. I walked 30 minutes to the bus stop, took the bus across town, and then walk another 30 minutes to get to work. Every day for break I would walk to Waffle house.

The first day I started I had to count the incoming money. It was easy task in my opinion but counting a lot of money repeatedly in one sitting wasn't as exciting as rappers made it out to be. I enjoyed working with my supervisors and my coworkers. They always kept me laughing. I'm glad I met them. They really valued me. I was always trying to have a positive attitude every day.

It was August 2019, and no one knew it at the time, but this was LSU's year to win the national championship. Every time anyone would talk about college football, I would bring up LSU. I rep-

DARNELLE CUYLER

resented them like I was their personal spokesperson. It got to the point that people started calling me Mr. LSU.

One of my supervisors pulled me to the side one day.

"You're always laughing and so happy. I don't know if you're going to be able to move up in this job because you don't show enough aggression."

My other supervisor said, "yeah, I don't know how you tell people 'no' with the biggest smile on your face. That's why I call you smiley."

"Well, I don't want to be rude to people."

It was a tough job because my supervisors, coworkers, and even myself would get cussed out every day. It was bad. I stayed positive because none of them knew that I was homeless with no job the last 6-8 months. They don't know how happy I was because my life started progressing since I didn't give up. I was happy that I started progressing with my life. I worked my ass off month in and month out with no signs of letting up. On the weekends I would run on the track at *Mike E. Long* stadium. On the weekdays, I would workout at my apartment gym every night.

I had to stay disciplined. I had to stay focus on my goals.

I been through some hard times, but I couldn't give up on myself. I tried to uplift and motivate my coworkers as much as I could. They were all shocked when I told them I graduated from LSU and FSU as a math major. They commended me for taking the road less traveled. Even though I finally had a job and had a place to live, I still wasn't satisfied since I wasn't working in my field of study. But I didn't dwell on that for too long.

Pick your head up and go harder.

I was riding the bus everywhere and it was getting exhausting depending on that for transportation. Whenever I felt too down on myself, I would plan a trip to Louisiana to see my family.

In October, I went to Louisiana to see the fam and watch the LSU football team play the University of Florida. As many times I have rode the greyhound, it was still long and draining. I never slept on the bus because it was just too dangerous to be that vulnerable on a bus full of strangers. If you're not careful and oversleep, someone will take your bag.

BE GREAT TODAY! NO DAYS OFF!

It was always good vibes whenever I got in town. Before we went to the tailgate to turn up for the game, I called Rayven and told her Happy Birthday. I never get to see Lyric and Rayven on their birthday so I would call and talk to them instead and send them some money if I had it.

When LSU beat UF, the town went stupid. It was another step closer to LSU going to the national championship game. I felt so refreshed going back to Florida after that. A weekend with the fam always fed my soul and rejuvenated my spirit. I was glad LSU beat UF because now I get to talk smack to one of my coworkers since he was a die-hard UF fan. I kept telling people that LSU was going to win the national championship this season, but nobody believed me.

My positive energy didn't change my circumstances. At least not yet.

"You need a car," one of my supervisors asked me.

"I can't afford one."

This was true considering I was still paying off one of my student loans that I had. However, she was persistent. She kept bringing it up and it was raising my anxiety a bit. I only make so much money, and with the bills I currently had, I was just getting by. She let me know that her, along with my coworkers, would help me get a car. I got a little aggravated because I didn't feel like anyone was listening to me or really grasping my financial status. And then I rode the bus home and honestly, it changed my mind. That shit legitimately sucked. I went to work and gave into them.

"Yeah, I'm ready to look at options for a car." I told myself I will just pay the loan off and use that money to pay my car payments. I knew November was days away and November was always good to me. I just prayed on it and then left it in God's hands.

November is here, and I was going to be better than I have been the past few months.

It's November, everything will fall into place. It always do. Keep the Faith.

This was a constant reminder to myself, and like clockwork, everything fell into place right on time. My family grew a little bit. Lyric had Londyn in the beginning of November. This was another reason for me to work harder. Another reason to pave the way. I

DARNELLE CUYLER

was proud. I uplift my nieces every chance I get since I don't get to see them often. I may not be there be physically but that is no reason for me to be absent in their lives.

Today it's November 9, 2019. This was the day I walked a couple miles to the post office to mail off my last loan payment for LSU. This was like an early birthday present for myself since my birthday was ten days later. I waited until they gave me confirmation of receipt that following Tuesday and they will proceed to show paid in full on my credit report. After I left the post office, I took the bus to a car dealership to talk about the process of getting a new car. After a few hours of waiting and paperwork, I left the same day with a new car. I was able to make car payments and car insurance. When I was leaving the dealership, everyone at the dealership were screaming happy birthday to me and congratulations.

I immediately went to hang out with Matt and Lamont right after so we can watch the biggest game of the century. LSU versus Alabama. The. Stadium was packed out with crimson, purple and gold showing across the stands. After watching LSU lose to Alabama eight years in a row, we all knew it was going to be different tonight. There was no way we were going to lose to Alabama tonight.

It's Forever LSU. LSU beat the Rolling Tides 46-41. I was going crazy! Everybody was going crazy on social media. When I left from hanging with Lamont and Matt I went home and ate some Oreos.

I'm not going to lie, I cried. I finally paid off my last loan for LSU, I didn't have to walk or ride the bus home because I got my first car all on my own, and LSU beat Bama. No matter how hard things get for me, November was always sweet to me.

I carried that momentum for the rest of the year.

I went back to LSU for thanksgiving. But this time, I wasn't riding the bus! I was in my car, cruising down I-10. I got there in half the time it usually took whenever I took the greyhound bus. I always go to Lois and Basem house. We always have Korean BBQ and steak. Basem and I would talk for hours about LSU winning the national championship because we called it before anybody.

BE GREAT TODAY! NO DAYS OFF!

When I left Louisiana, it was back to the grind. I continued to bring a positive attitude to work while dealing with customer hostility. I was grateful that I was working and going off the high of getting blessed in November.

December came and the grind continued. I went to visit home for Christmas. We all kept the peace and didn't bring up any negativity or caused any drama that happened in the beginning of this year. I haven't seen some of them since May, and others, longer than that. I was just happy to see my nieces for Christmas. After I returned to the Tallahassee to work for a bit, I drove down to Tampa to watch LSU play in their play-off game. They beat Georgia with no problem. I went to watch the next playoff game against Oklahoma with my LSU and FSU family and their friends. LSU quarterback threw seven touchdowns in the first half alone. We secured a spot for the national championship game!

Now the game plan was to get tickets to the national championship game. I kept telling Haley we have to go. It was tough because between requesting time off and trying to get limited tickets was a battle. The tickets were so damn expensive. Nevertheless, I was going to find a way to make it work and go to the game.

2020 was approaching. This was start of a new decade. I had to get my mind right and prepare for new beginnings. I set a few goals for myself. One of them was to see LSU win the national championship and start a scholarship fund for underprivileged students struggling financially during the semester.

The New Year came, and I spent it by myself in my apartment for a little bit. I drove down to Altamonte to see my family and left the same day since I didn't live or have anywhere to sleep. Trying to get the tickets for the national championship game was a mission and I was stressed out. I had to get a ticket to this game one way or another. A lot of people kept undermining the importance of this game because they didn't care as much as I did.

"That's so stupid to spend all that money on a ticket for one football game."

I didn't care. It's finally our time and I will see them see it through! One day during my lunch break, Emily and I were messaging each other about going the game. We were both having an anxiety attack because we needed to get tickets and it wasn't look-

DARNELLE CUYLER

ing too pretty. She messaged me the next day and it was the best thing I heard in a while.

"I couldn't risk it," she said. "I bought two tickets."

"YES," I screamed as I texted her back. "I'll pay whatever the difference is! We got to go!"

As soon as I clocked in for work, I requested time off so I can go to the national championship game. I knew I had to go. Even if I wasn't going to get that time off, I was going to that game to support LSU one way or another.

I don't care! It's *ForeverLSU*.

My team has been struggling too long! My job was so happy for me. They wanted LSU to win so I can shut the hell up about LSU football every week.

I packed my bags and drove out to Lois and Basem house in Louisiana. Basem and I were so hype that even the dogs were excited. Lois sat there and just laughed at us. I told them I got a ticket. The next day I drove down to *New Orleans*. I parked a mile away from the stadium where Cimajie was as well. I went to the stadium and saw Jeff & Nicole. I haven't seen them in years. I also saw a couple more people from LSU Urec and we were so excited to see each other. I went into the stadium and found my seat. The quarterback from LSU came out to *Lil Boosie Set It Off*.

"Dub," I said confidently. "We already won! It's over!"

The stadium just roared.

The national championship game in New Orleans, Louisiana on January 13th ,2020.

"Louisiana State University is your new 2019-2020 college football national champions!"

I was going crazy. I left the stadium with adrenaline rushing throughout my entire body and headed back to *Baton Rouge*. I saw Cimajie while I was walking to my car. I gave her a quick hug and kept it moving. She was with her people, and I had to go home so we couldn't stand in the road and cry about it for too long. The road going home was horrible. It was so foggy and dark on the highway. The only thing I had guiding me back to *Baton Rouge* was a vehicle with bright ass taillights. If the vehicle jumped of the cliff or crashed, I was going right with them because that's all I could was see. The vehicle was going so fast. We were going over 100 MPH easy for a good 10-15 minutes. Once I seen some streetlights, I knew I was back in *Baton Rouge*. I can find my way back from here. When I got back in Basem was so hyped that he was just yelling for a long period. I stayed up for a little while with Basem and talked about the game. We called the game since day one. I knew LSU was going to win because they had the exact same schedule they had when they won their last national championships.

A couple days later, I went back to Florida so I can get back to work. Things started getting crazy after that because the news kept talking about an airborne virus that was going around. This virus was known as the *Corona Virus* or *Covid-19*. Everyone everywhere was trying figure what was going on. Organizations started closing their offices, people were being furloughed, and people were losing their loved ones at a rapid rate. The bank that I worked out shut down two branches.

"Be happy you have a job."

As much as I hated that saying, they were right. From February to June, I worked in a different branch, and I had a different position. I didn't want to be there and because of the way I was onboarded on, I knew the workers at this branch were going to feel some type of way. I didn't want them to think I was trying to take someone's place or be something that I'm not. Unfortunately, this was the last time I saw all my coworkers at the same time. New hires were all brought in to work different positions. I worked as an ITM worker to continue help deal with transactions. I still had to keep a positive attitude because the people got nastier. It was because the situation everyone was in now.

It's the new normal.

People were getting sick and dying, and the government didn't have the best response or a suitable course of action. I was struggling to maintain my self-care because since the virus had spread, and more people were getting sick, there was an emergency order enacted that caused FSU campus to shut down. This meant no access to the gym nor the track. I needed to keep my mental game strong. I was grateful for the times Lamont and Chelsea would run with me. We'd talk about life and how we strive to do better and better others around us. We were witnessing more law

DARNELLE CUYLER

enforcement officers killing innocent black people but thank God it had national attention. It was still hard as an African American male that I can get killed at any moment by a cop and they would label me the bad guy. I tried to keep my mind away from thoughts like that and focused on my job.

I was working 50 hours a week. Every day we were open to help people complete their transactions. My new boss was telling me they didn't want me to get burnt out and that I should have a few days off. But they didn't know me. I was going to push through no matter what. My job consist of helping 40-50 people a day with their transactions. However, I was helping, on average, 100-120 people a day. Some days I went more than that. I didn't get tired, and I was trying to do all I could to pick up the slack.

I started running on the track at *Godby High School* to keep myself in shape and keep my mind right. Times were hard but I needed to go harder. I was working hard to put money aside because if anyone that I know and love were ever in need, they can call on me. I don't have much, but I can send what I can.

I was getting drained from being alone and working so much. I would talk to people, and they would talk so nasty to me and tell me crazy things day in and day out. I still had to have a positive attitude throughout it all no matter what. I had one lady get on the ITM with me and just talk. I knew she would request me because I was so nice to her, and she didn't have anyone to talk to. She told me that she was going to go kill herself.

"You don't have to do that. I know it's hard, but you have to keep living. I'm proud of you and I love you. You can come to the ITM and have them transfer you to me. I will talk to you every day, so you won't feel alone."

She started to cry and left. A few weeks went by and I felt sad because I was thinking about her and thought she killed herself, but she had got a job and was working. I was so happy when she told me that. I was still feeling down even after everything that was going on. I was trying to keep myself up.

One day I said I wanted to get a dog. The same day I seen on a social media post of my cousin selling puppies. They were rottweiler puppies. I always wanted to get me a rottweiler and I had

BE GREAT TODAY! NO DAYS OFF!

the money to get one. I kept thinking about it and contacted my cousin about the dogs. I asked if he still got a boy. He had one left. If the other person backed out, then I could have him. I waited and waited and until my cousin told me he was all mine. I paid him in full.

I was starting to feel better because I was getting a dog. I knew a dog would help me feel better mentally and allow me to be more productive for sure.

"What do you want to name your dog," my cousin asked.

"Well it's a Rottweiler," I said. "I can't give him a weak name. It has to go hard."

I started watching an LSU football game on *Youtube* and it came to me.

"J-Beaux," I said. "I'll name him J-Beaux."

On May 30th I drove down to Altamonte and picked up my dog. He was huge. I haven't been to Altamonte in a while. I saw some of my people, got some things I needed for my dog, and left. I met up with Nethaneel since we haven't seen each other since our time at LSU. That night I drove back to Tallahassee and the dog threw up in the car from motion sickness. I didn't even care. I was so happy that I got the dog. He gave me a reason to get up early. We went walking 4-5 times a day, even on the weekends. We were walking and running almost 20-30 miles a week. No matter how stressed I was, he was always down to run with me.

I was so grateful for J-Beaux. He was crazy, lot to handle because he was hyper, and always hungry. Shit, he sound like me. He was growing 10-12 pounds every three weeks. The amount of energy he had was insane. We would be up at 2am every morning for a good two months so he can go to the bathroom. The worst was when he'd take off running at full speed. I know a lot of people would think that's funny, but I promise it was heartbreaking. I would be tired and here he go, training for the Olympics. Over the summer, I took him to Tampa to see Haley, Nick, and Kelly. They loved him!. I didn't know that Tampa and St. Pete was one of the most dog friendly areas in the world. They treated J. Beaux like a god. I wish I could get that much love in my life too!

I always strive to go see my fam. It was always good vibes and a time for all of us to catch up. At my job, I was repositioned

DARNELLE CUYLER

back to my original position and kept working at the bank. We had a new staff and new protocols. I was a person that was used to adapting to change, but I knew I wasn't going to be working here much longer.

'I was back job hunting.

July and August were tough. I thought I'd land a new job before my lease was up, so I didn't renew it. I also had a dog and I wasn't trying to pay a hefty pet fee each month just to have him. I moved back in with Matt Hall. He insisted so we can grind together and he can hang out with J.Beaux. I told him I'd still pay him rent at full price. I don't like living off people or feel like I'm free loading. We were putting in work.

I loss three important people to me in the matter of a week. One of them was my mentor, Dr. Dowling, from LSU. The last time I spoke to him I was telling him that I was working hard and trying to start a scholarship fund for underprivileged college students like me. I didn't like how things were going. I hated the fact that I was working so hard and yet, tragedy was still finding its way to me.

Things didn't necessarily get better once September arrive. I kept having really bad migraines and it was had to sleep. The migraines were lasting for hours. I was struggling with this day and day out. I thought running would help, but it didn't. I was running 40-50 miles a week with J. Beaux and ended up straining one of his hamstrings. That didn't do anything but stress me out more. J. Beaux never whined about running until he was stuck in the house until he recovered. He was always down to run with me. I was drowning in my stress, and it was nothing that anyone could do. I was having headaches so bad that I was blacking out upstairs in the room. I would be so drained from being up all night and crying that when it was time to walk the dog, he stayed quiet so I can try to get some sleep. One day at work it got so bad to the point I had to go to the emergency room. They gave me prescription drugs, but it didn't work. It stopped the problem temporarily, but it made it worse once it started up again.

I couldn't help no one nor myself. I was still trying motivate others but it didn't feel right. It felt like I was faking it since I was altogether. I keep losing loved ones and had to deal with their deaths alone. I couldn't take any time off to grieve because I had to work. All my life I never felt like I had a shoulder to lean on and just cry. I was exhausted from struggling. The work environment was only making it worse. For some reason, my job was always on the line and I couldn't understand why. I was only valuable when it was convenient for them. I couldn't talk to anyone about my problems in the workplace because all they were going to do make me the problem. I have a dog but all I want to do is be alone all the time. I didn't have any motivation to do anything. To make matters worse, I'm homeless again. I have to live off one of my friends again. I already knew I had to leave this environment that I was in. I put in my two weeks and did all I could to stay strong. I was being discriminated against every day since. I stayed positive about everything until my last day.

Halloween rolled around and I wanted to do something to get out of my funk. So, I dressed J. Beaux was a garbage truck for Halloween because all he does is eat out of the damn trash cans on the sidewalk. Matt them wanted to celebrate but I wasn't trying to do none of that. I didn't have a reason to celebrate. The only good thing that happened to me in October was that my family grew a little bigger. Naomi was born. I stayed in my room and laid down. The headaches came and I started crying. I was sleeping on a Bingbag.

I'm 27 years old with two math degrees, yet I'm jobless and homeless. I cried harder. I struggle so much. I just wanted to know why this kept happening to me. This my seventh time being homeless in my life since I graduated high school. No one love or value me unless it's convenient for them. I don't like telling people my struggles because no one care, and I feel like it don't do anything but waste my breath. Then that's when a new spark erupted in me. It was right on time.

I had a pep talk with myself and it was just what I needed.

"November tomorrow! Everything will work out! We will go hard all month long. We will take advantage of every day. You will land a job. November never let you down before, it damn sure won't do it now."

DARNELLE CUYLER

The headache I had instantly started to die down. Although I still had headaches in November, they were nowhere near as bad as they once were. I started working out with Matt and Lamont. I was still job hunting. I was still running and praying to God that something will come. Tim was helping me out with job applications too. Prior to me quitting my job, I talked to Jorge about everything that was going on. He said he would reach out to some people. He posted on Facebook. I was a little upset because I didn't want my business out there like that, but I needed a job so fuck it. I was upset but then I reread his post and said, "fuck it", I need a job. He posted on LinkedIn as well. I was thankful for that. I was still cranking out job applications daily and Juliana had connected with someone that could possibly get me a job. I started to conduct interviews and I was feeling good about them. I just needed an opportunity to prove myself.

On November 17, J. Beaux and I drove to Louisiana.

We were going to celebrate my birthday and the wedding for Ally and Alex. This was a big weekend. We definitely intend on going hard but being safe as well.

He was throwing up all in the car again from motion sickness, but I wasn't tripping.

"Get it all out now because if you shit in my car, you're getting left on the highway. Everybody knows the rules on I-10. You don't stop in Alabama or Mississippi. It doesn't matter because we're not stopping!"

Thank God he slept in the car during that part of the ride. We got to the Louisiana in one peace. The fam was happy to see us. We stayed with Conor and Amy. They had a big field by their house that I can run J. Beaux through. We were running hard out there. I promise we was putting in work.

The next day I had training for another job interview I had. Everything was falling into place. I was eating out and eating sweets like crazy to the point I had a sugar headache. It's November 19th and I had my last round of interviews. The interviews went so well, and they all told me Happy Birthday. They had pretty much told me I got the job, but they will contact me the following week to let me know if I got the job or not. I felt so good. Then I

BE GREAT TODAY! NO DAYS OFF!

talked to all my family and friends, and they were all wishing me a Happy Birthday.

I went to this place called *Rouse* and brought different kinds of cakes. I brought a Red Velvet, Oreo, and a Cookie Cake. It was a great day. The next day the job called and offered me the job at 7:00 in the morning.

I accepted the job without hesitation.

Man, I was so happy that I contacted all of my friends and told them the good news. I went into the group chat with my brother and my cousins, Craig and James, and we talked about it. We always talked about the good times and the bad times in the chat, which always made us feel better a little bit at the end of it. I hung out with Conor & Amy, and we ate cake all day. J. Beaux and I did a lot of running in field because we were bored and were eating like crazy.

November 21, 2020, wedding time. I drove all the way to Natchitoches, Louisiana. It's far out on the countryside. I enjoyed the wedding and seeing my Urec family again. I was so happy. Booga really got married. I went back to *Baton Rouge* after the wedding because J. Beaux wasn't used to being alone for a long time, and Conor & Amy also stepped away from the house for a little bit. The next day, I spent some quality time with my family before driving back to Florida.

This weekend was bigger and better than I could ever imagined. I didn't expect to receive a job offer the same weekend as my birthday and Ally's Wedding.

One full tank got me to my destination without any hiccups along the way. I backed my car in and quietly went upstairs since everyone was sleeping.

Everyone was happy to see J. Beaux the next morning. I told them once I got a new job, I would take everyone to *Keke's* on me. Needless to say, I kept my word. A couple days later, Matt, Lamont, and I went to *Keke's* on me. For the next few days, I was preparing myself for the next transition. I was still waking up running and chilling at the crib. I was still staying to myself since I was still homeless and wasn't working yet.

One night, we were all sitting in the living room talking about how we wanted to be better and some things we can do to be

DARNELLE CUYLER

better. One of the things that was recommended was reading more. That idea wasn't for me since I wasn't an avid reader like that.

"I'm not a fan of reading," I said. "I'm a math major. Reading is a waste of my time."

Maybe one of them was talking smack or just didn't believe in my capabilities, but it was pretty random how we got to the next part of the conversation.

"So, you think you can write a book," one of them asked. "And publish it?"

I had full confidence in myself. "Yes, with ease."

Our conversation went further and I kind of felt like they were challenging me in a bit, in which they were. They challenged me to write a book and have it published by November 1, 2021. I was never one to back down from a challenge, so I rose to the occasion.

"Consider it done."

I took J. Beaux on a walk and as he was doing his thing, I kept thinking about the challenge and what I would write about. And then it hit me. This was a perfect opportunity to write about all of the obstacles I encountered in my life, at LSU, at FSU, and how in the end, no matter how hard things got, I never gave up. I conquered adversity and prevailed against all odds. Whether the books sales a lot or it doesn't, I want to use my story to motivate and inspire others that they have the capability to be better, and most importantly, no matter what life throws their way, they can make it.

Hell, if I can do it, they can too.

I'll even establish a scholarship fund at LSU and FSU for students in need and going through hard times financially and academically. I want to be a helping hand to those who struggled just like me during my time in school. I'll even use the some of the proceeds from the book to keep replenishing the scholarship fund. I won't half-ass the book and I'll give it all I got. I know I can't tell everything, but they'll have a better understanding of who I am, where I'm from, and how I overcame everything that stood in my way.

BE GREAT TODAY! NO DAYS OFF!

I finally moved away from *Tallahassee* and went to move into my new place. Tim helped me find a good place that was in a nice area, and Matt rode with me so he can help me move in. I planned on approaching this new job with a different mindset. I'm going to bring my absolute best at all times and be an asset to the company. I'm going to uplift and motivate my teammates every chance I get.

Before I could do that, I needed to let some things go that were holding me back from fully embracing my potential. Despite what my family and I been through in the past, I told myself I'll be the bigger person. I didn't want to hold grudges against them, so I decided that I'd only coming around during celebrations. That way we can all just keep the peace for at least a day. I won't forget the past, I'm just not letting it hold me back anymore. It was the only way I would be able to move forward in the future.

I came into 2021 with a lot of goals I wanted to accomplish. Despite everything going in the world right now, I knew that this year could be a big year for me. I just had to put in the work. After I got settled in, I let a few extra people know I got a new job and I was writing a book about my life.

"Don't work on the book unless you're feeling it," Julie told me. "You want it to be as authentic and as passionate as possible. Once you're done, shift your focus on getting a professional editor."

I kept that in mind while I was working on this book. I was losing sleep while I was writing certain chapters because I was stuck between remembering some painful memories and being completely transparent about my journey. As much as it hurts to remember, I remind myself that I'm no longer in that point of time in my life. I'm still standing, I'm still strong.

I realized that writing the book wasn't my only goal for this year. It was doing better overall and accomplishing other goals I haven't accomplished yet. I'm making it my mission to go back after those goals and doing more things that brought me joy. I promised myself that I was going train more and train harder so I can run at a few upcoming track meets. I was going to do everything I can to start my scholarship and be a beacon of hope for those who are struggling in their own journey.

Despite my current financial status, this was important to me. I had faith that everything will work itself out in the end. I

DARNELLE CUYLER

want to be able to help others that get overlooked, unsupported, and struggling to make ends meet. I wanted to show those individuals going through it, that we see them and we're there to help them. I wanted to show the world that the ones that aren't doing the best were still worthy of taking a chance on me. I remember nine years ago when I cried and begged the bursar office to stay at LSU. Now I can turn around and help pay students tuition for them to continue their education at LSU. What's even better is not only I can do it at 1 university, but both of the institutions I graduated from.

No matter what's going on in my life, I'm still going to motivate others to be better and accomplish their goals. I'm still trying to be the biggest hype man and number one fan to my loved ones and friends. I promised myself that no matter how hard or even how much I work, I will make time to attend birthdays, weddings, or any event that allows me to spend time with them.

I'm a man of my word. When I say I'm coming, I'm coming!

This year I will be an all-around better person. I'm still going to put up shots for Andrew and Zach. I'm still going to keep the promises I made to them both. I'm also going to work on my speaking ability so I can better myself as a motivational speaker. That way, when it's time to give speeches, I can do it without worrying if I'll do well. I will make the most out of every day I'm blessed to live through. No matter how hard things get I will keep standing, I will keep fighting, I will keep uplifting others, and I will be strong.

Every day I will live by my motto.

Be Great Today. No Days Off.

After Thoughts

I want to say thank you for taking time out of your busy schedule to read my book. Just know the contribution you made in purchasing this book will go to Darnelle Cuyler's Hardship Scholarship Foundation at Louisiana State University and Florida State University. I tried to be as transparent with you as possible. Thank you for reading about my life. I was told not to write the book if I wasn't going to give it all I got.

As you can tell by now, I give everything all I got. Always remember this, give everything you have in this life.

I know after reading this, a common question that a lot of people will ask is if I could speak to my younger self, what would I say? But truthfully, I already did. I spoke to my younger self when I was 19 years old running in *The Trenches*. I saw myself sitting on the side of the road in a puddle of my own tears. I was complaining about life, cursing God, and making promises at the time that God made me stand on. I couldn't watch myself have a pity party any longer.

"Get up and go home! We're coming back tomorrow and I'm taking over!"

It bothered me watching myself complain about my circumstances because the pain and fear of not making it was so great, that I could feel my younger self succumbing to it. That would've changed the whole trajectory of my life if I gave in to that fear. He doesn't know what he's capable of yet. He doesn't know he's fighter, an overcomer, or a graduate. He doesn't know how great he is or even how great he can be. He doesn't know it yet.

But he will.

DARNELLE CUYLER

The next day I watched my younger self come back to *The Trenches* and run. After while, he sat down in the same spot yesterday and cried a bit.

"Get up," I yelled at him. "I told you I was coming back today. Get up!

The tears faded away. He got up.

I started motivating myself and thinking about all the hardships that I was about to endure. Do you really want to go to Louisiana? Do you really want to deal with the fact that you will struggle for years before it gets better? The answer was yes for both questions.

"You will get out of here and you will go to LSU! You will graduate and you will make it! I'm going to show you how to have faith! Just because you're struggling right now doesn't mean you're not going to make it. When we're done here, go home, email LSU, and wait for them to respond."

No amount of adversity will steer you off this path. Not only will you achieve your goals, but you will also do more than you've ever expected. Some of your family and friends won't have your best interests at heart. The support level will be slim to none, but you can't give up. I will teach you have to love unconditionally and know that there are people out there that will love and support you unconditionally. I promise you will work so hard that you will no longer have to depend on others. You'll be able to hold your own weight and then some. You'll be grateful for the times you were in a puddle of tears instead of a puddle of blood. You'll be one of the greatest to ever make it out of *Altamonte Springs, Florida*.

Every day will be an opportunity to be great! Every day will be an opportunity to get better.

BE GREAT TODAY! NO DAYS OFF!

BE GREAT TODAY! NO DAYS OFF!

Credits:

Edited by: William Bodden Jr.
Book Cover by: Jordan Douglas
Photography by: Corey Nelson and Matthew Bisignano

Golden
Productions

www.FilmDen.Media

WILLIAM BODDEN